Well-Handicapped Horses

HOW TO IDENTIFY UNDERRATED HORSES ON THE FLAT

JON GIBBY Bsc Econ (Hons).

ACKNOWLEGEMENTS

I would like to express my thanks to my family for their encouragement and support, particularly to my wife Helen for putting up with me locking myself away in the study for hours on end whilst penning this book.

Special thanks to my brother Mark for his input. His great enthusiasm for horse racing remains a source of inspiration and I acknowledge the part he has played in developing some of the ideas in this book.

Thanks to Julian Brown for bringing everything together and for his continuing support.

Published in 2010 by Raceform Ltd
Compton, Newbury, Berkshire, RG20 6NL

A catalogue record for this book is available from the British Library

ISBN 978-1-906820-53-4

Cover designed by Tracey Scarlett
Interiors designed by Fiona Pike

Printed in the UK by MPG Books Ltd, Bodmin, Cornwall

Contents

Chapter One

Moving On

It is eight years since my first book *Betting on Flat Handicaps* was published and inevitably a lot has changed during that time. I argued then that the success of a particular betting methodology is normally transient and that in order to remain ahead of the game it is necessary to adapt to new realities as they become manifest. Since that time I have had to evolve my approach to winner finding because, as I predicted, the profitability of my old method has gradually and irrevocably declined.

My knowledge of draw bias used to give me a significant edge over most other punters. I was able to simplify the selection process by eliminating horses that had little chance of winning on account of their draws and my edge was such that there were occasions when the horses that I eliminated included the first five or six in the betting. More often than not I was right to discard them and on some occasions I could have made a profit simply by backing every remaining runner.

The fact that so many horses remained well fancied despite facing almost insurmountable draw biases proved that the majority of punters had no grasp of the subject. Instead they preferred to back horses that had performed conspicuously well on their last run and relied on the old pounds per length calculations to predict which of the horses that were renewing old rivalries would prevail. Their calculations ignored the impact that not only draw bias, but also pace bias, may have had on the past performances of the horses in question, as well as the extent to which they would affect their performance during the race itself. While the majority of the crowd remained ignorant about the influence such biases had on the outcome of races, those possessing a sound knowledge of the subjects were in an enviable position.

That position of advantage has not endured in the face of the increasing availability of well researched material detailing the effects of the draw. Following on from the publication of books on the subject written by the likes of Graham Wheldon and David Renham, the *Racing Post* introduced its excellent Topdraw service. Furthermore, websites have appeared that provide draw statistics and discussions about the subject have become commonplace on the various internet forums and chat rooms. Bit by bit, punters and pundits alike have become more au fait with the subject and even the presenters on the BBC, Channel 4, attheraces and Racing UK (some of whom used to exhibit mild contempt for the 'draw boys') now routinely discuss it. Bias-savvy punters influence the odds available on the betting exchanges, inflating the odds about poorly drawn horses and shortening the odds of those that are well drawn and the occasions when horses at the head of the market can be eliminated on account of their draws have become considerably less frequent.

In an interesting article on his website Drawn2Win, David Renham used the example of two typical Beverley sprint handicaps that were staged six years apart to argue that the market has now caught up with anyone still seeking to profit from backing well drawn horses. The first race he highlighted was run on 13 April 2005. It was a twenty runner sprint handicap run over Beverley's five furlongs (renowned as possibly the most biased course and distance in the country, where the high draws hold a significant advantage over those drawn low). The result was as follows:

POSITION	HORSE	DRAW	SP
1st	FONTHILL ROAD	17	7/1
2nd	PHILHARMONIC	19	6/1
3rd	THE LORD	20	9/4
4th	NATIVE TITLE	11	10/1

Predictably the first three to finish were drawn high, but they were also relatively well fancied with prices ranging from 9/4 to 7/1. These prices were notably shorter than in a comparative twenty runner handicap run over the same course and distance six years earlier on 8 May 1999. The result on that occasion was as follows:

POSITION	HORSE	DRAW	SP
1st	BLACK ARMY	20	12/1
2nd	LEGS BE FRIENDLY	19	16/1
3rd	NIFTY NORMAN	14	9/1
4th	PIGGY BANK	18	20/1

Renham drew the following conclusions from the difference between the two results: 'Big difference here, with the three highest drawn horses (who happened to come first, second and fourth), being offered at 12/1,

16/1 and 20/1. Having the three highest drawn horses all at double figure odds six years on just does not happen – regardless of form etc. The draw bias is so well known now, that the prices of the best drawn horses are arguably much shorter than their true odds. Going back to the April 2005 race, the prices of the top three drawn horses were 9/4, 6/1 and 9/1. All single figure odds and, one of them, at the amazingly short price of 9/4 in a twenty runner handicap! Clearly the market has caught up – the prices of the well drawn horses are much shorter than they would have been a few years ago. Gone are the days of big prices on the best drawn horses at Beverley.

'Interestingly, in the 1999 race Dominelle was sent off at odds of 7/2 despite being drawn in stall seven. By comparison the shortest price of those drawn in stalls one to nine in the 2005 race was a massive 22/1. Furthermore, in the 1999 race only two horses drawn in the lowest nine stalls were bigger than 25/1 whereas in the 2005 example, eight out of the nine were 40/1 or bigger!' Renham's conclusion was that the market has caught up: 'The diminishing prices of well drawn horses at draw biased tracks have generally squeezed out any value for us, the punters. Indeed these days, it could be argued that well drawn horses are often poor value.'

In addition to the fact that the prices of well drawn horses have contracted other developments have impacted on the usefulness of draw statistics. Many of the old sprinkler watering systems once used by racecourses have been replaced by new equipment that is designed to ensure that water is dispensed more evenly across the whole width of the tracks. The effectiveness of the old sprinklers that were situated in the middle of courses was limited and in many cases not enough water reached the outer and inner rails. As a result the ground was faster next to the rails than it was in the middle at many tracks. This led to the existence of predictable and consistent draw biases of varying significance at most of our courses. Although this was beneficial to punters like me it was understandable that many within the racing community did not welcome it. Owners and trainers complained that their runners often had no chance of winning on account of being drawn on the wrong part of the track and that it was unfair that they should waste time and money on watching races that, from their point of view, were non-events. Although I have some sympathy with such objections I am yet to be convinced that a bias free surface can be delivered by either the latest watering systems or by work to improve track drainage. I would argue that such remedial work more often than not results in the bias shifting to a different part of the track or becoming more transient and this leads to a state of confusion that serves only to inflate the profits of the bookmakers.

When an established draw bias exists at a course the jockeys are aware of it and most of them attempt to keep their mounts on the faster strip of ground. Once a bias starts to shift to a different part of the track it usually leads to a state of confusion among those that wear the size five hats. Although you may know where the best strip of ground is as a result of your analysis of recent results, more often than not the jockey on your selection will have a different opinion. At one stage during the 2009 Flat season it became apparent that the traditional strong inside rail bias at Beverley had temporarily disappeared and that it was the horses that made their run towards the centre of the track in the home straight that usually prevailed. However, old habits die hard in this game and the majority of jockeys ignored what was obvious and continued to head for the inside rail whenever they could. Trying to second guess them proved to be nigh on impossible and for the first time in many years I found it difficult to predict how races at this course would unfold. Clearly, the change in bias from the inside rail to the centre was not providing the level playing field desired by owners and trainers and the consequence was that winner finding had become harder for punters.

At some meetings the opinion of the jockeys regarding where the best ground was seemed to change from race to race, particularly at the wide, galloping tracks such as Ascot and Newbury where they regularly partook in a game of 'follow the leader'. A definite trend emerged during 2009 for the runners to shun the rails in favour of the centre of courses, but there was little consistency.

When the draw factor plays no part in a race, big-field handicaps in particular become a difficult medium to profit from. The exposed runners in these races are usually accurately handicapped to hold a similar chance at the weights and it is hard to differentiate between them other than by their suitability to the going, the course and the distance and most punters reach the same conclusions from this information. There is no doubt that the BHB handicappers have continued to improve their skills over the years and their analysis of the form of exposed horses is normally hard to argue with. They now take into account all of the factors that can affect a horse's performance, including any draw or pace bias, and adjust their ratings accordingly. Their dedication to accuracy is illustrated by the following extract taken from an article on the BHB's website that explains the job of a handicapper;

'Even the simplest calculations of each performance will take into account the distance of the race, the going, the weight carried, the immaturity of the horses, any apprentice allowances, the distance the horse won by or was beaten by and the quality of the opposition. In reality, calculations are never that simple ... There are so many factors to be taken into account. Horses are slowly away, unsuited by the draw, raced too keenly, hampered or get unbalanced in the race. Things might not have been to the horse's liking – the going, the track, the distance, the pace of the race and so on. The job of the Handicapper is to consider all these variables. The skill of the Handicapper is the interpretation of form. To help him he will go through the recordings of every one of his races again and again. The Handicappers maintain a database, with every run of every horse, the level of performance decided by the Handicapper, together with notes on every race and every performance.'

There is little point in trying to outsmart the Handicappers when it comes to rating a horse's performance using the traditional pounds per lengths calculations because they are taking all the relevant factors into account and are spending much of their time watching and replaying recordings of every race to ensure that they do not miss anything of significance. However, their job is to rate what they see horses do on the racetrack, rather than to speculate about their potential and this is an important distinction. Although they can take into account how easily a horse wins a race and factor in whether it started slowly, whether it was badly drawn or whether it was impeded when assessing its performance they are supposed to measure what they see. If a horse that is bred to stay two miles has its first three runs over five furlongs, and is totally outpaced as a result, it has to be rated on the form it has shown over five furlongs and it is not the Handicappers' job to speculate about the level of form the horse might achieve at a later date when allowed to race over two miles. Likewise, if a horse has its first three runs on ground that it detests and as a consequence finishes well beaten, it is not the Handicappers' job to guess what the horse might be capable of on a different surface. Most young horses improve as they strengthen and mature but the scope of such potential improvement can only be guessed at and once again it is not the role of the Handicappers to make predictions of this kind and factor them into their ratings. Punters, however, are free to speculate and to attempt to quantify the latent inherent ability of a horse that has not yet manifested itself on the racetrack. Those that become skilled in this art will make money because horses that are well ahead of the handicapper normally win or go close when conditions are in their favour.

In *Betting on Flat Handicaps* I explained how the method of selection I used involved choosing two or three handicaps each day which were likely to be affected by either a draw or pace bias. I eliminated those runners that were disadvantaged by the bias and then used other factors to reduce the remaining runners down to the live contenders. Over the last few years I have moved away from this labour intensive method of selection. I no longer sit down in the morning for three or four hours to analyse handicaps with a view to identifying the likely winners. Instead, the majority of my form study involves looking at the results of recent races in both the *Weekender* and on the *Racing Post* website with a view to identifying well-handicapped horses and keeping a list of them to follow. Len Ragozin, the American speed ratings guru, once wrote: 'The day that I stopped comparing horses with each other and started comparing them with themselves was the day I started to make money from betting.' Like Ragozin, I have learned to stop comparing horses to one another and instead I seek to identify those that have been underrated by the Handicapper. When my analysis is correct I do not need to concern myself too much with the opposition because under the right circumstances genuinely well-handicapped horses are hard to beat.

I was interested to read in a recent edition of the *Weekender* that Tom Segal (the esteemed Pricewise of the *Racing Post*) has a similar approach to handicap races. In an article in which he argued that ante-post betting can give a punter an edge over others, he wrote: 'The same rules apply to big handicaps. Many people will spend hours trawling through the form trying to find an edge, but for me the bigger the field the shorter the time it takes to find a bet because I'm simply looking for an unexposed horse. These big fields are chock full of exposed horses who we all know lots about. If the handicapper and most punters can't split about ten of them then I certainly wouldn't be able to either. On the other hand if there is a horse that hasn't shown his hand yet, I'm always interested. Of course there are going to be loads of times when you are on a horse that isn't well handicapped or doesn't have the ability you expect, but it often works the other way too. Basically, it's a good idea to be the first one in on any bet you have and that usually means going against the grain or betting ante-post.'

The game has changed significantly in the last decade and unless you go against the grain or interpret form differently to others you will struggle to make a profit. As the influence of the internet has grown there is now an almost limitless supply of information available to punters and they are using that information to shape the market via the exchanges. In the face of such strong competition, finding and maintaining an edge over the public has become more difficult. Even the professional gambler Alan Potts has found the going tough over the last couple of years. In an interview with *Smartersig* in April 2008 he stated that he had lost £19,000 over the preceding six months and that he had been forced to change his approach; 'Five years ago, the high stake single win bet at "value" prices was still my staple, but the internet was changing the world, the on course market was suffering and I could see that I needed to alter my approach. Now, I've given up the high stakes single win, mostly because I could no longer find the value, such has been the impact of the exchanges. I work almost exclusively with short priced horses on Betfair, because that is where the liquidity is greatest and where an edge can still be found. If this losing run continues for a few more months, I'll have to think again!' It would appear that another professional gambler, Dave Nevison, has also been finding things tougher than they used to be because during a recent TV appearance he described himself as being 'potless'.

During the same interview with *Smartersig* Potts was asked what he considered to be the key characteristics needed to become a successful professional gambler and he replied; 'Flexibility – what worked before doesn't work now, what works now probably won't work by 2012.' Back in 1983 the American speed figure guru Andrew Beyer made a similar point in his excellent book *The Winning Horseplayer*: 'There are no immutable truths, no absolute rights or wrongs. Certain systems may produce profits for a while, but as the betting public catches on to them the odds drop and they eventually cease to work.' For many years Beyer could have made a profit by betting blindly in every race on the horse that had earned the highest of his speed figures last time out, but that situation changed permanently after he agreed to provide the *Daily Racing Form* with his figures for inclusion in its form guides. It was not long before they ceased to be profitable and Beyer soon recognised that a more individualist approach to the puzzle of winner finding was required if he was to stay ahead of the crowd. He became a convert to the art of 'trip handicapping' which involved interpreting form and reaching subjective conclusions. When he looked at a race Beyer wanted to know which of the runners were favoured or disadvantaged by the way it unfolded, which of the runners had encountered bad luck or an ill-judged ride, which were affected by the prevailing pace and draw biases, which lost ground racing wide on the turns, which had shown signs of poor temperament or which had shown guts and tenacity. He wanted to identify those horses that had performed better than the bare form suggested. If his opinion about the merits of a horse's performance contradicted that of the betting public at large there were profits to be had.

This type of analysis does not lend itself to the bandwagon effect that inevitably impacts on prices because as Beyer noted: 'horseplayers ... don't like the subjectivity and the seeming imprecision of making ... judgements. They are instead enchanted by numbers, by mathematical approaches to the game that purport to turn the art of handicapping into an exact science. So much of their wagering is based on statistical methods that a skilful watcher can find edges with which to beat the game.'

Subjectivity has become the guiding principle behind my methodology and I have become less interested in anything that is well understood by the betting public. I now concentrate almost exclusively on unexposed horses that are open to improvement. Most punters find this type hard to fathom and that is what makes them attractive to me as a betting medium. I know that when I successfully interpret their past performances and identify those that are better than their bare form has been rated I have an edge over the opposition. Such horses are by definition well-handicapped. Unless I can satisfy myself that a horse is well-handicapped I will not bet on it – hence the title to this book.

Chapter Two

Speed Figures and Ratings

Speed figures based on the official handicap scale are an excellent tool for identifying well-handicapped horses and the Topspeed ratings published in the *Racing Post* and *Weekender* remain integral to my methodology. These weight adjusted figures convert the time it takes a horse to cover a particular distance into a rating. A horse that is awarded a Topspeed figure of 80 has produced the same adjusted time that a horse with an official rating of 80 should be capable of achieving. As long as the going allowance and the standard times used to produce the figure were accurate you can assume that the horse has not been overrated, but it could potentially be better than the bare rating suggests. If the horse in question subsequently returns to the track with an official rating below 80 you know that it is well-handicapped.

Form ratings are more likely to overrate horses than speed figures and a form rating higher than a horse's official mark does not necessarily prove that it is well-handicapped. Slowly run races in particular are often overrated because the dynamics of such contests do not properly test the ability of the contestants. A horse's ability or class is best quantified by considering both its stamina and speed and its rating should ideally be a reflection of how fast it can run and how long it can maintain its speed for. Because stamina is rarely an issue in slowly run races form ratings become little more than an expression of tactical speed and track position, rather than overall ability or class. Although accurate speed figures are worthless as a measure of ability in slowly run races, at least they never overrate the contestants and that is an important distinction to make between the two.

The relationship between slowly run races and suspect form ratings is particularly apparent in the results of Conditions races, which often bring horses of widely different abilities together on similar weight terms. A good example is provided by the career record of the filly Ermine And Velvet who was unraced as a two-year-old. After belatedly making her racecourse debut she had the usual three runs in maidens and on the evidence of those she was no more than a moderate handicapper in the making. She had been unfancied on each occasion and the best speed figure that she had achieved was just 69. On her third run she was awarded a form rating of 77 by RPR and that matched the initial official rating she was subsequently allotted by the Handicapper.

ERMINE AND VELVET (C E Brittain) Nayef (11.1f) – Ermine (Cadeaux Genereux (7.8f))								3-y-o
DATE	DIST/ GOING	RACE TYPE	RESULT	COMMENT	SP	OR	TS	RPR
26/09/09	8f Gd	H'cap	8th	tracked leaders	66/1	89	67	83
13/08/09	7f GF	Maid	2nd	led	6/4	89	53	77
10/07/09	8f GF	H'cap	8th	chased leader	50/1	91	55	85
25/06/09	7f GF	Listed	11th	prominent	20/1	93	40	65
05/06/09	7f Gd	Listed	2nd	chased winner	33/1	77	72	88
16/05/09	7f GS	Maid	2nd	chased leaders	11/1	-	69	77
29/04/09	8f St	Maid	9th	led	14/1	-	32	39
17/04/09	7f GS	Maid	4th	chased leaders	33/1	-	56	71

It was something of a surprise when she appeared among the contestants for a Listed race at Epsom on her next start on 5 June 2009. The race contained horses rated 105, 102 and 100 and on the bare form Ermine And Velvet looked to have no realistic chance of winning, an assumption that was reflected in her odds of 33/1. However, the early pace in the race turned out to be moderate and on a speed favouring track such as Epsom it was likely that the front runners would hold a significant advantage and so it proved. Soon after the start Ermine And Velvet settled in second place behind the leader Ocean's Minstrel who was rated 102. Neither was challenged for their positions and when the pace finally quickened in the last few furlongs nothing was able to produce enough tactical speed to overtake them and they held their positions throughout.

On the face of it Ermine And Velvet appeared to have improved dramatically on what she had achieved previously. The Handicapper responded by hoisting her official rating to 93 whilst the producers of the *Racing Post* form ratings awarded her a figure of 88. However, as you can see from the above table she had clocked a speed figure of only 72 – five pounds below her official rating of 77. In fact there was no hard evidence that she had improved. She had demonstrated that she had a certain amount of tactical speed, but not that she could sustain her speed for long enough over the seven furlong trip to justify the lofty ratings awarded to her by the Handicapper and RPR. It was likely that she had simply been flattered by having raced prominently in a moderately run race on a speed favouring track. The fact that the race was moderately run was reflected in the winner's speed figure of 83 which was nineteen pounds lower than its official rating.

Had Ermine And Velvet been held up in the rear in the same moderately run race and finished where she did, I would have had few doubts about the validity of the ratings awarded to her by the Handicapper and RPR. Although there would be suspicion that she might not be able to reproduce the form in a strongly run contest over the same distance, she would nevertheless have demonstrated exemplary tactical speed by passing several horses rated over one hundred in the sprint to the line. Only a top class horse would be capable of producing the necessary acceleration and the filly would have deserved a rating of at least 93 but probably higher. However, the likelihood was that she had been flattered by her proximity to much better horses and so it proved. She failed to win in four subsequent starts and was well beaten in two handicap races. The nearest she came to breaking her duck was in a maiden race at Salisbury on 13 August 2009 for which she was sent off the 6/4 favourite, but she only managed to come second despite having the race run to suit. The highest speed figure that she achieved in those four runs was a lowly 67. After her defeat in the Salisbury maiden the *Racing Post* analyst remarked that: 'She was not good enough to score despite having set the pace and got the rail, and is clearly not up to her current rating, with the 77 she was given prior to that Listed second looking a truer reflection of her ability.'

Some years ago I decided to produce my own speed figures for all-weather racing that were based on the official handicap scale and weight adjusted in the same way as Topspeed figures. After extensive research carried out over a period of weeks I was confident that I had produced some very accurate standard times and that my figures would be both unique and profitable. However, my sense of anticipation turned to one of disappointment almost as soon as I started calculating the figures. It quickly became apparent that all the effort I had put in had not provided me with an edge over the opposition because my figures were invariably either the same as Topspeed's or within one or two pounds of them. I quickly decided that the time and effort involved in producing the figures could be better employed doing other things, but it proved to me that Topspeed's figures are hard to better.

Even when the standard times are well researched speed figures will only be accurate if the all important going allowance correctly represents the impact that underfoot conditions had on the final times. The process of determining going allowances will always remain a matter for conjecture and mistakes of varying magnitude are inevitable. Any significant mistake has its consequences, but those that cause horses to be overrated have the biggest impact on my methodology because they may lead me to mistakenly believe that a horse is well-handicapped. With that in mind I go carefully through the results in the *Weekender* each week to check whether any errors have been made and this process has taught me not to take every figure at face value.

By way of an example have a look at the results of the seven races run at Sligo on 30 September 2009:

SLIGO 30/09/09

Good to yielding (yielding in places) changing to yielding (soft in places) after race four.

Going Correction: -0.15s per furlong (Gd)

RACE WINNER	RACE TYPE		WINNING DISTANCES	COMMENT	OR	TS
THUNDER BRIDGE	2-y-o	maiden	13L, 3L, 3L	tracked leaders	-	101
FOOTPRINT	2-y-o	handicap	1¾L, 1¾L, 1½L	chased leaders	69	62
FAST LIGHTNING	3-y-o +	handicap	1¾L, 3L, ½L	in rear	63	45
KARMA	3-y-o	maiden	1L, 9L, 2L	mid-division	-	42
TIN TOWN BOY	3-y-o +	handicap	4L, 2½L, 1¾L	in rear	75	8
LEAH CLAIRE	3-y-o	handicap	1¼L, 3L, 2½	in rear	48	-
SECOND GLANCE	4-y-o +	maiden	7L, 7L, 1¼	tracked leaders	62	7

The performance that caught my eye immediately was that of the two-year-old debutant Thunder Bridge who had clocked an extraordinary speed figure of 101. It is extremely rare for a two-year-old to record a speed figure of over one hundred on its debut and if it was believable then the colt was likely to be a force to be reckoned with in the Classics next year and could be expected to progress to a rating of 120 or higher. On the face of it the high figure appeared to be reinforced by the fact that Thunder Bridge won impressively, trouncing the rest of the field by thirteen lengths, and by the fact that he had been awarded an RPR of 105, but I was not convinced. Although there was no mention of the weather conditions at Sligo in the *Weekender* it appeared that it had probably begun to rain at some stage during the meeting due to the fact that the official going description changed from good to yielding, to yielding after race four. Under such circumstances you would expect the speed figure compiler to factor the change into the going correction but in this case a figure of -0.15 seconds per furlong had been used to calculate the figures for the entire meeting. As the ground softened over the course of the afternoon the final times became progressively slower and that is reflected in the speed figures which steadily declined from a hundred and one down to seven.

In this case there were no race reports to refer to for clues about the strength of the early pace in the races, but it was nevertheless possible to make some informed guesses. To begin with I suspected that the first contest had been overrated. Thunder Bridge had not been entered for any of the big races and a check of Steve Taplin's book *Two-Year-Olds of 2009* revealed that although the horse's trainer had discussed the prospects of thirty-eight of his youngsters he had not mentioned Thunder Bridge. I also noted that the horse had been born on 1 January 2007 which is the best possible date of birth for a two-year-old and it meant that he had held a significant advantage over most of the opposition in terms of his physical and mental maturity. I suspected that the colt was probably not top class and if that was the case then the 101 rating he had been awarded was not believable. I also thought it highly unlikely that the last two handicaps on the card had been slowly run. In both of these contests the fields had finished well strung out and it was significant that the two winners had made progress from the rear of the field to win. These are usually signs that the pace was strong. When there is a slow pace in a handicap the field normally finishes in a bit of a heap and those that raced up with the pace or chased the leaders generally account for the majority of the first five to finish. In these two examples most of those that raced prominently finished well beaten and the evidence suggested that the winning speed figures of eight and zero were well wide of the mark.

I concluded that the second race was probably the slowest but that this had been masked by a subsequent deterioration in the going. Not only were the winning margins the smallest on the day but the winner had chased the leaders in the early stages, the leader had finished second of the fifteen runners and the horse that chased the leader finished fourth. If I was right then the figures for the entire meeting were inaccurate, but without access to a set of standard times for each class of race I was not able to rework the figures to reflect my interpretation of the deteriorating underfoot conditions. However, I was pretty sure that the going had been faster than -0.15 seconds per furlong during the first race and possibly the second but that it had then become progressively slower than -0.15 seconds per furlong over the course of the afternoon. Although Thunder Bridge had probably achieved a decent level of form I suspected that it was significantly lower than the speed figure of 101 and the RPR of 105 indicated and I decided that I would not back him until such time that he proved he was deserving of those inflated figures, particularly as he was sure to be well fancied on his next outing.

He was the well backed 6/4 favourite when he reappeared on 26 October 2009 in a Group 3 contest at Leopardstown, but he proved disappointing. Despite conditions being similar to those that he had encountered at Sligo he only managed to come fifth, recording a Topspeed figure of 81 and an RPR of 100 in the process. He did not appear to have any excuse as he was well positioned during the race, but he could not find any extra inside the final two furlongs. It seemed that the 101 Sligo figure had indeed overestimated his potential.

Going corrections can be miscalculated for a variety of reasons. Perhaps the most obvious of these is a lack of uniformity in the going. This might be caused by either the ground becoming progressively wetter during a rainy day or by it becoming gradually drier during a sunny one, but not exclusively so. Most Flat courses have both a straight track as well as a round one and races are contested on different sides of the straight track at the same meeting. This causes problems for speed figure compilers because the going is seldom exactly the same on both sides of the course. For example, at Ripon most sprint races of fourteen or fewer runners unfold towards the stands' side rail because the starting stalls are positioned against it. However, races of a mile or more take place on the round course and when the runners exit the final turn into the home straight they race against the far rail. More often than not the going is faster against the far rail than it is on the stands' side, as can be seen by looking at the results of the Ripon Great St.Wilfrid handicap over the last six years. This six furlong Heritage handicap usually has over twenty runners and the field invariably splits into two groups. In the last six years all of the winners have raced on the far side. In four of those years the stands' side group finished a long way behind the far side with the gap ranging from four and a half lengths (equivalent to 13lbs) to a massive nine and a quarter lengths (equivalent to 28lbs). This sort of discrepancy occurs regularly at our tracks and is a major hindrance to the accurate compilation of speed figures.

Ideally it is best to create a separate going correction for races on the straight course and another for those on the round course. However, as a rule, going corrections become less accurate the fewer races they are based on and when there are only one or two races to work with they are unlikely to be reliable. This problem is particularly acute at Sandown which has a totally separate five furlong track. On those occasions when only one five furlong contest takes place at one of their meetings the going correction is inevitably not much better than a stab in the dark and the resultant speed figures should always be treated with caution. Southwell's All-Weather five furlong track provides similar problems for figure compilers. The most reliable speed figures are likely to come from tracks where all of the races are run on the same part of the course such as Lingfield (AW), Wolverhampton, Chester, Warwick and Pontefract.

Speed figures also struggle to quantify times when all, or nearly all of the races at a meeting are run in the same way - in other words when they are all slowly run or all strongly run. When that happens the going correction will overestimate the slowly run races and underestimate the fast ones by assuming that they were all averagely run. This scenario happens most often on slow or heavy ground because the jockeys often set off at a slower pace than normal in order to ensure that their mounts are able to see out the distance on the stamina sapping ground. If one of the races is run at a moderate but nevertheless a faster pace than the others, the winner is likely to attract a high speed figure that is not merited. In reality it has not run particularly fast but has simply run faster than the other winners who crawled round the track. For this reason it is never a good idea to accept high speed figures that were achieved on heavy or soft ground at face value and I am wary of concluding that a horse is well-handicapped on the basis of one. It is harder to spot whether all the races at a meeting were strongly run, but it is bound to happen from time to time, particularly at those tracks where it is established that early speed is an advantage.

In order to avoid being deceived by over-inflated speed figures I have devised some simple rules that highlight those occasions when the going correction may have been miscalculated. I look to see which of the winners at each meeting have recorded Topspeed figures that exceed their official ratings and I then focus on their races. I am particularly interested in the results of handicaps because the official ratings of the runners are normally a more accurate guide to their current level of ability than they are in sellers and claimers. If a race was genuinely run in a fast time I expect to see that the field finished more strung out than usual and that there was at least one gap of two lengths or more between two of the first four to finish. The rationale behind these rules is that in a genuinely fast run race the runners rarely finish in a heap behind the winner.

I become suspicious if too many of the runners in a race achieve a Topspeed figure that exceeds their official ratings. In my opinion only a handful of runners usually reproduce their best form in a race and only a certain percentage of them are likely to be well-handicapped. I therefore distrust the Topspeed figures for any handicap race of fifteen or fewer runners in which the fourth horse home clocked a figure higher than its official rating, or the fifth horse in races of sixteen runners or more. Have a look at the following two examples:

LINGFIELD 15/08/09

DORMANS PARK HANDICAP   6f (good to firm)

HORSE	DISTANCE	COMMENT	OR	TS
GWILYM	-	trckd ldrs; led 1f out; r.o strly	63	73
GHOST DANCER	1¾	hld up rear; hdwy 2f out	60	65
PEOPLETON BROOK	5	hld up rear, hdwy 2f out, outpcd	56	46
BATELEUR	¾	in touch; outpaced fnl f	66	54
SAM'S CHOICE	2¼	in touch	64	45
BOLLIN FRANNY	¾	led until 1f out, weakened	48	27
CHARLES DARWIN	3½	in touch	64	32
DYNAMO DAVE	¾	soon behind	50	16
METROPOLITAN CHIEF	2¼	held up in rear	48	7
SWEET KISS	nse	with leaders; weakened 2f out	54	12
SUPER FRANK	1¾	always behind	66	19
SHERJAWY	11	in touch	58	-

Gwilym achieved the highest speed figure in relation to his official rating of all the winners on the Lingfield card and both he and Ghost Dancer were likely to be well-handicapped if the figures were accurate. This race had all the hallmarks of a strongly run contest. The two pace setters finished well beaten and weakened once headed, having gone off too fast. The field was strung out and there was a big gap of five lengths between the two well-handicapped horses and the others. Furthermore, as you would expect in a strongly run race some of the runners made good progress from the rear as the leaders tired. I had no doubt that the speed figures were merited and that assumption was reinforced when I looked up the past form of Gwilym because not only had he previously had an official rating of 72 during 2007 but he had also twice clocked speed figures in excess of 73. The Handicapper elected to raise him only five pounds to 68 and I was pretty sure that he remained well-handicapped now that he had returned to form. He next ran in a five furlong handicap at Newmarket but was pulled up after reportedly losing his action. However, he did win his next race; a six furlong handicap at Wolverhampton at the attractive odds of 11/1, clocking a speed figure of 72 in the process.

Ghost Dancer was another exposed horse who appeared to have returned to form. He too had previously been officially rated in the seventies so a figure of 65 was certainly believable. Surprisingly, the Handicapper elected to keep Ghost Dancer's rating unchanged on 60 so the gelding had at least five pounds in hand. He failed to capitalise next time out at Goodwood when he came fourth after hanging right when making his challenge, but he made no mistake on his following outing at Warwick when he won at 11/4.

Compare that race to the following nine furlong handicap run at Sandown on 13 August 2009:

SANDOWN 13/08/09

DAYTONA AT SANDOWN HANDICAP				9f (good)
HORSE	DISTANCE	COMMENT	OR	TS
ETHIC'S GIRL	-	midfield; led 1f out; kpt on well	69	81
BROUHAHA	¾	trckd leading pair; went 2nd 2f out	74	84
MEFRAAS	2¼	rear; prog over 1f out; too much to do	74	80
SUMMER WINDS	¾	with ldr; led 4f out to 1f out	83	87
LATIN SCHOLAR	½	held up midfield; kpt on from 1f out	76	79
ADMIRAL DUNDAS	¾	trckd ldrs; one pace	78	80
AWATUKI	8	in touch	66	50
TILOS GEM	11	led to 4f out	77	37
CANONGATE	13	held up in last	85	14

Ethic's Girl achieved the highest speed figure in relation to her official rating of all the winners on the Sandown card, a figure that suggested that she was twelve pounds ahead of the Handicapper. However, unlike the previous example this had some of the hallmarks of a race that had been overrated. The main giveaway was the fact that the first six horses to finish had all been awarded a speed figure higher than their official ratings and it was unlikely that the third horse Mefraas would genuinely have been six pounds ahead of the Handicapper having been beaten by three lengths. It was improbable that sixty-six percent of the runners were well-handicapped and it broke my rule (explained above) regarding the fourth horse in a nine runner race. Furthermore, the first six to cross the line were more tightly grouped than I would expect to see in a race that had supposedly been run in a fast time and two of the three runners who set the pace in the early stages managed to finish in the first four. A check of the records of the winner and the second revealed that Ethic's Girl's previous highest speed figure had been 74 and Brouhaha's best turf figure from eighteen runs had been just 64, although he had clocked one standout figure of 81 on Polytrack. This provided further evidence that the race had been overrated.

There was no doubt that the speed figures were far too high and I suspected that, on what was a hot summer's day, the ground had dried out significantly over the course of the afternoon. The race in question was the last one on the card and was therefore probably run on the fastest ground. The going correction figure of +0.02 seconds per furlong for every race did not reflect the drying conditions. The figure should have been different for each of the six contests, perhaps progressing from a minus figure to a significantly bigger plus figure than +0.02 by the time of the last race.

I concluded that a speed figure of 74 was more appropriate for Ethic's Girl, the same as her previous best. After the race her official rating was raised to 75 whilst Brouhaha's was raised to 78 and consequently neither could be described as being well-handicapped. The horses that took part in the race had another twenty-nine outings between them before the end of the season, but only one of them managed to win. That dubious distinction went to Admiral Dundas who managed to scrape home in a Hamilton claimer on 20 September 2009. Ethic's Girl had a further six runs and her best subsequent speed figure was 76. There was no doubt that the Sandown race had been overrated and the dismal strike rate of the runners thereafter confirms how important it is to identify those races that are incorrectly assessed by the speed figure compiler.

The meeting held at Southwell (detailed below) is worth examining because like the Sandown card the times of the handicaps became quicker in relation to the official ratings of the winners, but on this occasion I drew a different conclusion as to the merit of the figures.

SOUTHWELL (AW) 05/12/09

Standard Going Correction: 0.16s per furlong

RACE WINNER	RACE TYPE	BEATEN LENGTHS	*RACING POST* PACE COMMENT	OR	TS
MERRION TIGER	H'cap 14f	7, 2½, 2¼	Pace was only fair	50	38
DOCTOR ZHIVAGO	Maid 8f	2, 6, shd	They went a fair pace	-	60
FELDAY	H'cap 6f	½, ½, 3½	Didn't hang about	90	69
LUCKY PUNT	H'cap 11f	5, 2½, 1¼	Moderate pace	84	63
SHADOWS LENGTHEN	H'cap 11f	9, 1¼, 4½	Set sound pace	65	60
SAUTE	H'cap 14f	4, 8, ½	Went good gallop	58	72

A look at the speed figures in relation to the official ratings of the winners showed that after taking the class of each race into consideration the last two were significantly faster than the others. This is best seen by dividing the official ratings of the winners into their speed figures to give a percentage. The percentages for the handicaps in race order were as follows; 76%, 77%, 75%, 92%, and 124%. Importantly, these percentages factor class into the equation and they reveal that the first three handicaps were run in similar relative times but that the last two were progressively and significantly faster. Had the track become quicker over the course of the afternoon, or was the huge speed figure recorded by Saute believable? According to the *Weekender* the weather that day had been fine and dry. If the track had been turf then it would have been likely that the ground had dried out over the afternoon and that conditions had become quicker as a result. However, Fibresand does not tend to become faster in dry weather and is more likely to speed up on a rainy day as a result of the water compacting down the deep and loose surface.

As always, the *Racing Post* analyst's comments provided some valuable clues which suggested that the last two races were strongly run. The one anomaly was the comment 'they didn't hang about' referring to the six furlong handicap because the overall time was slow. I concluded that the runners in that race may simply have given the visual impression that they had gone off quickly because they were the highest rated horses on the card and by definition they could be expected to travel faster than the other significantly inferior animals on show. The fact that the runners in that race finished closely bunched in relation to the other contests (only seven lengths covered the entire field) suggested that it was moderately run and that was backed up by the class adjusted percentage figure of 77.

All the evidence suggested that Saute's speed figure was believable and if it was correct then both he and the second horse Dart were well-handicapped. At the time of writing Saute had not run again but Dart reappeared at Southwell on 22 December 2009 when she ran in a handicap over the same distance. Amazingly she had been dropped one pound to a mark of 55 (I really have no idea what the Handicapper was thinking about when he concluded that Dart had run below form on 5 December 2009) and if her speed figure of 64 last time out was correct she was nine pounds ahead of the Handicapper.

When I checked her career record I became convinced that she was well-handicapped and I felt sure that she would win. She had won twice before at Southwell when under the care of James Fanshawe and had clocked speed figures of 72 and 65 at the same venue. She had been rated as high as 70 as recently as January 2009 and had only had six runs since that time. She had had a mid-summer break after being transferred from Fanshawe's yard to that of Sue Lamyman so it was reasonable to conclude that she had needed her first two runs for her new handler. She was presumably fully fit last time out and the evidence suggested that she had rediscovered her best form.

She was up against a well fancied favourite in the shape of Merrion Tiger, who had won over course and distance last time out by nine lengths and he was the choice of all the attheraces pundits. However, he made limited appeal to me because he had been raised by nine pounds to a mark of 59. In twenty career outings his highest ever speed figure was a lowly 50 and on the balance of his form he did not look as well-handicapped as Dart who was available at 4/1 and was the clear value in the race. The result never looked in doubt and the mare proved that she had indeed been well-handicapped by beating the in-form Merrion Tiger by two and a half lengths. The first three pulled clear and there was thirteen lengths back to the fourth horse.

Although Dart had run seventeen times prior to her victory and was fully exposed I was prepared to back her because there was a valid explanation as to why, after so many runs, she was suddenly ahead of the Handicapper. In her case she had dropped a long way in the weights and now that she had returned to her best following a switch of stables she had pounds in hand of the opposition. She proved that when she also won her next race over the same course and distance by three lengths off a mark of 61 and then came a gallant second under the welter burden of ten stone, two pounds to the improving Russian Music off a mark of 66.

There was no doubt that the 64 speed figure that she had been awarded on 5 December 2009 had been an accurate assessment of the ability she had demonstrated that day.

Rating horses according to their finishing positions is often unsatisfactory because the resultant figures may not reflect what actually happened during a race. Until such time as we have access to reliable sectional times for each horse in a race, quantifying the true merit of their performances will remain impractical. However, it is nevertheless worth thinking about how a race unfolded and to consider how some of the contestants should perhaps be rated differently. By way of example, have a look at the result of the following seven furlong handicap run at Musselburgh on 11 August 2009:

MUSSELBURGH 11/08/09

TOTEEXACTA HANDICAP (3-y-o)   7f (good)

HORSE	WINNING MARGINS/FORM SUMMARIES		OR	TS	RPR
DARK MOMENT 9-3	-	hld up midfield; nt clr run over 2f out; chsd ldr 1f out; styd on wl to ld nr finish	58	27	65
MS SOPHIE ELEANOR 9-7	½	led; qcknd 4f out; hdd nr finish	62	30	68
CILS BLANCS 9-4	2	chsd ldrs; effrt 3f out; kpt on same pce	59	22	59
GEMS STAR 8-6	½	trckd ldrs; effrt 3f out; kept on	47	8	46
MORE TEA VICAR 8-9	1½	hld up in detached last, kpt on fnl 3f	50	7	45
HOSANNA 9-0	2¼	chsd ldrs; effrt 3f out; wknd 1f out	55	6	44
MEYDAN STYLE 8-6	12	t.k.h; trckd ldr; wknd 2f out; sn bhd	47	-	3
HINDFOOT OAK SIOUX 9-0	2	s.i.s; effrt 3f out; sn bhd	55	-	6

It is clear from the winner's Topspeed figure of 27 and from the form summaries that the race was slowly run for the first three furlongs before developing into a three furlong sprint. In other words there was almost a separate race within the race. In fact the leader Ms Sophie Eleanor quickened the pace four furlongs from home but the majority of the other runners were asked for their effort three furlongs out. Interestingly, RPR elected to use three pounds per length to rate each horse, whereas Topspeed used two and a half pounds per length. The winner was allotted an RPR of 65 and that assessment appeared to be based on the assumption that the third horse had run to its official mark of 59. All of the other runners were then given a rating in line with the distances that they either beat, or were beaten by the third horse Cils Blancs. However, neither of the ratings reflected what actually happened in the race.

At the moment when the contest turned into a three furlong sprint some horses were better positioned than others. The leader Ms Sophie Eleanor was ideally positioned at the front of the field. By setting a slow early pace she had conserved her energy and it was unlikely that she would weaken significantly in the closing stages. The three horses in the worst positions when the pace quickened were Dark Moment, More Tea Vicar and Hindfoot Oak Sioux. The latter finished well beaten and can be ignored, but the bare ratings did not reflect the meritorious achievements of the other two. Without sectional times it is not possible to measure exactly what they did achieve, but having viewed a video of the race I estimated that Dark Moment was positioned around four lengths behind the leader at the three furlong pole and that More Tea Vicar (who was 'detached in last place') was around seven lengths behind the leader. That being the case, in the three furlong sprint to the line Dark Moment made up four and a half lengths on Ms Sophie Eleanor, and More Tea Vicar made up three and a half lengths. Because the race effectively turned into a three furlong sprint it could be argued that a more appropriate scale to measure performance would be around three and a half pounds per length rather than two and a half or three. If you assume that the in-form leader Ms Sophie Eleanor ran to her mark of 62 then it is logical to award Dark Moment (who was arguably four and a half lengths superior to her) a rating of 74 (4.5 x 3.5 = 16 (rounded up), 16 + 62 = 78, minus the four pound difference in weight carried = 74). On the same basis you could argue that More Tea Vicar, who made up three lengths on the leader, deserved a rating of around 60.

Significantly, Dark Moment had been fitted with cheekpieces for the first time prior to the Musselburgh race and that provided a tangible explanation for his sudden apparent improvement. His projected rating of 74 suggested that he was well-handicapped when he reappeared at Newcastle on 14 August 2009 under a penalty that had raised his mark to just 64. Although he was stepping back in distance to six furlongs I was unconcerned because he had displayed fine speed in the final half of the seven furlong Musselburgh contest. Thankfully, he managed to come out on top of a tight finish to the Newcastle race and was returned at 5/1.

According to his projected rating he was still well-handicapped when he reappeared five days later at Hamilton on a mark of 70 and he duly landed the hat-trick at odds of 4/1, clocking a speed figure of 74 in the process.

More Tea Vicar ran twice more before the end of the season and the way that she performed made a projected rating of 60 look fanciful. However, you can see that in the previous year (when she was under the care of Richard Fahey) she had earned an initial official rating of 70 and clocked a Topspeed figure of 63, so she has proven herself capable of running to that sort of mark in the past.

MORE TEA VICAR (Patrick Morris) Bahhare (10.3f) – Grand Splendour (Shirley Heights (12.3f)) 3-y-o **OR 45**							
DATE	DIST/GOING	RACE TYPE	RESULT		ODDS	OR	TS
04/09/09	Lin 7St	H'cap	10th	10L	40/1	48	14
24/08/09	Ham 8Hy	H'cap	7th	21L	18/1	48	-
11/08/09	Mus 7Gd	H'cap	5th	4L	33/1	50	7
30/06/09	Ham 8GF	Maid	6th	19L	50/1	60	-
31/03/09	Fol 10GS	H'cap	8th	68L	18/1	62	-
20/02/09	Wol 9St	H'cap	6th	18L	12/1	65	-
21/12/08	Grl 8St	Maid	5th	7L	16/1	70	63
10/12/08	Sth 8St	Maid	5th	17L	15/2	-	1
15/11/08	Grl 8St	Maid	3rd	½ L	20/1	-	56
03/11/08	Wol 7St	Maid	5th	6L	40/1	-	49

Her best two runs had come over eight furlongs as a two-year-old and on the occasion of her third at Great Leighs she had stayed on well under pressure in the closing stages. It is evident from her breeding that she probably needs a minimum of ten furlongs and indeed three of her dam's progeny have won or placed over that distance. It is possible that the heavy ground was against her on 24 August 2009 and the seven furlongs at Lingfield on her last start almost certainly would not have suited. She has dropped five pounds in the ratings since her run at Musselburgh and may well be capable of springing a surprise if she is stepped up in distance next season. Clearly, her overall profile is regressive and such horses should normally be avoided. However, I cannot help concluding that she has had few opportunities at middle distances so I shall keep a watch on how she is campaigned from now on, and having watched the video of the Musselburgh race there is no doubt that she stayed on well for pressure in the closing stages. Ten furlongs on Polytrack might prove to be her optimum conditions.

Form ratings and speed figures are not just devalued by their inability to reflect how races unfold - they have other flaws too. Perhaps the main one of these is the assumption that the scale used to adjust ratings in line with the distances that horses finish in relation to each other is applicable under all circumstances. In my opinion this is wrong because winning distances are not purely a reflection of one horse's superiority over another. In practice they vary significantly as a consequence of the impact that the going, the pace of a race or the configuration of a course has on the stamina of the horses. In general terms, the greater the test of stamina the bigger the winning distances become and unless this reality is factored into the various pounds per length scales that are used they will not be accurate under all circumstances.

Consider the differences between the all-weather courses at Lingfield and Southwell. The former has a fast Polytrack surface, tight turns and a short run in. Races there tend to be relatively slowly run and they develop into sprint finishes. All of these factors mean that the majority of the races run at Lingfield do not place an emphasis on stamina and as a result bunch finishes are the norm. By contrast the deep Fibresand surface at Southwell and the galloping nature of the course place a much greater emphasis on stamina and as a result the runners become more strung out. Despite this obvious difference, the distances between horses at both tracks are routinely converted to ratings using the same pounds per length formulae. A possible consequence is that winners are awarded form ratings that are too high in Southwell races and too low in Lingfield races. For example, in seven furlong handicaps at Southwell the third horse is beaten by three lengths on average, whereas at Lingfield the average distance is only 1.6 lengths. If handicap races were rated using the third horse as the starting point, the winners at Southwell would on average be rated 3.5lbs superior to the winners at Lingfield (1.4 lengths x 2.5lbs = 3.5lbs). The ratings compilers get round this problem by using horses other than the third as their starting point, but in my opinion that is not ideal.

This problem becomes greater in line with the distances of the races. For example, in sixteen furlong handicaps at Lingfield the third horse is beaten by 2.8 lengths on average, whereas at Southwell the average distance is eight lengths. Working to the usual scale of 1lb per length and rating the race through the third horses the winners at Southwell would on average be awarded a form rating 5.2lbs higher than the winners at Lingfield. The impact that such discrepancies have on the efficacy of form ratings should be obvious.

Winning margins also vary significantly in races run over the same course and distance on account of differences in the going. When the ground is on the soft side of good the winning margins (or beaten lengths) are on average significantly bigger than on fast ground because the stamina of the runners is tested to a much larger degree. For example, in ten furlong handicaps run at York on ground that is softer than good, the third horse is on average beaten by 4.4 lengths, whereas on good to firm ground the average margin is 2.75 lengths - a difference that equates to 3.3lbs. It is generally accepted that soft ground form does not work out as well as fast ground form and the difference in average beaten lengths is certainly one of the explanations for why that is so.

Using *Raceform Interactive*'s data search facility I calculated the mean number of lengths that the third horse finishes behind the winner at each distance on each type of going. As you can see the distances vary significantly and I believe that this should be accounted for if ratings are to presume to be accurate.

THE MEAN NUMBER OF LENGTHS THAT THE THIRD HORSE FINISHES BEHIND THE WINNER ON DIFFERENT TYPES OF GOING						
DISTANCE	HEAVY	SOFT	GOOD/SOFT	GOOD	GOOD/FIRM	FIRM
5f	2.7	2.3	1.75	1.55	1.55	1.5
6f	2.6	2.5	2.2	1.95	1.8	2.0
7f	3.3	2.75	2.0	2.0	2.0	1.8
8f	4.0	3.0	2.8	2.0	2.0	2.2
10f	3.3	3.1	3.0	2.1	2.6	3.0
12f	5.9	3.3	3.0	2.75	2.3	3.6
14f	7.3	5.0	3.5	3.2	3.1	3.4
16f	8.7	3.75	4.1	3.3	2.7	5.0

Predictably, the average beaten lengths decrease in a linear fashion as the going changes from heavy to good/firm, but surprisingly increase again as the going changes from good/firm to firm. I can only surmise that this anomaly is caused by the fact that a high proportion of runners do not act on genuinely firm ground and thus the finishes are less competitive than normal. These days of course genuinely firm ground has been eliminated by the increased use of watering.

I made some minor adjustments to the figures to make them more linear and uniform in appearance and although I am no statistician I would suggest that the table below is more accurate:

DISTANCE	HEAVY	SOFT	GOOD/SOFT	GOOD	GOOD/FIRM	FIRM
5f	2.7	2.3	1.75	1.6	1.5	1.6
6f	2.9	2.5	2.0	1.8	1.7	2.0
7f	3.3	2.75	2.2	2.0	1.9	2.1
8f	4.0	3.0	2.6	2.1	2.0	2.3
10f	4.7	3.4	2.8	2.3	2.2	2.6
12f	5.9	3.8	3.0	2.7	2.5	3.0
14f	7.3	4.2	3.5	3.0	2.8	3.5
16f	8.7	4.6	4.0	3.4	3.1	4.0

I have converted the average number of beaten lengths into the following pounds per length scale which takes account of the impact that the going has on winning distances:

GOING ADJUSTED POUNDS PER LENGTH SCALE						
DISTANCE	HEAVY	SOFT	GOOD/SOFT	GOOD	GOOD/FIRM	FIRM
5f	2.1	2.4	3.2	3.5	3.7	3.5
6f	2.0	2.2	2.7	3.0	3.2	2.7
7f	1.5	1.8	2.3	2.5	2.6	2.4
8f	1.1	1.4	1.6	2.0	2.1	1.9
9f	1.0	1.3	1.5	1.9	2.0	1.75
10f	0.9	1.2	1.45	1.75	1.9	1.6
11f	0.8	1.15	1.4	1.65	1.75	1.3
12f	0.7	1.1	1.3	1.5	1.6	1.4
13f	0.6	1.0	1.2	1.4	1.45	1.3
14f	0.5	0.9	1.1	1.25	1.3	1.15
15f	0.45	0.8	0.95	1.1	1.2	1.0
16f	0.4	0.7	0.8	1	1.1	0.8

I assumed 'good' going to be the norm and in the corresponding column you will find the standard pounds per length conversion scale. Working from that scale I made the necessary adjustments so that at each distance the average number of lengths between the winner and the third horse always converts to the same number of pounds, irrespective of the going. For example, over seven furlongs on good ground the third horse is on average beaten by two lengths. Two lengths multiplied by the standard conversion rate of 2.5lbs per length equals five pounds. Therefore, the average rating awarded to the third horse on all other types of going in seven furlong races should equal five pounds. Because the third horse is on average beaten by 3.3 lengths on heavy ground over seven furlongs a more appropriate conversion rate is 1.5lbs per length (1.5 x 3.3 = 5lbs). Using this adjusted scale to produce form ratings means some of the anomalies that currently exist are ironed out.

If the third horse in a sixteen furlong race on good ground is awarded a form rating of 80 the winner will on average be awarded a rating of 83 (3.4 lengths x 1lb = 3lbs), but on heavy ground that increases to 89 (8.7 lengths x 1lb = 9lbs), a significant and unjustified difference of six pounds. Using my conversion table both of the winners would be rated 83, arguably a more satisfactory outcome.

The table below shows the adjusted scales that I have devised for the all-weather tracks using the same method. It is interesting to note the striking similarity between heavy ground on the turf and Southwell's Fibresand circuit, both of which provide a searching test of stamina.

ADJUSTED POUNDS PER LENGTH SCALES FOR THE ALL-WEATHER								
	SOUTHWELL		LINGFIELD		KEMPTON		WOLVERHAMPTON	
DISTANCE	AVERAGE DISTANCE BETWEEN THE WINNER AND THIRD/REVISED SCALE		AVERAGE DISTANCE BETWEEN THE WINNER AND THIRD/REVISED SCALE		AVERAGE DISTANCE BETWEEN THE WINNER AND THIRD/REVISED SCALE		AVERAGE DISTANCE BETWEEN THE WINNER AND THIRD/REVISED SCALE	
5f	2.0L	2.8	1.7L	3.3	1.75L	3.2	2.0L	2.8
6f	2.75L	2.0	1.7L	3.2	1.75L	3.1	2.0L	2.7
7f	2.85L	1.75	1.7L	2.9	2.0L	2.5	2.25L	2.2
8f	3.3L	1.3	1.8L	2.3	2.2L	1.9	2.3L	1.8
9f	-	-	-	-	-	-	2.6L	1.6
10f	-	-	1.85L	2.2	2.3L	1.75	-	-
11f	4.4L	1.1	-	-	2.4L	1.7	-	-
12f	4.65L	0.9	2.0L	2.0	2.5L	1.6	3.0L	1.35
13f	-	-	2.2L	1.8			-	
14f	5.2L	0.7	-	-	-	-	3.5L	1.1
16f	8.0L	0.4	2.8L	1.2	3.2L	1.1	5.0L	0.7

I would argue that the above scales gives better results than the standard one and that they produce more consistent ratings, but I have little doubt that many of you will consider me a heretic! By way of an illustration to back up my assertion have a look at the chart below which details the record of the mare Dart on the twelve occasions she has visited Southwell's all-weather track. It draws a comparison between ratings calculated using my scale and those of RPR:

DART'S CAREER RECORD AT SOUTHWELL(AW)						
DATE	DISTANCE	POSITION	OR	MY RATINGS	RPR	STANDARD SCALE
05/01/10	14f	2nd	66	67	73	68
01/01/10	14f	1st	61	68	72	73
22/12/09	14f	1st	55	66*	68	75*
05/12/09	14f	2nd	56	62	67	66
11/11/09	14f	7th	59	51	47	46
18/10/09	14f	4th	63	50	42	39
29/01/09	14f	5th	70	62	61	57
01/01/09	14f	2nd	67	69	72	70
09/12/08	14f	4th	67	67	72	67
10/11/08	16f	1st	63	64	73	66
28/10/08	14f	4th	63	61	65	60
12/12/07	11f	1st	63	63*	78	65*

With the exception of the two ratings marked with an asterisk (which were rated around the fourth horse) all of my ratings assumed that the third horse had run to its handicap rating and used that as the starting point for the ratings. As you can see mine are more in line with Dart's official ratings than the RPR figures and are less prone to big fluctuations. The figures in the 'Standard Scale' column are worked out in the same way as those in the 'My Ratings' column except that they have been calculated using the standard pounds per length scale rather than mine. Once again they are arguably less consistent and in my opinion they overrate Dart's performances on 22 December 2009 and 1 January 2010. I might be proven wrong, but I would not expect to see Dart winning a handicap race off a rating of 75 anytime soon. I should point out that I do not keep my own set of ratings because it is too time consuming, but when I am looking at past results I am more likely to use my scales to inform my opinion about whether any of the contestants are well-handicapped.

My scale does not work with speed figures. On soft or heavy ground they cause beaten horses to be awarded inflated ratings whenever the winner records a high speed figure. This is caused primarily because speed figures rate the winner first and then work downwards but there is no doubt that the standard scale better reflects the time that each horse takes to cross the line. I do not think that it is right to expect one scale to fit both types of rating because they are different. Speed figures are a measure of how quickly a horse completes a race, whereas form figures measure where they finish in relation to each other and there is a subtle difference between the two.

THE IMPACT OF WEIGHT ON RATINGS

There is some evidence that the effect of weight is not as great as the theory suggests and it is doubtful whether one pound in weight consistently equates to one point on the official handicap scale. Have a look at the table below:

WIN RATIOS IN RELATION TO THE WEIGHTS CARRIED IN HANDICAPS			
WEIGHT CARRIED	ALL-AGED	THREE-YEAR-OLDS	TWO-YEAR-OLDS
9-12 - 10-00	1.35	-	-
9-9 - 9-11	1.20	-	-
9-6 - 9-8	1.20	1.40	1.55
9-3 - 9-5	1.10	1.20	1.50
9-0 - 9-2	1.00	1.10	1.20
8-11 - 8-13	0.95	1.00	1.10
8-8 - 8-10	0.90	0.95	1.00
8-5 - 8-7	0.85	0.90	0.90
8-2 - 8-4	0.80	0.80	0.80
7-13 - 8-1	0.75	0.70	0.60
7-10 - 7-12	0.60	0.60	0.50
7-7 - 7-9	0.50	0.40	0.30

As you can see the win ratios in each category increase in line with the weight that horses carry in handicaps. This should not be the case because in theory weight adjustments are designed to ensure that all horses have the same chance of winning irrespective of where they are on the handicap scale. However, it is clear that the best horses win more often than they should and that weight is not as effective as the theory suggests.

Based on my research I estimate that weight is only about three-quarters as effective as it is assumed to be, but its effect does vary depending on the conditions. It has more effect on soft or heavy than on fast ground and it has more effect when a race is strongly run than when the pace is pedestrian. Because its actual effect varies it is difficult to assess its impact from one race to another and for that reason I choose to ignore that the theory is flawed. Reducing the effect of weight by a quarter does not make much difference to the ratings in normal handicaps so I do not bother to make any adjustments. However, when it comes to amateur races I do. In these races horses have to carry up to twelve stone and the big weights they carry skew speed figures significantly. Research that I have conducted shows that the Topspeed figures awarded to the winners of amateur races are on average six pounds higher (in relation to their official rating) than in normal handicaps and I always reduce their speed figures by that amount. If you consider that runners in these events carry about twenty-eight pounds more than in normal handicaps you can see that six pounds is roughly a quarter of the additional poundage that they carry.

Chapter Three

Pace Handicapping

I make no apology for once again dedicating a chapter to the subject of pace handicapping and for going over some of the ground that I covered in my first book, because quite simply this one would be incomplete without it. Those without an understanding of how pace shapes and influences the outcome of the majority of races will struggle to unravel the complexities of form and their calculations will be inaccurate and based on false assumptions.

When trying to predict the outcome of a race it is important to consider the running styles of the contestants in order to draw conclusions about which horse is likely to lead, how strong the early pace will be and in races that take place on a straight course where the early leader is likely to be situated on the track. When you foresee the answers to these questions the task of finding the winner is made significantly easier. Unfortunately, the answers are harder to predict than they used to be because connections are now more likely to study the running styles of the contestants and to formulate a plan to overcome or exploit the way in which the race is likely to develop. However, when it comes to reviewing the result of a race these questions are usually easy to answer and it is possible to make accurate observations as to how a race unfolded and how that either helped or disadvantaged the contestants. This information can then be used to identify those horses that have run better than their finishing positions suggest and also to highlight horses that should be opposed next time out because they were flattered by the result.

One way of predicting which horse will lead and whether the pace will be strong or slow is to award 'speed points' to each runner in a race. I have adapted a method that was originally developed by the American, William Quirin, which involved awarding each horse points in accordance with their early position in a race. Our different form summaries mean that it is not possible to tell how far behind the leader each horse was but it is possible to get a good idea of their position by interpreting the race comments and speed points can be allocated accordingly. I have adapted Quirin's method to suit our form summaries and I use the first comment a horse is given for each of its last three races. In other words if the description was 'held up rear, pushed along to lead halfway, weakened final furlong' the relevant comment is 'rear' and if the description was 'prominent, effort to lead three out, ridden clear final furlong' the relevant comment is 'prominent'. I then award speed points to each horse as follows:

Four Points: made all, led
Three Points: with leader, pressed leader, pressed winner
Two Points: speed, prominent, close up, chased winner, chased leader, tracked leader, tracked winner, with leaders.

If a horse has raced less than three times you should add the highest single figure that it has achieved to its total either twice, or three times. For example, if a horse has raced only once and 'made all' its total would be twelve rather than just four. The horse with the most cumulative points is the one that is likely to lead.

The distance of the qualifying race needs to be considered. If a horse has been racing over shorter trips it may have been unable to race as prominently as usual because it lacked the speed to keep up over the shorter distance. While if it has been racing over longer trips it will have found it easier to take an early lead. It is a good idea to deduct a point for each furlong that the horse is dropping back in distance and to add a single point if it is stepping up in trip.

Once you have allocated each horse speed points it is a good idea to arrange them in the same way that the starting stalls are numbered, with high numbers on the left and low numbers on the right (as shown below) in order to make it clear where the early pace is situated on the track.

STALL	13	12	11	10	9	8	7	6	5	4	3	2	1
POINTS	0	3	12	8	2	0	0	2	0	2	2	0	0

In this example the horse in stall eleven would be the most likely to take the lead but may be challenged for it by the horse in stall ten. If this pace configuration related to a race that was due to be contested on a straight course with no significant draw bias it is very likely that those drawn high would dominate the finish. Under these circumstances it is a significant advantage to be drawn next to the early leader and it is surprising how many times the winner is drawn in one of the three stalls either side of the pace-setter, particularly when the leader is pressed by another runner drawn next to it. In races on straight courses it is common to see a field of runners take on a shape akin to an arrow head with the early pace-setter at the tip. More often than not the winner will be situated near the 'tip' or, if held up early, will be further back but following a similar path to the leader. The further down either 'edge' of the arrow head a horse is positioned the less chance it has of winning and in the above example I would heavily downgrade the chances of those runners drawn in the lowest two stalls, particularly the horse in stall one. Unless there is a draw bias in favour of the high numbers I would also downgrade (but to a lesser extent) the chance of the horse in stall 13, especially if the runners are tending to congregate away from the rails towards the middle of the track. Not only do horses drawn widest of all see too much daylight but if they are also drawn away from the pace they are likely to get too far behind in the early stages and then struggle to make up the ground.

It is easy to confuse a pace bias with a draw bias and it is unwise to jump to conclusions about the possible existence of a strong draw bias on the evidence of just one or two races, without firstly considering the impact that pace may have had on the results. The meeting that took place at Leicester on 26 October 2009 provides a good example of how things can change from race to race and how pace bias is often the single most important factor influencing the outcome of races contested on a straight course.

STALL	15	14	13	12	11	10	9	8	7	6	5	4	3	2
POINTS	0	3	3	12	3	1	0	4	0	2	0	2	0	0
		Won		Led										

The speed point chart for the first race of the meeting at Leicester indicated that the majority of the early pace was drawn high and that Baby Judge was likely to take an uncontested lead from stall twelve. I should point out that there were many non-runners at this meeting and that explains why some stall numbers are missing in the speed points charts.

The result (reproduced below) shows that although Baby Judge enjoyed an uncontested lead he failed to take advantage, having appeared not to see out the seven furlong trip. The first and second places were filled by horses that were drawn within three stalls either side of him and they had benefitted from the tow that Baby Judge had given them into the race.

HAYMARKET NURSERY HANDICAP (DIV I)

7f (GOOD TO FIRM)

DIST	HORSE	DRAW	EARLY PACE COMMENT	SP	OR	TS
-	HOUSE RED	14	prominent, stayed on	10/1	62	60
½	POWER OF DREAMS	9	held up, hdwy 2f out	7/1	63	59
4½	BABY JUDGE	12	soon led, hdd fnl f	7/1	58	43
hd	KNOWLEDGEABLE	8	outpaced, r.o fnl f	25/1	47	31
1	CRUSHING	11	held up, hdwy 1f out	3/1F	64	45
1½	ORPEN ARMS	6	prominent, wknd fnl f	7/1	60	37
½	BRAMSHILL LADY	10	prominent, wknd fnl f	25/1	65	41
¾	RAINSBOROUGH	15	chased leaders, wknd	10/1	64	38
shd	BRING SWEETS	2	mid-division	9/1	49	23
½	DRINKING BUDDY	5	rear	40/1	57	29
6	IZUIZORIZUAIN'T	4	chased leaders	11/2	58	14
1	WELSH LEGACY	3	prominent	66/1	50	3
1½	ARGYLL	13	mid-division	25/1	56	5
10	BA JETSTREAM	7	outpaced	33/1	53	-

As you can see, the first five home were drawn in stalls fourteen, nine, twelve, eight and eleven and it would have been reasonable to conclude after the race that a strong draw bias in favour of the high numbers was operating on the straight course, particularly as there was a four and a half length gap between the horse that finished second and the third. However, the fact that the early pace was drawn high should have warned punters to exercise caution before leaping to conclusions.

The speed point chart for the second race (over seven furlongs) was relatively uninformative because on this occasion there was no confirmed front runner. The probable early leader was the filly Rosiliant from stall nine and the rest of the pace appeared to be evenly spread across the track. After the result of the first race it would have been reasonable to assume that Rosiliant would be taken over towards the far side (high) by her rider and that high numbers would once again dominate.

STALL	14	13	12	11	10	9	6	5	4	2	1
POINTS	2	0	4	0	1	7	4	0	3	0	0
							Won			Led	

However, such speculation proved to be irrelevant because it was Dixie

Bright from stall two who took the early lead and maintained it for nearly six furlongs. This time it was the low numbers that were towed into the race and in a complete reversal from the opening contest it was those runners drawn high on the wide outside that were never able to get into contention. The first three to finish were drawn in stalls six, two and one and once again it was either the leader, or those drawn within three stalls either side of the leader that dominated the race.

HAYMARKET NURSERY HANDICAP (DIV II)
7f (GOOD TO FIRM)

DIST	HORSE	DRAW	EARLY PACE COMMENT	SP	OR	TS
-	DREAM NUMBER	6	Tracked ldrs, r.o	11/2	65	56
1	DIXIE BRIGHT	2	Led, hdd 1f out	33/1	58	46
½	CUTS BOTH WAYS	1	Rear, r.o u.p fnl f	15/2	50	37
1½	MINI MAX	4	Behind, r.o fnl f	22/1	60	43
¾	ROSILIANT	9	Chased ldrs	20/1	58	39
6	PUSH ME	13	Rear, hdwy 2 out	7/2	64	28
½	MR HARMOOSH	10	Prominent	3/1	64	27
¾	BOJANGLES ANDREWS	5	Prominent	12/1	50	11
3½	DISPOL KABIRA	11	Held up	25/1	47	-
7	THEWINNATAKESITALL	12	Held up	16/1	56	-
14	REGAL RAVE	14	Rear	6/1	59	-

The speed point chart for the third race suggested that King's Sabre would lead from stall eleven and, if so, the low numbers were likely to have the advantage.

STALL	18	17	16	15	14	13	12	11	9	8	6	3
POINTS	0	2	0	2	4	4	0	9	2	0	0	2
			Won	Led								

As it transpired the connections of King's Sabre decided to hold him up in the early stages and it was Lady Florence from stall fifteen who took the lead and maintained it for nearly six furlongs.

GUMLEY CLAIMING STAKES

3 & 4-y-o   7f (GOOD TO FIRM)

DIST	HORSE	DRAW	EARLY PACE COMMENT	SP	OR	TS
-	RIOLIINA	16	Chased ldrs, r.o wl	33/1	75	55
3¼	PIAZZA SAN PIETRO	8	Held up, hdwy 1f out	4/1	68	53
1½	STRATEGIC MOVER	17	Chased ldrs, styd on	9/1	69	44
1	LADY FLORENCE	15	Led, hdd 1f out	8/1	63	45
3½	KERSIVAY	12	In touch, wknd fnl f	7/2F	72	45
¾	STAND IN FLAMES	13	Mid-division, wknd	17/2	58	27
1	ALAN DEVONSHIRE	3	Prominent, lost place	18/1	58	36
1¼	HAY FEVER	18	Prominent, wknd	20/1	62	27
¾	JEREMIAH	9	Rear	12/1	67	29
1¼	ISLAND CHIEF	14	Chased ldr, wknd	5/1	71	26
12	DEPORTISTA	6	Mid-division	100/1	-	-
¾	KING'S SABRE	11	Prominent, wknd	14/1	58	-

Once again the early pace had a decisive influence on how the race unfolded and this time it was the high numbers that benefitted from receiving a tow from the front runner. The highest rated horse Rioliina won at 33/1 having had the 'box seat' behind Lady Florence for most of the race before striking for home over one furlong out. The likelihood that there was a bias favouring those drawn next to the pace was given further credence by the fact that four of the first six to finish were housed within two stalls either side of the leader.

The fourth race was for two-year-old maidens and not many of them had had more than one or two runs. As a result the worth of the speed chart as a predictive tool was significantly compromised and there was little way of knowing before the race how it would unfold.

STALL	10	9	7	6	5	4	3	2	1
POINTS	2	0	0	0	0	4	0	0	0
					Won				Led

In the event it was Rolling Hills who took the early lead from stall one but the lead was to change hands several times during the race. Galatian from stall four took over at the head of affairs after two furlongs and then the winner Deacon Blues from stall five took and maintained the lead two furlongs from the finish. The fact that there was no long time leader muddied the pace picture but there is little doubt that the low numbers held an advantage with the first three home being drawn in stalls five, one and three. The two horses that were drawn wide in the highest stalls struggled to get into the race and their performances could be excused.

EBF FOSSE WAY MAIDEN STAKES

2-y-o   6f (GOOD TO FIRM)

DIST	HORSE	DRAW	EARLY PACE COMMENT	SP	OR	TS
-	DEACON BLUES	5	tracked ldrs; r.o	7/4	-	71
1¼	ROLLING HILLS	1	led; hdd 4f out; styd on	25/1	-	67
nk	HUMIDOR	3	tracked ldrs; no extra fnl f	3/1	-	66
shd	VANILLA RUM	7	prom; outpcd 2f out; rallied	20/1	-	66
½	GALATIAN	4	chsd ldr; led 4f out; hdd 2 out	7/1	-	64
1¼	MINT WHIP	9	s.i.s; outpcd; r.o well fnl f	22/1	-	55
nk	ORCHID WING	2	held up	13/2	-	59
8	MASTER OF SONG	6	s.s; hdwy ½ way; wknd 2 out	100/1	-	34
1½	LADY SLIPPERS	10	rear	6/1	-	24

Under the circumstances the debutante Mint Whip performed with credit having run on well on the outside in the closing stages and although she is seemingly bred for speed she gave the impression that she should improve for a step up in distance next year. Despite starting slowly and then being disadvantaged by two biases she managed to clock a speed figure of 55 on her debut and should therefore be capable of winning off a mark in the low sixties.

The fifth race on the straight course was another race for two-year-old maidens and once again the speed point chart was of little value because the runners did not yet have established running styles.

STALL	12	11	10	9	8	7	6	5	4	3	2	1
POINTS	4	0	0	0	0	0	0	0	2	0	0	0
		Led								Won		

As it turned out it was the horse with the highest number of speed points, Caramelita who took the early lead, but once again there was no long term leader during the race and the lead changed hands three times. Adventure Story (from stall ten) took over from Caramelita after one furlong and she was subsequently headed by the winner Miss Zooter (who started in stall three) with over three furlongs remaining. Whenever the lead changes hands in this manner it is hard to be dogmatic about which part of the draw was favoured by the way in which the race unfolded, but given that the first two leaders and all those that raced prominently were drawn high I would have expected the high numbers to have been favoured. With that in mind I considered that the performances of the low drawn duo Miss Zooter and Kenyan Cat could be rated a bit better than the bare form.

HOBY MEDIAN AUCTION MAIDEN FILLIES STAKES

2-y-o   6f (GOOD TO FIRM)

DIST	HORSE	DRAW	EARLY PACE COMMENT	SP	OR	TS
-	MISS ZOOTER	3	chasd ldrs; led 3f out; ro	7/1	-	58
4	ADVENTURE STORY	10	prom; led 5f out to 3 out	13/8	-	45
1¼	KENYAN CAT	4	rear; hmpd; r.o fnl f	9/1	-	42
½	CARAMELITA	12	led 1f; chsd ldrs; no ex	11/2	73	40
nk	TRADE NAME	7	hdwy 5f out; styd on	15/2	-	39
6	KENSWICK	6	mid-div; wknd 1f out	8/1	-	20
¾	CATAWOLLOW	1	s.s; outpcd; nvr nrr	66/1	-	18
¾	SUZI'S CHALLENGER	11	prom; wknd 3f out	66/1	-	15
2½	VIA AURELIA	8	prom; wknd 1f out	8/1	-	7
1¼	KEEP SILENT	5	mid-div; sn behind	66/1	-	3
½	FARMERS DREAM	9	prom; wknd 2f out	40/1	-	1
nse	SOSTENUTO	2	rear, wknd ½ way	66/1	-	1

The final race on the Leicester card to be run on the straight course was an all-aged handicap for amateur riders. In a race full of exposed horses with established running styles it was likely that the speed point chart would be a useful predictive tool.

STALL	18	17	16	15	12	11	10	9	7	6	2	1
POINTS	0	2	0	5	0	0	2	8	5	0	4	1
							Won	Led				

A One took the lead as expected from stall nine but he struggled to maintain it for long because he was racing from ten pounds out of the handicap and was outclassed. He was headed by Camerooney (from stall fifteen) after only one furlong but that horse's lead did not last long before Castano (from stall twelve) took over at the head of affairs four furlongs out. Castano was subsequently headed by the winner Realt Na Mara two furlongs from the finish. The pace picture was once again muddled as a consequence of there being no sustained front runner and although the first and the second were drawn within three stalls either side of the early leader I suspect that was simply a coincidence. When the front runner does not lead the field for the majority of a race it is usually unwise to conclude that there was a pace bias in favour of horses drawn next to it.

AMATEUR JOCKEYS ASSOCIATION INSURE THEIR MEMBERS

HANDICAP 3-y-o and up   7f (GOOD TO FIRM)

DIST	HORSE	DRAW	EARLY PACE COMMENT	SP	OR	TS
-	REALT NA MARA	10	prom; led 2 out; pushed clear	8/1	65	78
4	IRON OUT	6	mid-div; headway 4 out; ran on	11/4	67	67
¾	SAIRAAM	17	mid-div; headway ½ way	9/1	55	53
3¾	CAMEROONEY	15	prom; led 5 out; headed 4 out	16/1	55	41
1¾	CASTANO	12	chased ldrs; led 4 out til 2 out	10/1	56	36
2	OCEAN LEGEND	2	held up; styd on; n.d	9/1	68	42
2	KHESKIANTO	7	prom; ridden 2 out; wknd	14/1	60	28
6	EFIDIUM	18	rear	25/1	68	16
6	WEST END LAD	11	rear	10/1	69	-
1½	A ONE	9	led; hdd 5 out; wknd ½ way	66/1	55	-
4	AVEROO	16	prom; rdn ½ way; wknd	10/3	61	-
55	CANARY GIRL	1	outpaced	66/1	55	-

All of the races run on the straight course were won by a horse that had either been prominent or had chased the leaders in the early stages and it was likely that a track bias favouring early pace had been in existence. The result of the mile handicap run on the round course during the same afternoon was also dominated by horses that had raced prominently. Whenever early pace is favoured on a straight course the runners drawn next to the early leader have an advantage because they are likely to be towed into a prominent early position by the pacesetter. Horses drawn away from the pacesetter invariably appear to get outpaced in the early stages and they find it hard to make up ground on a track that is offering no assistance to runners attempting to come from behind.

The horses that were both held up and drawn away from the pace had virtually no chance of winning at Leicester on 26 October 2009. Having reached this conclusion I reviewed the result of each race on the straight course and looked to see whether any horse had performed with credit in the face of both biases. Those that met the criteria were:

Race 1:   Bring Sweets
Race 2:   Push Mc
Race 3:   Piazza San Pietro
Race 4:   Mint Whip (already discussed above)
Race 5:   Kenyan Cat
Race 6:   Ocean Legend

Having examined the career records of the qualifiers I quickly decided that Piazza San Pietro and Ocean Legend were of no interest to me. Piazza San Pietro was fully exposed having had eighteen runs and his two victories had come in a seller and a claimer. The fact that he had run in another claimer at Leicester suggested that his connections did not think that he was well-handicapped on a mark of 68. Ocean Legend had had thirty-two runs and was fully exposed. He had a very poor strike rate, having only won twice during his career, and there was nothing in his record to support the view that he might be well-handicapped.

Bring Sweets on the other hand had the profile of a potential improver now that he was competing in handicaps. His first three runs had been over five furlongs and he had been consistently outpaced over that trip. It was therefore interesting that he appeared to have come in for some support prior to his handicap debut in the opening seven furlong contest. Considering that his form was woeful and that he had been off the track for 147 days (during which time he may have been gelded) it was surprising that he had opened at odds of 6/1 before drifting out to 9/1. That suggested somebody thought he was well treated on a mark of 46. Although his supporters never looked like collecting they were possibly unlucky because Bring Sweets never had a chance after being held up from a low draw and he wasn't helped by the fact that his apprentice rider not only put up 3lbs overweight, but also managed to drop his reins when asking Bring Sweets for an effort over two furlongs out.

Bring Sweets clocked a modest speed figure of 42 when he ran over the inadequate trip of five furlongs on 8 May 2009 and his current mark of 46 looks potentially lenient if he does improve for stepping up in distance.

Although this cheap purchase is no doubt very ordinary I suspect that he can win a race or two from his lowly handicap perch, but given his breeding and overall profile he is likely to be no better than a selling plater.

Push Me was definitely of interest. She had already come to my attention when winning a seven furlong Wolverhampton seller on her debut. On that occasion she had done well to overcome a wide draw and also to make headway from the rear of the field to win readily in what was a moderately run race. She travelled strongly through the race that day and only needed a little encouragement from her rider to beat a 64 rated rival with some authority. The victory had clearly been expected by her connections because they backed her from 16/1 into 11/1 and after the race her trainer reported that: 'She's a nice filly and works well at home. She'll want a bit of cut when she goes on turf. It's just a shame about the big Rule 4.'

That victory qualified her for a handicap mark and although her initial rating of 64 looked fair I decided not back her on the fast ground at Leicester in view of her trainer's comments about her needing cut in the ground. However, after she performed better than her finishing position suggested my interest in her was heightened. I was convinced that she was better than her form made her look and having been beaten by ten lengths the odds about her were likely to be generous next time.

On 2 November 2009 she returned to Wolverhampton to contest another seller over seven furlongs. She had a decent draw in stall six and although she faced a 70 rated rival, as well as three others that were rated a couple of pounds higher than her, I felt pretty sure that she could beat them. Contests of this type are usually full of crocks and quitters but Push Me was a lightly raced winner and she had already demonstrated that she was capable of knuckling down at the business end of a race. As I suspected, the merit of her past form had been obscured and I was able to get on at 12/1 – a price I considered to be too generous. Unfortunately, there was no happy outcome because things did not fall for the diminutive filly during the race. For the first three furlongs she travelled well but disaster struck when she was sandwiched between bigger looking rivals and stumbled four furlongs out. Although she dropped back at that stage she had enough in hand to come powerfully back into the race. As she exited the final turn her rider found himself short of room and then made the mistake of switching towards the inner rather than pulling to the outside where he would have benefitted from a clear passage and the better ground. Once she found room she powered home but was never going to catch the winner who had obtained first run on her. She closed the leader down to be beaten just under a length at the line but the bird had flown. I have no doubt that with better luck she would have won comfortably.

Kenyan Cat was given an initial official rating of 68 following her run at Leicester. She may be able to win off that sort of mark but she hardly looks thrown in considering that her best speed figure to date has been the 42 she clocked at Leicester. Although she finished half a length in front of the 73 rated Caramelita that day the latter appears to have been overrated. The fact that that filly has raced five times but has yet to run in a handicap suggests that her trainer does not feel she is capable of winning a handicap off her current rating. Although Kenyan Cat is better than she has shown and should improve for a step up to one mile there is insufficient evidence to suggest that a mark of 68 is lenient. Furthermore, because she has finished third or fourth on each occasion she has run she has shown a little too much to the Handicapper and is unlikely to be much of a price on her handicap debut.

THE IMPACT OF PACE ON RACES RUN ON A STRAIGHT COURSE

Pace invariably has a say on the outcome of big field handicaps that are run on straight courses and this is particularly true when they are staged at Newbury. I am always interested in the three-year-old handicaps that are staged at the Berkshire course in the first few months of the season because they are full of unexposed types that hail from the top stables and you can guarantee that they will produce plenty of future winners. By correctly assessing the impact that pace has on these races you should be able to identify which of the runners are worth following and which should be avoided.

DUBAI DUTY FREE FINEST SURPRISE HANDICAP							
7f GOOD/SOFT (0-95, 3-Y-O)							
DIST	HORSE	DRAW	EARLY PACE COMMENT	ODDS	OR	TS	No. OF RUNS
-	MAKAAMEN	15	Made all	10/1	90	80	2
1¼	WANNABE KING	4	Mid-division	10/1	84	71	2
nk	FAREER	3	Chased leaders	10/1	87	73	3
½	FELDAY	13	In touch	11/2	84	69	4
1	TRUISM	7	In touch	11/1	83	65	2

shd	BRIEF ENCOUNTER	6	In touch	14/1	83	65	3
1	KEY SIGNATURE	8	Mid-division	16/1	83	62	5
3¼	DALRADIAN	9	In rear	20/1	81	51	5
¾	CLOUDY START	1	Chased leaders	11/2	88	56	4
2¼	INDIAN ART	5	Chased leaders	25/1	88	49	8
1¼	BABYCAT	14	With leader 1f	40/1	90	48	5
1½	SAUCY BROWN	12	Rear	18/1	94	47	7
nse	NOVERRE TO GO	11	Chased leaders	11/2	89	42	6
nk	SILVER GAMES	16	Rear	33/1	89	41	5
6	TIMETEAM	2	Rear	25/1	88	23	12
2¼	DADDY'S GIFT	10	Rear	16/1	89	17	13

The above handicap was staged on 17 April 2009 and it featured a good number of lightly raced runners from the top yards. You can see from the right hand column that the race was dominated by the unexposed horses and those that had had six or more runs were uncompetitive. Basically, the more runs that a horse has the more exposed it becomes and the more likely it is that the Handicapper will have accurately assessed its ability. A horse that has been accurately assessed is invariably vulnerable to horses that have had four or less runs because the chances are that at least one of them will have been underrated by the Handicapper and will simply be too good for it.

As is usual when a race is full of unexposed types that are yet to form established running styles the speed point chart was unlikely to be particularly useful. The chart below shows that there was no established front runner in the race and that the pace was spread evenly across the width of the course.

STALL	16	15	14	13	12	11	10	9	8	7	6	5	4	3	2	1
POINTS	0	4	2	1	1	6	1	0	2	0	0	3	6	2	0	4
		Won														

It was Makaamen from stall fifteen who took the early lead and proceeded to make all. He was half-heartedly pressed for the lead by Babycat who exited from stall fourteen but the early pace was not strong as the *Racing Post* analyst highlighted: 'This looked a quality handicap beforehand, but it was ruined to an extent by a very moderate early pace which didn't quicken noticeably until approaching the last quarter mile. As a result of the slow tempo, several of these were inclined to take a pull, especially Saucy Brown, Noverre To Go and Indian Art. The field raced in a bunch straight down the middle of the track. When there is such a slow gallop on, the best place to be is usually at the front and in the case of Makaamen that was certainly true.'

The lack of early pace meant that those horses that were held up in mid-division or behind were disadvantaged. The front runner was able to stay on strongly towards the finish having conserved valuable energy in the first part of the race and it was unlikely that anything would be able to come from the mid-division or behind to win unless it was ahead of the Handicapper. Because the horses that set the early pace were drawn high those drawn low were at a disadvantage, although the impact of the bias would have been more significant if the early pace had been stronger.

Over the last five years there have been twenty handicap races with between fifteen and sixteen horses run over seven or eight furlongs at Newbury and the results confirm how hard it is for a horse to win if it is drawn well away from the early leader. Thirteen of the twenty winners either made all (only one made all) or were drawn within three stalls either side of the initial leader and that equates to an impact value of 1.44. In other words they won forty-four per cent more often than they should have. Furthermore, there were forty-seven handicaps of fifteen or more runners that were contested over the same course and distances in the last five years and the results prove that any horse drawn more than eight stalls away from the initial leader is seriously disadvantaged. Out of a total of 850 runners 266 were drawn more than eight stalls away from the leader (31%) but they accounted for only six of the forty-seven winners (12.7%). That equates to an impact value of 0.4, or put another way they win sixty per cent less often than they should.

Newbury is far from atypical in this respect because similar impact values apply at the other wide galloping flat tracks where the draw bias is transient and usually insignificant. At Redcar for example, in all handicaps run over the straight course with seventeen or more runners, the impact values relating to the winner being drawn within three stalls either side of the initial leader are 1.4 in races over seven and eight furlongs and 1.5 in races over five and six furlongs. A total of 1,222 February 2009 runners competed in these races of which 378 (31%) were drawn more than eight stalls away from the initial leader. Those 378 runners accounted for twelve of the sixty-four winners (18.7%) and that equates to an impact value of 0.6. These significant biases are stronger than the majority of the draw biases you will find detailed in an appendix to this book. Importantly, they are not widely understood by the betting public and that fact alone makes this information worth knowing. In his book *Enemy Number One* professional gambler Patrick Veitch emphasized that it is this sort of information that punters should aim to exploit: 'By realising that you are seeking to back a horse with underestimated factors and bet against a horse with overestimated factors you will start to acquire the right mindset.'

The two horses that had performed well against the underestimated Newbury pace biases were the seasonal debutantes Wannabe King and Fareer, particularly the former who displayed good speed in the closing stages to come from an unpromising position to narrow the gap behind the winner to just over a length. He was a relatively late foal having been born on the 11th of April and had had just two previous runs. He probably had more maturing to do than many of his contemporaries and was clearly a colt with potential, particularly as he was likely to improve for what was his first run of the season. I concluded that he was well ahead of the Handicapper.

Fareer was also of interest. He had only run three times but was already a winner having won a two-year-old maiden on fast ground at Doncaster over six furlongs. Like Wannabe King he was also a late foal (he was born on the 29th of April), so the likelihood was that he had further improvement in him, particularly as the Newbury race was his seasonal reappearance. Although his performance in the Newbury race had not been as eye-catching as Wannabe King's the likelihood was that he was better on faster ground and it was interesting that Richard Hills had elected to ride him rather than Hamdan Al Maktoum's other runner – the winner Makaamen. Although jockeys do often choose the wrong horse to ride, the possibility existed that Fareer was the better horse but had not been able to show it due to a combination of the good to soft ground, a lack of fitness and the way in which the race unfolded.

Makaamen was the sort of horse that I am happy to oppose the next time they run. Although he won readily enough, he enjoyed the run of the race out in front and was almost certainly flattered by the result. Although he had scope for further improvement, having only raced three times, I felt that he might struggle to overcome the five pound rise that he was subsequently allotted by the Handicapper. He had been foaled on the 25th of January and had benefitted from being physically more mature than most of his rivals in the Newbury race. Furthermore, I suspected that Barry Hills did not hold Makaamen in particularly high regard because he had not given the colt any big race entries and his comment after his charge had won a Doncaster maiden on its second start was the less than bullish: 'I haven't any particular race in mind for him, we'll see how the Handicapper treats him.' The evidence suggested that Hills saw Makaamen as no more than a handicapper and the fact that the colt drifted in the betting from 15/2 to 10/1 on his handicap debut at Newbury indicated that connections did not believe he was particularly well treated on an opening official rating of 90.

Makaamen's next race came in a seven furlong handicap at Haydock on 23 May 2009, run on heavy ground. He was sent off the 5/2 favourite that day but was well beaten after taking a keen hold in response to his rider's attempt to restrain him in the early stages. Although comparisons between the Haydock race and the Newbury one are fairly pointless on account of the heavy ground, it was no surprise to me that Wannabe King (who re-opposed on three pounds better terms) was able to turn the form around with Makaamen by a total of seven lengths, despite having been badly drawn in relation to his rival. After his disappointing performance at Haydock, Makaamen was subsequently gelded. Although this operation can sometimes help a horse by improving its temperament it is important to understand that it also signals that the trainer considers it to be short of top class. If a trainer believes that a colt is potentially capable of winning a Listed or Group race he or she is unlikely to recommend that it should be gelded because it may acquire some stud value in due course. Makaamen did not run again until 10 October 2009 when he once again performed poorly, finishing a well-beaten twelfth after going too fast too early in what was a strongly run contest.

Wannabe King was presumably held in high regard by his connections because he held an entry for the Irish 2000 Guineas. Whilst that was probably too ambitious his Newbury performance suggested he was better than his official rating of 84 – although it was likely that he would probably need fast ground to prove the point. I backed him on his next start which came in an eight furlong Windsor handicap on good to firm ground. Although he did not have the best of draws from stall five I was prepared to overlook that slight negative because I felt that he was well enough handicapped to overcome the bias. He was supported from 5/1 into 4/1 but finished a disappointing sixth after not getting the run of the race. Any chance he had effectively disappeared when his jockey elected to steady him and take him back towards the rear after two furlongs, having raced prominently to that point. The first three to finish were all drawn high and they raced prominently throughout. Wannabe King was asked for an effort two furlongs from home but he had been set too much to do and never looked like getting back into contention.

I did not support him on his next two starts because they came on heavy and soft ground and I felt he would be unsuited by the conditions. Despite my reservations he ran with credit (finishing fourth on both occasions), particularly as he had been poorly drawn in one race and had had no chance in the other due to having been held up in a slowly run affair that was dominated by those that raced prominently.

The ground was good to firm for his next run which came on 29 July 2009 at Redcar and I backed him at 6/1. There were only six other runners and I considered that those odds were far too generous. Unfortunately, Wannabe King let me down once again by finishing second. Although I was disappointed by his defeat I had no cause to alter my view that he was well-handicapped because once again he did not enjoy the run of the race. I had not anticipated that he would take the early lead for over a furlong at Redcar (before racing prominently throughout) and I felt that the change in tactics backfired. In my opinion he had seen too much daylight too early and as a result he had not finished the race as strongly as he otherwise would have. Nevertheless, he had probably been beaten by a decent horse and the fact that the field was strung out like washing behind him did nothing to dissuade me from my belief that he was on a favourable handicap mark.

Although my patience was wearing thin with the colt I decided to persevere with him when he next ran in a Windsor handicap on 10 August 2009. On this occasion he had been fitted with first-time cheekpieces (which I hoped would sharpen him up) and he had the decent draw of stall ten of ten. With the ground again riding fast, conditions were in his favour and I was happy that he represented value at 4/1. For once he enjoyed the run of the race. He tracked the pace on the inside from his high draw and travelled conspicuously well throughout. When he was asked for his effort he quickly asserted and put the race beyond doubt before sauntering home three lengths ahead of the second.

I backed him again when he reappeared ten days later at Epsom. For the second successive time he was well drawn having been allotted stall one on this turning left-handed track and I felt that a six pound rise in his rating was unlikely to stop him now that he had returned to winning ways. I was happy to take odds of 7/2 because everything was in his favour. He once again enjoyed the run of the race on the inside and when a gap opened in the final furlong he only had to be shaken up to win with more ease than the half-length winning margin suggested.

Although he was raised a lenient looking three pounds for that victory I declined to back him on his next outing which came in an eight furlong handicap at Ripon on 31 August 2009. I took the view that the good ground there was not as fast as Wannabe King liked and he also had a bad draw in stall six of sixteen. A check of past results revealed that no horse had won an eight furlong handicap in the last five years when positioned eleven or more stalls away from the inside rail. Furthermore, Ripon's round course heavily favours horses that race prominently (mainly because it is vital to race next to the inside rail up the home straight) and I anticipated that Wannabe King would not only get behind in the early stages as a consequence of his wide draw but would also lose ground on the turn. I envisaged that he would then be disadvantaged by having to make his challenge towards the outside in the straight. I considered that 6/1 overestimated his winning chance and I decided to sit the race out. I was left to rue that decision because Wannabe King won with consummate ease! He was always travelling well and showed a bright turn of foot to close on the clear leader in the straight before going on to win by three lengths. He recorded a speed figure of 100 at Ripon and finished the season officially rated 103 – nineteen pounds higher than the mark he had run off at Newbury on 17 April 2009. He had one more run which came in the Cambridgeshire on 3 October 2009 but although he was well supported from 11/1 into 8/1 to win this annual thirty-two runner cavalry charge, he failed to see out the stiff nine furlongs and weakened one out. Notwithstanding that performance I was encouraged enough by the way that he easily overcame the strong Ripon draw bias on 31 August 2009 to believe that he has the potential to win some decent races next season, particularly if he strengthens up over the winter.

I did not have to wait long to benefit from placing Fareer on my list of horses to follow after the Newbury race. He reappeared on 7 May 2009 in a Chester handicap run over seven and a half furlongs on good to firm ground. He was likely to prove better suited to the underfoot conditions than he had been at Newbury and he had a decent draw in stall three so I decided to back him at 4/1. He was held up early, but fortunately the pace was strong and when he was switched to the outside entering the straight he came with a storming run to win with authority by over a length, despite drifting over towards the inside rail.

I declined to back him next time he ran because the going was heavy for the Betfred Silver Bowl at Haydock and I was confident that he would be unsuited to it. He ran well enough under the circumstances to finish fifth of fifteen, particularly as he met with interference during the race. Although I got that decision right I unfortunately also declined to back him on his only other outing of the season when he contested the Britannia Handicap at Royal Ascot run on good to firm ground. He was drawn in stall fifteen of thirty and I thought that he would struggle to win from there because in the equivalent race for older horses the previous day (the Royal Hunt Cup) the first three to finish had been drawn one, five and four. In the event Richard Hills restrained Fareer after the start and then switched him over to the stands' side. Despite losing ground as a result of that manoeuvre it worked in Fareer's favour because he benefitted from being held up in what was a strongly run race. As the front runners tired he cut through the pack and managed to prevail by a head in a driving finish to land odds of 20/1, having been as big as 33/1 at one stage. Needless to say I was gutted to have missed out on such a big priced winner but it will not be the last time that my reverence for draw bias proves to be detrimental rather than an advantage! Fareer clocked a speed figure of 97 that day and ended the season officially rated 100 – thirteen pounds higher than he had been at Newbury on 17 April 2009.

The only other horse that I decided to follow from the Newbury race was Cloudy Start. He had already come to my attention when he was given an official rating of 88 after clocking a speed figure of 91 in a Redcar maiden on his final start as a two-year-old. Although he appeared to be potentially well-handicapped on that evidence I had no interest in backing him at Newbury on his seasonal debut on account of the fact that he was starting on the wide outside from stall one. Over the last five seasons only 4.5% of runners that have exited from stall one in seven and eight furlong handicaps run on Newbury's straight course have managed to win. This compares poorly to the strike rates of stalls numbered two to four, which are 9.9%, 11.8% and 9% respectively. This often overlooked bias is found on most other straight courses and has nothing to do with the ground that the horses exiting from stall one race on. At Newbury the stalls are invariably positioned against the stands' rail with the highest numbered berth sited next to it and this means that the position of stall one on the track changes significantly in line with the number of runners. I believe stall one fares badly because horses racing on the wide outside see too much daylight. Furthermore, the early pace invariably develops away from them and they find themselves at the bottom edge of the arrow head formation that routinely takes shape in these races.

Any horse that overcomes this Newbury bias is likely to be well-handicapped. Only three horses have managed to do it in the last five years and they were Rydal Mount, Folly Lodge and Quintrell. Rydal Lodge went on to win again two races later off a ten pound higher mark so had obviously been well treated when winning at Newbury. The rider of Folly Lodge overcame the bias by immediately switching his mount right across to the stands' rail after the start and Quintrell was a filly that hated to be crowded and actually needed to race away from her rivals in order to produce her best form. From stall one she was able to race in splendid isolation and as such it was the perfect stall for her to start from. Cloudy Start finished ninth but I knew that his poor showing could be ignored, particularly as it was his seasonal debut, and the next time he ran in a handicap he won at 10/1.

As a footnote to the Newbury race it is worth mentioning that ten of the sixteen horses who took part went on to win later in the season and between them they won fifteen races. The three runners that I put on my list of horses to follow won seven of the fifteen. It is always worth paying particular attention to the result of any competitive early season three-year-old handicap run at one of the grade one tracks because they invariably contain unexposed types that go on to win plenty of races and a good proportion of the better handicaps.

PACE AND THE DRAW

Where a strong draw bias exists on a straight course do not expect the location of the early leader in the starting stalls to make a significant difference to how the race unfolds. For example, in five furlong handicaps of fourteen runners or less run at Thirsk, you can be pretty sure that the early leader will move across to the favoured stands' rail irrespective of its position in the starting stalls and as a consequence the traditional bias in favour of the high numbers is invariably reinforced by the fact that the early leader will either already be drawn high, or will tack across soon after the start to tow the high numbers along. Those runners drawn out wide that lack the speed to get to the stands' rail, but nevertheless race middle to stands' side, find themselves racing on the slower ground and away from the pace and as a consequence they struggle to make an impact. Any horse that is able to win under such circumstances is likely to be ahead of the Handicapper. In fact, in the last five years, only Westbrook Blue has managed to win when racing middle to stands' side after exiting from one of the lowest four stalls. He proved that he had been well-handicapped by going on to win his next race by two lengths off an eleven pound higher mark (at the generous odds of 15/2). The other low drawn winners during this period overcame the bias by crossing to the far rail and most of them 'made all'.

The location of the early pace can be important in sprint races at Thirsk (and at other tracks where racing next to either rail on the straight course is an advantage) but only on those occasions when field sizes are large enough that the runners extend from one side of the course to the other. In these circumstances the field often splits into two groups with one racing against the far rail and the other racing against the stands' rail. If the ground is similar next to either rail the winning group will more often than not be the one that is taken along at the fastest pace in the early stages by its leader. However, if the ground next to one of the rails is significantly faster than the ground next to the other rail the location of the early pace is unlikely to have a bearing on the result and the horses racing on the better ground will usually dominate the finish.

The table below demonstrates the relationship that often exists between a horse's draw, the early position that it assumes in a race and the impact that that position has on its chance of winning. The stalls closest to the inside running rail are usually a significant advantage to front-runners where there is only a short distance to the first turn and this is certainly the case in six furlong races at Catterick. Not only do the front-runners benefit from taking the shortest route home, but they are more likely to find themselves enjoying an uncontested lead when they exit the turn into the home straight. Any horse that attempts to press a well drawn front runner on the outside inevitably has further to travel round the bend than its well drawn rival and more often than not it will fall a little way behind it by the time they exit the turn. As a result the front-runner may then benefit from an uncontested lead for much of its run up the home straight. This is particularly significant at Catterick because the fastest strip of ground is usually against the inside rail and in order to get past the front-runner any challenger has to switch out on to the slower ground.

PACE AND THE DRAW IN 6f RACES AT CATTERICK
(ON GOOD OR GOOD/FIRM GOING)

STALL	RUNNERS THAT WERE HELD UP IN MID-DIVISION OR BEHIND % OF RUNNERS THAT ARE HELD UP	WIN RATIOS		STALL	RUNNERS THAT CHASED THE LEADERS % OF RUNNERS THAT CHASE THE LEADERS	WIN RATIOS		STALL	RUNNERS THAT LED OR RACED PROMINENTLY % OF RUNNERS THAT RACE UP WITH THE PACE	WIN RATIOS	
1	34	0.0		1	48	2.7		1	18	1.8	
2	40	0.0		2	32	1.0		2	28	3.5	
3	44	1.5	0.5	3	36	0.0	2.0	3	20	0.0	2.1
4	32	1.0		4	44	2.9		4	24	1.5	
5	47	0.0		5	33	2.9		5	20	3.4	
6	48	0.0		6	33	0.0		6	19	0.0	
7	34	1.0		7	46	2.1		7	20	0.0	
8	39	0.8	0.4	8	26	0.0	0.9	8	35	1.8	
9	32	0.0		9	36	0.0		9	32	0.0	
10	50	0.0		10	21	2.3		10	29	0.0	0.6
11	47	1.4		11	32	0.0		11	21	3.1	
12	46	0.0	0.6	12	23	0.0	0.9	12	31	0.0	
13	55	0.0		13	45	0.0		13	0	NQ	
14	60	0.0		14	40	4.0		14	0	NQ	

Where there is a short run to the first bend horses that usually lead or race prominently are at a big disadvantage if they are drawn towards the outside. Ideally a front-runner needs to lead without going flat out, but in order to get to the front before the bend from a high draw they invariably go too fast too early. This early exertion inevitably affects their ability to finish a race strongly and only front-runners of extra quality and stamina can overcome such a disadvantage.

Front-runners are usually prisoners to their running style and most jockeys make a frantic bid to get over to the inside rail before the turn. You can see that the percentage of horses that lead or race prominently from each stall goes up significantly the wider out that they are drawn. In fact many of the runners that would usually chase the leaders in the early stages either race more prominently than they normally would, or are taken back towards the rear of the field. The figures prove that such tactics are self-defeating because the winning record of poorly drawn prominent runners is less than half as good as those drawn low.

The table also highlights the problems faced by horses that are drawn in the lowest two stalls and are held up. The efforts of the jockeys drawn out wide to improve their positions before the first turn leads to a scramble for the inside rail and this invariably causes scrimmaging. In the battle for the best early positions it is the horses on the inside that get barged against the inanimate running rail and then find themselves shuffled right back to the rear of the field. Once they get behind they struggle to get back into the race at this speed favouring track.

The combination of a speed favouring track and a short run to the bend means that it is the well drawn horses that either race prominently or chase the leaders that do best with win ratios of 2.1 and 2.0 respectively. Which of the two groups prevails is normally decided by the strength of the early pace. If several horses vie for the lead the pace is likely to be unsustainable and they usually weaken quickly in the final couple of furlongs. In these circumstances it is the horses that sit in behind the leaders near to the inside rail that have the box seats. They conserve energy in the early stages by saving ground on the bend and by not engaging in the fight for the lead and that allows them to come through and pass the weakening leaders with ease in the closing stages. Any horse that wins in this manner is likely to have been flattered and its performance should be downgraded.

The table below shows how the dynamics change in handicap races run over seven furlongs at Catterick:

PACE AND THE DRAW IN 7f RACES AT CATTERICK
(ON GOOD OR GOOD/FIRM GOING)

RUNNERS THAT WERE HELD UP IN MID-DIVISION OR BEHIND				RUNNERS THAT CHASED THE LEADERS				RUNNERS THAT LED OR RACED PROMINENTLY			
STALL	% OF RUNNERS THAT ARE HELD UP	WIN RATIOS		STALL	% OF RUNNERS THAT CHASE THE LEADERS	WIN RATIOS		STALL	% OF RUNNERS THAT RACE UP WITH THE PACE	WIN RATIOS	
1	24	1.7		1	47	0.9		1	29	2.2	
2	38	1.1		2	33	1.9		2	29	2.9	
3	40	0.0	0.8	3	37	0.6	0.7	3	23	1.8	1.6
4	41	1.0		4	39	0.0		4	20	1.0	
5	47	0.5		5	25	0.0		5	28	0.0	
6	42	1.5		6	36	2.9		6	22	1.0	
7	52	1.3		7	22	1.0		7	26	2.7	

8	38	0.0	**0.9**	8	32	1.4	**1.4**	8	30	1.5	**1.6**
9	55	0.4		9	26	0.9		9	19	1.2	
10	49	1.0		10	35	0.0		10	16	1.6	
11	66	1.2		11	17	1.5		11	17	1.5	
12	45	0.7		12	30	2.1		12	25	0.0	
13	59	0.7	**0.7**	13	28	0.0	**1.6**	13	13	6.0	**1.7**
14	75	0.5		14	19	4.1		14	6	0.0	
15	68	0.0		15	12	0.0		15	20	2.5	
16	86	0.0		16	14	0.0		16	0	0.0	
17	89	0.0	**0.0**	17	11	0.0	**0.0**	17	0	0.0	**0.0**
18	25	0.0		18	25	0.0		18	50	0.0	

The additional furlong before the bend significantly alters which draws and which running styles are favoured. There is no longer a frantic contest for the early lead and those drawn higher than stall five are more likely to be able to either lead or race prominently without having to be hustled into using too much energy too early. The impact that this has is remarkable and you can see that the horses that race prominently after breaking from stalls one to fifteen have a very similar strike rate.

The extra distance of the race places more emphasis on stamina and the horses that are held up have a better record than they do over six furlongs. When the early pace is too strong it is the horses held up towards the rear that usually come through in the closing stages, whereas in six furlong contests it is those that chase the leaders that benefit the most. Without the rush for positions before the first bend there is less early scrimmaging in seven furlong races and those drawn in the lowest two stalls that are held up fare much better. They do not get so far behind early on and the extra distance means that they have a better chance of picking up the leaders in the home straight. Remarkably, their win ratios improve from **0.0** and **0.0** to **1.7** and **1.1**. These biases are replicated at most other tracks with similar configurations and it is important to understand the impact that they have on results.

It is also important to recognize that many of our tracks suit one particular running style more than others and when you look at past results you should look out for horses that have bucked a track bias, particularly if they overcame a disadvantageous pace at the same time. For example, I consider Ripon to be the track that most favours front runners and if I see that a horse has come from behind to win there I give it extra credit and if the pace of the race was slow I will be particularly interested in the horse in question because to overcome two biases it would probably have had to be well-handicapped. Likewise, if a horse wins from the front at Newbury and the race was run at a strong pace it will have overcome two biases and is likely to be better than the bare form. The table below shows which courses favour early speed in races of up to eight furlongs and they are listed in order from Ripon down to Newbury.

FAVOUR SPEED	AVERAGE	DO NOT FAVOUR SPEED
RIPON	AYR	LEICESTER
FOLKESTONE	SANDOWN	BEVERLEY
WARWICK	NEWMARKET (ROWLEY)	CARLISLE
HAMILTON	THIRSK	DONCASTER
CHEPSTOW	REDCAR	SALISBURY
CHESTER	NEWMARKET (JULY)	YARMOUTH
CATTERICK	GOODWOOD	YORK
EPSOM	NOTTINGHAM	PONTEFRACT
LINGFIELD (TURF)	WINDSOR	BATH
NEWCASTLE	HAYDOCK	ASCOT
MUSSELBURGH	BRIGHTON	NEWBURY

Chapter Four

Utilizing the Effect of the Draw

Prior to watching the attheraces coverage from Lingfield on the afternoon of 15 September 2009 I had no intention of placing a bet in the Felbridge Nursery Handicap. However, after witnessing the preceding EBF Maiden Stakes for two-year-old maidens I began analysing the race afresh.

DIST	HORSE	DRAW	COMMENT	SP	TS	OR
–	MAGICIAN'S CAPE	11	Raced against near side rail	9/1	65	79
¾	SWIFT RETURN	10	Raced against near side rail	4/1	63	73
1	ANOTHER MAGIC MAN	9	Raced one off near side rail	25/1	60	71
1½	SANTA MARGHERITA	8	Raced against near side rail	66/1	51	62
3	HALYARD	6	Raced towards outer	4/1	48	59
1¼	AGENT ARCHIE	4	Tracked leaders on outer	25/1	45	56
hd	AL DAFA	5	Soon led group that raced wide	10/11	44	56
¾	ELTHEEB	2	In rear of group that raced wide	16/1	42	54
½	SPRING HEATHER	7	Raced towards near side	16/1	36	48
2	GRAND MARY	1	In rear of group that raced wide	25/1	31	43
7	SEFTON PARK	3	With leaders out wide	66/1	16	30

EBF MAIDEN STAKES
7f (GOOD TO SOFT)

The above result seemed to prove that a strong bias in favour of the horses that raced hard up against the stands' side rail was in play. As you can see the three horses that raced next to it finished first at 9/1, second at 4/1 and fourth at 66/1. Furthermore, the third horse raced one off the near side rail and ran better than his odds of 25/1 suggested he would. Significantly, the well backed 10/11 favourite Al Dafa finished well beaten after leading a group of runners that raced wide throughout. The group that raced wide finished over six lengths behind the winner and in view of the fact that it contained the favourite and one of the joint second favourites I concluded that there was a significant bias at work.

I was pleased to discover that three of the four highest drawn runners in the following Felbridge Nursery Handicap were outsiders in the betting because as long as they raced next to the favoured stands' rail there was every chance that these relatively unexposed two-year-olds would finish close up, irrespective of their odds. I decided that I would combine the four highest drawn in a combination forecast and I subsequently backed Dragonessa to win at 12/1 and Lairy to win at 16/1 after there was an avalanche of money for the pair of them. Clearly, I was not alone in having spotted the bias and unfortunately by the time the race started their odds had contracted to 10/1 and 9/1 respectively, shredding my potential big forecast payout in the process!

FELBRIDGE NURSERY HANDICAP
6f (GOOD TO SOFT)

DIST	HORSE	DRAW	COMMENT	SP	TS	OR
-	DRAGONESSA	10	Raced just off near rail	10/1	51	52
¾	LAIRY	12	Raced against near side rail	9/1	42	45
½	BELL'S OCEAN	2	Raced widest of all	6/1	64	68
½	CHANDRAYAAN	11	Raced towards near side	5/1	56	62
1¾	SILVEE	13	Raced against near side rail	20/1	35	46
1¾	DO MORE BUSINESS	5	Raced towards outer	15/2	49	66
nk	KAPELAD JUNIOR	6	Raced towards outer	13/2	45	63
1½	WING OF FAITH	7	Raced just off near rail	4/1	37	59
nse	MRS PUFF	8	Raced towards outer	16/1	30	52
5	SUPER DUPLEX	9	Raced against near side rail	20/1	30	68
4½	EVERGREEN DANCER	4	Raced towards outer	12/1	4	57
12	ARKELLION	3	Raced towards outer	16/1	-	56

The race unfolded as I had hoped with my selections either racing next to, or one off the rail. Thankfully the jockeys on most of their rivals did not seem to have taken the previous result on board and several of them were happy to race towards the middle of the track rather than attempting to tack over to the rail and cause crowding in the process. As a consequence my selections enjoyed the run of the race and although Bell's Ocean did his best to spoil things by running an excellent race to finish third, (despite racing widest of all throughout) a positive result never looked in danger. The forecast paid 101/1 (just over 8/1 for each unit of my stake) but may have paid over 400/1 if the odds of the first two had remained at the opening show of 16/1 and 25/1.

The following race was an apprentice handicap over six furlongs. Once again I had had no intention of getting involved in it but, buoyed by my earlier success, I decided to look at it again. The opening odds about the three highest drawn in this nine runner contest were 3/1, 6/1 and 16/1. Try as I might I could not bring myself to back the 16/1 shot Pocket's Pick who was still a maiden after fifteen runs and was clearly regressing badly despite the recent application of various forms of headgear. His official rating had dropped steadily down from an opening 83 to 65, but his last three speed figures had shown a similar pattern, deteriorating from 54 to 45 to 33, suggesting that he was unlikely to be competitive off a revised mark of 65. In the end I decided that I would simply back the in-form Merry Diva who had the best draw of all. Amazingly, the race was won by Simple Rhythm who broke from stall two and proceeded to make all down the centre of the track! She finished a head in front of Reject and a further three quarters of a length in front of the unfortunate Merry Diva, both of whom raced hard up against the stands' rail. The *Racing Post* analyst reported that: 'Merry Diva ... had to squeeze between Riflessione and the stands' rail over a furlong from home and, considering how close she got once through it, she would have gone very close to winning with a clear run.'

On the evidence of the day's racing Simple Rhythm had performed a minor miracle to win a handicap by bucking a huge bias the way she had and it was clear to me that she must have been a well-handicapped horse. However, my assumption was not immediately confirmed by an examination of her record which showed that she was relatively exposed, having had twenty-one races up to that point. Nevertheless, there were several clues that suggested that her mark of 64 was potentially lenient. She had at one point been rated as high as 79, but of more significance was her record on soft ground. Apart from her debut (when she was probably not ready to win) she had encountered soft ground on only one other occasion and had won. Furthermore, she had also had one outing on Southwell's Fibresand surface (which is considered to equate to soft ground) and had won on that occasion too. Clearly, she was a different filly when there was give underfoot and this was proved beyond doubt by her performance in the Lingfield race. I added her to my list of horses to follow and I could not wait to back her when she next encountered a soft surface.

Her next start was in a Kempton (AW) claimer but I was prepared to let her go unbacked because in my opinion Polytrack equates to a fast surface on the turf. Thankfully she finished well beaten. On 28 September 2009 she ran in a Brighton handicap but once again I declined to back her because I thought that the good to firm ground was sure to be against her. I was stunned when she won the race readily having been sent off at odds of 8/1. Following that victory her rating was raised to 71, but I felt that she could win off that mark as long as she had soft ground.

Just over a week later she reappeared in an apprentice handicap at Nottingham and thankfully the ground was riding good to soft after an inch of overnight rain. In view of the fact that she was in such good form I could not understand why she was available at 14/1 and I could only presume that most punters considered that she was too high in the ratings. Now that she had the ground she required to reproduce her best form I reckoned she would prove to be well-handicapped and so it turned out. She took the lead over two furlongs out, burst clear in emphatic fashion and despite drifting right across to the far rail she won readily by two lengths. Her victory confirmed that she had had pounds in hands of her rivals when she bucked the strong draw bias at Lingfield on 15 September 2009.

I would not normally entertain backing a horse that has run twenty-four times because invariably they are fully exposed. However, in the case of Simple Rhythm I was prepared to be flexible because all the evidence suggested that she was a different filly when there was some cut in the ground and with a career record of three wins from four on that surface I took the view that her potential on soft ground had not yet been fully revealed.

Having reviewed the results from the straight course at Lingfield on 15 September 2009 I identified a total of eight horses (in addition to Simple Rhythm) that merited further investigation due to the fact that they had been disadvantaged by racing well away from the favoured stands' rail. Whenever, the true merit of a horse's performance has been masked by a bias I am interested in it because it may mean that the Handicapper underestimates it, and it nearly always means that it will be available at bigger odds next time out than it otherwise would have been! If it is an unexposed potential improver then it may be added to my list of horses to keep an eye on. That does not mean that I intend to back it next time it runs. In fact I might not back it at all, or I might subsequently remove it from my list. Much depends on how it is campaigned and how the

Handicapper assesses it. For example, if a horse comes to my attention on its second outing it may cease to be of interest to me if it runs conspicuously well on its third run and as a result is given an opening official rating that I do not consider to be lenient.

Of the eight runners referred to earlier that were disadvantaged by the draw there was a group of four that raced towards the centre of the course in the seven furlong maiden won by Magician's Cape, which I will come to later. The other four were Bell's Ocean, Bawaardi, In The Mood and Black Stocking. Bell's Ocean had now run well despite having been poorly drawn on her last three runs. However, I was not particularly taken with her overall profile because she had already run nine times and was starting to look exposed for a two-year-old. Furthermore, I suspected that she may actually have benefitted from being drawn on the outside on her last three runs. She was a very small looking filly and I reckoned that she was the sort who would have problems whenever she encountered fields of over ten runners and was drawn in the middle, or whenever she was drawn towards the inside on a turning track. Because of her diminutive size she was likely to come off worst in the bumping and barging that inevitably occurs when so many runners are fighting for the shortest route home against the inside rail. I noted that her only victory had come in a five runner contest and there was little doubt in my mind that she needed to have plenty of space around her in order to perform to her best. I therefore decided not to add Bell's Ocean to my list.

The other three had all competed in the same seven furlong maiden race and it was hard to know what to make of the form. Firstly, the time of the race had been moderate with the winner Bawaardi clocking a speed figure of only 51 and secondly, the value of the form was questionable in view of the fact that the poor 48 rated maiden Commandingpresence finished third, ahead of both In The Mood and Black Stocking. However, I considered that the proximity of Commandingpresence could possibly work in their favour because all three of them were now eligible for their first official rating and there was a chance that they might get in lightly if the Handicapper considered that the 48 rated horse had run to form. I was a little disappointed when I discovered that Bawaardi had been rated 73, In The Mood 65 and Black Stocking 55, because I had anticipated ratings that were about five pounds lower. However, I decided that I would place Bawaardi and In The Mood on my list of horses to follow. Both of them had been returning from long absences but still came in for good market support and I reckoned that they were better than they had shown to date. In particular I anticipated further improvement from Bawaardi after I read that he had been gelded since his last run.

I was not so keen on Black Stocking. She had clearly been difficult to train and had not raced as either a two-year-old or as a three-year-old. Such a delay always raises doubts in my mind and furthermore, the evidence suggested that she was probably a one-paced plodder. Last time out she had been described as having 'plugged on' on fast ground (a comment that is excusable on soft ground but not on fast in my opinion) and in the Lingfield race she had 'stayed on steadily' in the final two furlongs. There was a chance that she could improve for a longer trip but I decided that the right thing to do was to have no further interest in her because one-paced plodders do not win many races.

In The Mood was the first to run again. He reappeared in a one mile handicap at Salisbury and given that he had 'plugged on' last time out over seven furlongs on good to soft, I was confident that the extra furlong and stiffer track would suit. As I had anticipated, the merit of his previous performance appeared to have been overlooked and I was more than happy to back him each way at 11/1 even though he could have had a better draw than stall two of eleven. Soon after the start he was quite badly bumped, but from then on he pretty much enjoyed the run of the race. A furlong out he was in the lead and appeared to be going well under Alan Munro but unfortunately he drifted towards the centre of the track together with most of the other runners and the one horse who stuck to the far rail, Dichoh, managed to stay on from an unpromising position to pip him on the line. I concluded that that was probably as good as he was because after a relatively slow early pace he had been ideally placed to take advantage but had failed to deliver. At one stage it looked as if he would be able to accelerate away from the field from his prominent position but his finishing effort ultimately proved to be a bit disappointing and he appeared to be just as one-paced as the 'plugged on' comment had suggested. As there had been no real excuse I decided to remove him from my list as I could no longer argue that he was well-handicapped, particularly as he was raised a pound following that defeat. Furthermore, he was likely to go off at relatively short odds on his next appearance following such a narrow defeat and it was doubtful that he would represent value.

Bawaardi returned to the track on 12 October 2009 when he competed in a seven furlong handicap at Salisbury on soft ground. I had decided to back him but the results of the three preceding races caused me to change my mind. Sometimes when the ground is on the soft side at Salisbury low numbers can hold an advantage and I was therefore not too concerned that Bawaardi was drawn in stall five of sixteen. However, in the preceding three races the first two to finish were drawn 15 and 16 out of 16, 14 and 13 out of 15 and 12 and 8 out of 12. The evidence suggested that there was a strong bias in favour of those that raced against the far rail and under the circumstances it would have been madness to ignore it and to go ahead with my plan to back the gelding. Considering that he was carrying a pound overweight he ran quite pleasingly to finish sixth despite racing well away from the rail and having been held up at the rear in what turned out to be a fairly slowly run affair. To date he has not run again but he remains on my list and I am pretty sure that he can win off his current mark when conditions are in his favour.

Of more interest to me were the group of four that had raced towards the centre of the track in the seven furlong maiden won by Magician's Cape (the result of which has been reproduced above). This group had included the hot favourite, in the shape of Godolphin's Al Dafa, who was sent off at 10/11. I was interested to see that he had been beaten by two horses that had also raced in the centre group and they were Halyard and the previously unraced Agent Archie. Eltheeb was also of interest having finished only three quarters of a length behind the favourite.

I expected the debutant Agent Archie to improve on what he had achieved in the race because John Best's horses usually come on for their first run and when I looked him up in Steve Taplin's book *Two year Olds of 2009* I was intrigued to discover that he had cost $180,000 as a yearling; that his trainer had given him a four star rating (out of a possible five) and had made the following remark: 'Owned by Dave Gorton who did so well with Square Eddie last year. At this stage I would say that he is a better specimen than Square Eddie and that whatever he does he finds easy.' When I looked up Square Eddie on the *Racing Post* website I discovered that he was a Group One winner in America and that he had been rated 116. If the assessment of his trainer was right then Agent Archie had to be worth following, particularly now that the merit of his debut had been masked by the Lingfield draw bias!

I did not have to wait long before my judgement was put to the test because he reappeared eight days later in a nine furlong maiden at Goodwood. He was well drawn in stall nine of ten on what is a turning right-handed track and as he had shown some speed on his debut it was likely that he would make full use of his advantageous draw by racing prominently. There did not appear to be much in the way of opposition and it was a debutant of Richard Hannon's that was sent off as the 3/1 favourite. I was pretty sure that Agent Archie was good enough to win, particularly as he had had the benefit of a previous run and now had a good draw. Under the circumstances I considered that 4/1 was a fair price and so it turned out. Robert Winston bounced him out of the stalls, got across to the inside rail and Agent Archie proceeded to make all to win by one and a half lengths. The Handicapper reacted by allotting him an initial rating of 75 and I suspect that that could prove to be lenient. Agent Archie's sire has a stamina index of 12.1f and his dam's only other offspring won over ten furlongs, so the likelihood is that he will really come into his own once he is stepped up to twelve furlongs and beyond. When that happens I will be staggered if he cannot win off a mark of 75.

Halyard had cost 58,000gns and was another who appeared to be held in some regard by his trainer (Walter Swinburn). A check of his entries revealed that he was thought good enough to be entered for the £250,000 Tattersalls Timeform 3-y-o Trophy, which is a race run over ten furlongs. The stamina indices of his sire and dam sire were 10.4f and 9.6f respectively so it was likely that middle distances next year would be his game. He had had one previous run and had made an eye catching debut at Sandown, making good late headway after losing any chance of winning by starting slowly. Given his profile and the fact that he had won the race that took place down the centre of the track at Lingfield he too had to go on my list of horses to follow. Clearly, much depends on his next outing and how much of his ability is revealed to the Handicapper but I will await the publication of his opening official rating with interest.

Eltheeb was another expensive purchase, having cost 150,000gns, and was also presumably thought to have potential given that he had been entered in both the Derby and the £250,000 Tattersalls Timeform 3-y-o Trophy. However, I was not particularly taken with what he had achieved to date and I concluded that his future would initially lie in modest handicaps once he was allotted an official rating. He had been well beaten by fifteen lengths on his debut and his odds of 50/1 that day suggested that he had not been setting the gallops alight at home. Prior to the Lingfield race he was once again unfancied at 16/1 and to my mind he had all the hallmarks of a horse being prepared for modest handicaps. For that reason I elected not to back him when he ran in another maiden on 7 October 2009. He was once again unfancied at 25/1 and thankfully finished well beaten.

It was then a question of awaiting the Handicapper's assessment of Eltheeb's first three runs. When I saw that he had been rated 60 I felt pretty sure that he had been presented with a winning opportunity. His breeding suggested that he would come into his own once he was stepped up in trip to around nine or ten furlongs and having taken into account his purchase price and his big race entries I felt that he would prove to be better than 60 in due course. His trainer John Dunlop had awarded him three stars in Steve Taplin's book and had described him as being: 'A big, tall colt but a good mover – one for the second half of the season.' This description strongly suggested that the colt would improve with time as he strengthened up and I liked the fact that he was a good mover which is normally a sign of a decent animal.

Having decided to add him to my list of horses to follow at this stage I was left somewhat bemused when I discovered that his next engagement was in a maiden race at Brighton rather than in a handicap! The trip was once again eight furlongs and I felt that Eltheeb would find it an inadequate test of stamina on such a sharp track. I declined to back him at odds of 50/1 as I could not be sure about the level of opposition he was up against. Unfortunately, he ran reasonably well to finish third to an unraced Godolphin horse but he proved that his opening mark of 60 had been lenient by clocking a speed figure of 65. The *Racing Post* analyst reported that: 'Eltheeb kept on gamely under pressure and turned in by far his most encouraging effort so far. He already looks in need of a stiffer test and should build on this.'

I was disappointed that John Dunlop had opted to run his colt in another maiden race. Once you have managed to secure your charge a favourable official rating why risk it in this way? There is always the danger that your well-handicapped horse will finish close up to a decent type and that its official rating will be hoisted in consequence and it was no surprise when Eltheeb's rating was subsequently raised from 60 to 68. Eight pounds is equivalent to four and a half lengths in a race over ten furlongs so there was no doubt that his chance of winning a handicap had been negatively affected. Despite this I opted to keep the colt on my list in the expectation that he would be put away until next season. Hopefully he will be gelded and will strengthen up considerably over the winter and, if so, I feel that he is still capable of winning a handicap or two over middle distances off his revised mark, which is low for a horse with his connections and profile.

The beaten hot favourite Al Dafa was another horse in the race with a Derby entry and clearly has plenty of potential. His finishing position did not reflect his true merit because Dettori did not give him a hard race once it became obvious that the group in the middle had no chance with those next to the stands' rail and I believe that he will develop into a useful sort once he is stepped up in trip. However, I did not put him on my list because I doubt whether he will remain with Godolphin (as he is probably not well enough thought of to warrant another year under their care) and there are too many imponderables surrounding his future at present.

Another good opportunity to exploit a draw bias occurred during Ayr's Gold Cup meeting on 19 September 2009. Over the preceding two days it had become evident that there was a strong bias operating on the straight course in favour of those that raced towards the far side of the track. Things are often not straightforward with respect to the draw at this meeting and in the past the advantage has seemed to switch from the far side to the stands' side from one race to the next and any bias probably had more to do with where the pace setters were situated rather than any difference in how the ground was riding. At this meeting however, the evidence had become overwhelming and all three of the sprint handicaps prior to the Saturday had been won by a low drawn horse. After the first four to finish in the Ayr Silver Cup on the Saturday were drawn 2, 3, 11 and 5 out of twenty-five runners there was no longer any doubt that anything that raced against the unfavoured stands' rail was doomed. I was therefore intrigued to see that in the following Group 3 race for juvenile fillies all of the fancied runners were drawn in high numbered stalls and with the stalls positioned in the centre of the track there was a good chance that the field would split and the fancied runners would elect to race against the stands' rail.

On the form figures, and in a race in which all the contestants were carrying level weights, this looked a formality for Beyond Desire who was officially rated 105, ten pounds ahead of her nearest rivals Conniption and Jeanie Johnston. However, they were drawn in stalls 14, 13 and 11 respectively and one of the 94 rated runners – Hairspray – was drawn in stall 12. The only runner rated within twenty pounds of Beyond Desire drawn low was She's A Character – officially rated 94 and drawn in stall two. However, I was not taken by the form of She's A Character and I suspected that she had been overrated following an impressive debut victory. Although she had been quickly raised in class to Group company following her maiden win at Doncaster she had failed to make any sort of impression and as you can see below her speed figures suggested that she had done nothing to deserve her lofty rating of 94. I noted that she had only been given three stars by her trainer in Steve Taplin's book and the fact that she was available at 33/1 despite being officially the highest rated of the low drawn runners spoke volumes about her chance. I felt sure that she could safely be eliminated from further consideration.

| SHE'S A CHARACTER (R A Fahey) Invincible Spirit (7.6f) – Cavernista (Lion Cavern (7.8f)) OR 94 | | | | | | |
DATE	COURSE/ DISTANCE	RACE TYPE	OUTCOME	SP	OFFICIAL RATING	TOPSPEED
03/09/09	Sal 6Sft	Listed	7th 12L	10/1	97	29
29/07/09	Goo 7Gd	Group 2	6th 5L	16/1	-	70
19/06/09	Asc 6GF	Group 3	4th 6L	11/1	-	64
06/06/09	Don 6GS	Maiden	1st 5L	7/1	-	73

Of the others that were drawn low I dismissed both Catbells, who had had three runs but had only managed a personal best speed figure of 54, and also Eternal Instinct who despite having had nine runs had only managed a moderate personal best speed figure of 75. Of those that were in the bottom half of the draw that left only Astrophysical Jet, Distinctive and Midnight Martini and to my eyes Astrophysical Jet stood out. She had had just the one run but had been pretty impressive when winning a Nottingham maiden by three lengths despite having lost ground at the start and also having been hampered in the early stages. The fact that she had started at odds of 5/1 on her debut for the Ed McMahon stable suggested that she was well thought of and the fact that she was able to record a Topspeed figure of 80 first time out marked her out as being potentially decent.

Distinctive had also shown plenty of promise in her two outings to date. On her debut she had finished a promising third at York after losing any chance of winning by rearing at the start and she followed that by winning 'readily' at Redcar on 29 August 2009. She clocked a modest speed figure of 71 that day but she was open to improvement and the manner of her victory suggested that she was capable of a lot better.

The other contender was Midnight Martini and I found her the hardest to weigh up. She had run five times and had improved each time, culminating with a decent win in the Doncaster Sales race at York, which was worth a massive £147,000 to the winner. However, there was little doubt in my mind that she had had the run of the race on that occasion, having benefitted from racing prominently from a high draw on a day when there had been a strong tail wind in the straight (four of the first five to finish had been prominent in the early stages of the race). My doubts about the merit of the form were supported by the fact that she had clocked a modest speed figure of 76 at York and that her previous best had been 69. I noted that after her previous win at Thirsk in August her trainer Tim Easterby was quoted as saying: 'I think the world of Midnight Martini', but although I have a lot of respect for his opinion I concluded that she was probably not good enough to compete with what I thought were a couple of lightly raced 'improvers' in the shape of Astrophysical Jet and Distinctive. Furthermore, of the three she had the worst of the draw in stall seven so I decided to eliminate her from further consideration.

Having concluded that Astrophysical Jet was the most likely winner I backed her each-way at 12/1 and I also combined her with Distinctive in a reverse forecast. When the race started I was delighted to see that the field split into two with all the fancied runners heading for the stands' rail as I had anticipated. My selections headed for the favoured far rail and it was soon apparent that they were some way ahead of their rivals.

LAUNDRY COTTAGE STUD FIRTH OF CLYDE STAKES
(GROUP 3) 6f GOOD

DIST	HORSE	DRAW	COMMENT	SP	TS	OR
-	DISTINCTIVE	3	Raced far side	33/1	95	80
3¾	MIDNIGHT MARTINI	7	led far side	12/1	83	84
nk	ASTROPHYSICAL JET	1	Raced far side	10/1	83	-
shd	BEYOND DESIRE	14	Led stands side	Evens	82	105
¾	CONNIPTION	13	Raced stands side	7/1	80	95
3¾	CATBELLS	5	Raced far side	40/1	68	-
shd	ETERNAL INSTINCT	4	Raced far side	100/1	68	78
nk	JEANIE JOHNSTON	11	Raced stands side	20/1	67	95
1	SHE'S A CHARACTER	2	Raced far side	33/1	64	94
3½	MUSIC SHOW	10	Raced stands side	5/1	53	89
3¾	CLASSLIN	8	Raced far side	200/1	41	-
3½	AMARY	9	Raced stands side	22/1	29	90
6	HAIRSPRAY	12	Raced stands side	28/1	9	94

When Astrophysical Jet took the lead from Midnight Martini a furlong out I was sure that I would land a major forecast payout because

Distinctive was beginning to finish strongly from the rear and the far side still held a sizeable advantage. Unfortunately, although Distinctive forged clear to win by nearly four lengths at 33/1, Astrophysical Jet suddenly began to tire in the closing stages and the horse that she had seemingly left for dead a furlong out, Midnight Martini, managed to claw her way back into contention and snatch second near the finish. I was thankful that Astrophysical Jet managed to hold on to third place, because the stands' side runners were closing fast in the final stages but I was left to rue what might have been. With the benefit of hindsight perhaps I should have included Midnight Martini in my reverse forecast bet and a win or each-way bet on Distinctive would not have gone amiss! In my experience it is a lot easier to narrow a field down to the genuine contenders than it is to maximise profits by making the right bets and this is still an area that I need to improve upon.

The race provides an excellent illustration of the influence that the draw can have on the outcome of a race. If you ignore the performance of the winner Distinctive and assume that Midnight Martini ran pretty much to her mark of 84, the result suggests that the far rail had an advantage that was equivalent to around twenty pounds. You might think that that sounds far-fetched but this assumption was certainly verified by the result of the preceding Ayr Silver Cup handicap in which the stands' side runners finished nearly six lengths behind those that raced on the far side. Working to three pounds per length, six lengths equates to nearly eighteen pounds.

Obviously it is extremely difficult for a badly drawn runner to overcome such a bias and this is particularly true in handicap races because the levelling effect of weight usually ensures that none of the runners has enough in hand over its rivals to overcome a disadvantage equating to eighteen pounds. Exposed horses have no chance of overcoming a strong bias but, from time to time, you will encounter a lightly raced 'improver' that has been thrown into a handicap with a very lenient official rating that does have that sort of amount in hand, but they are few and far between. In non-handicap races things are often not so straightforward, because whenever there are lightly-raced and unexposed types in a race it is difficult to predict just how much improvement they are open to. Without the levelling effect of weight one or two of them might have enough in hand to buck the bias.

Of course most draw biases are fairly insignificant in comparison to the one at Ayr and are easier to overcome. It is a good idea to try and form an opinion about the strength of a draw bias and how its strength might be expressed in terms of pounds and lengths. If I have identified a well-handicapped horse that is poorly drawn I have to consider whether it has enough in hand to be able to overcome the bias. Not so long ago I would have put a line through any horse that was badly drawn but I now recognize that there is a trade off to be had in respect of the draw and the odds that are available about a horse because the new generation of punters are happy to oppose anything that is badly drawn. If I believe that my selection has enough in hand to overcome a well established draw bias I will consider backing it if I believe that I am receiving significantly better odds about my selection than would have been the case if it had been better drawn.

Where a strong bias has been in evidence it is always worth taking a look at the runners that were badly drawn to see whether any of them might be worth following. I was particularly interested in the result of the two-year-old contest won by Distinctive because it featured several lightly raced types that were likely to be progressive. Of those that had been badly drawn the one that really caught my eye was Conniption. This filly had already come to my attention on her debut when she won most impressively at Newbury. That day, despite having been slowly into stride and looking a little green she had quickened in fine style over a furlong from home and won easing down by four and a half lengths. Two things marked that performance out as being special. Firstly, she had recorded a Topspeed figure of 90 which is a figure seldom achieved by any horse on its debut. Secondly, despite her inexperience she had managed to quicken off a strong pace and that is normally the mark of a serious horse. However, I am always suspicious of high speed figures that are recorded on soft or heavy ground so I decided that I would reserve judgement before concluding that she was a star in the making. On the plus side there was no doubt that she was she well bred having cost her connections 225,000gns and her trainer Brian Meehan clearly held her in high regard having described her as 'a lovely filly'.

CONNIPTION (B J Meehan) Danehill Dancer (8.0f) – Showbiz (Sadler's Wells (11.3f)) **OR 94**							
DATE	COURSE/DISTANCE	RACE TYPE	OUTCOME		SP	OR	TS
30/10/09	Nmk 6Gd	Listed	4th	3L	4/1	95	72
19/09/09	Ayr 6Gd	Group 3	5th	5L	7/1	95	80
03/09/09	Sal 6Sft	Listed	5th	3L	15/8	-	61
17/07/09	Nby 6Sft	Maiden	1st	4½L	12/1	-	90

At the time of writing her career record is as above. On the evidence of her breeding it is likely that she will need at least one mile to be seen at her best and being out of a Sadler's Wells mare she should appreciate some cut in the ground, as her opening victory seemed to confirm. I have no doubt that she appreciated the extra test of stamina provided by the soft going at Newbury and that she found six furlongs on good ground too sharp on her last two runs.

On her second start she encountered soft ground at Salisbury so had no excuses on account of the underfoot conditions. However, she was the most inexperienced of the contestants that day and that proved to be her downfall. After initially pulling hard in a slowly run race she then veered across to the far rail when asked for an effort and effectively threw the race away. Just prior to veering to her right she had looked the likely winner and there was no doubt that she was better than the basic result suggested.

Considering that Ayr's sharp six furlongs on good ground was never going to play to her strengths on 19 Spetember 2009 she performed with credit against the huge draw bias there. She managed to finish less than a length behind the 105 rated Beyond Desire and four lengths ahead of the next finisher on the stands' rail – the 95 rated Jeanie Johnston. The stands' side form suggested that Conniption should be rated 103 or higher, rather than 95 and given that she had achieved a speed figure of 90 on her debut, despite being eased down and starting slowly, I was confident that a projected rating of 103 did not flatter her and that she could prove to be better than that when stepped up in trip.

Oddly she was kept to six furlongs for her final outing as a two-year-old which came at Newmarket on 30 October 2009 and I declined to back her as a consequence. Despite the fact that six furlongs on good ground was an insufficient test for her, she once again performed with great credit. She lost ground when dwelling at the start and was held up at the rear in what was a moderately run contest. When she was belatedly asked for her effort two furlongs out she was initially short of room but when an opening came she 'quickened between horses' in eye catching fashion. However, the leading trio had got first run on her and because of the moderate pace in the race they were never going to come back to her. She finished fourth, but I was impressed by her performance. The fact that she had quickened when asked for her effort, despite running over an inadequate trip again, reinforced my belief that she will be a force to be reckoned with next season.

Incidentally, the strength of the bias at Ayr during the Gold Cup meeting was subsequently highlighted by the result of the Group Two Rockfel Stakes which was staged at Newmarket on 17 October 2009. The race saw a rematch between the Ayr winner Distinctive and Music Show who had finished over thirteen lengths behind the former last time out, but had had the massive disadvantage of racing next to the stands' rail. The Rockfel was over seven furlongs rather than six, so direct comparisons between the two races are unsatisfactory, but it came as no surprise to me that Distinctive flopped at Newmarket despite being one of the joint second favourites because she had been flattered by the Ayr result. I was surprised that Music Show was able to improve enough to win the Rockfel at 25/1 and I had no financial interest in her but I was less surprised that she was able to achieve a twenty six lengths turnaround in the form with Distinctive as prior to the Ayr race she had been rated 89 whereas Distinctive had been rated 80 and it was always likely that the latter's revised rating of 101 might overestimate her achievements.

Appendix A to this book contains up to date and comprehensive draw figures and I strongly recommend that you get into the habit of using them. Where there was sufficient data I was able to produce draw figures for the individual stalls as well as average figures for groups of stalls. In my opinion this extra detail is important and gives my figures an edge over others that divide the statistics into three groups (Low, Middle and High). Expressing draw bias in this fashion is unwieldy and it can be misleading. For example, if you look at the chart relating to Southwell (AW) you will see that in six furlong races the average figure for the low numbers is 1.0 which suggests that there is no bias. However, in reality stall one and to a lesser extent stall two are poor draws with individual figures of 0.3 and 0.7 respectively. Personally, I would not entertain backing a horse other than a front runner that has drawn stall one, unless it has at least ten pounds in hand. Without being alerted by the individual draw figure the chances are you would remain unaware of the strength of the bias.

Due to space constraints I have not produced figures for the long distance races but you should be aware that strong biases do exist even in races over extreme trips, particularly those containing large numbers of runners. The Cesarewitch, the Ascot Stakes and the Northumberland Plate are three examples that spring to mind. Basically, when betting in any race not covered by my statistics you should refer to Topdraw in the *Racing Post* for pointers.

Chapter Five

Two-Year-Olds

As someone who concentrates almost exclusively on unexposed or well-handicapped horses you would expect that a large proportion of my bets would be placed on two-year-olds but that is not the case. In fact, for a variety of reasons I place relatively few bets on them.

During the first few months of a season two-year-old races tend to be won by one of three types; the obvious 'form' horses that are sent off at restrictively short odds, debutants, or horses that improve dramatically for the experience of having had a run or two. Experience has taught me that I struggle to make a profit in this sphere because the odds about the form horses are too short and the successes of the other two types are often difficult to foresee. Later on in the season the nursery handicaps begin to be staged and although they are full of unexposed and potentially well-handicapped horses there are usually too many of them contesting each race and it can be hard to separate the wheat from the chaff. Too many of them will either be trying a new distance or will be encountering different underfoot conditions and most of them will be open to significant improvement simply because they are so inexperienced. These contests also often include horses that have won their only race to date and trying to accurately quantify their ability is notoriously difficult.

When I have identified a horse that I believe to be well-handicapped I hope to back it when it takes on more exposed opponents, but such opportunities do not often occur in nurseries because there are too many lightly-raced types among the runners. Occasionally I will back a two-year-old in a handicap if I know from its speed figures that it has been significantly underrated by the Handicapper, but as a rule I restrict myself to analysing the results of two-year-old races with a view to identifying horses to follow as three-year-olds. From July onwards I endeavour to identify the best of the two-year-old crop with a view to backing them ante-post for the Classics because there is often significant value to be had in the ante-post markets when you become familiar with what to look for.

I do not pay much attention to two-year-olds during the first few months of the season because those that run early on are not normally the type that I am looking for. A high proportion of them are the precocious sprinting stamp of horse that will often do best in their first season and then gradually deteriorate. They are physically and mentally ahead of most of their peers and they are trained to take advantage of the superiority they hold in the early stages of the season. By the end of the season most of them will have raced numerous times and become fully exposed. These precocious sprinting types are often compact in shape and they lack the physical scope that is necessary if they are to improve as they mature. When they begin their three-year-old careers most of them hold no secrets from the Handicapper and that is a problem because unless they have progressed physically they will struggle to win. This is exacerbated by the likelihood that they will not improve if stepped up in distance because most of them are not bred to stay. Their handicap ratings usually have to drop significantly before they are able to win a race and it is not uncommon for them to draw a complete blank in their second season.

The lack of progress made by early season types in their second season and beyond is illustrated by the following list of all the two-year-olds that have won either a Group or Listed race at Royal Ascot since 2003 and then remained in training after their first season. Royal Ascot takes place during June and most of the contestants in the juvenile events are the best of those that have already raced. As you can see from the table only a few of them went on to repeat or better what they achieved at Ascot in their subsequent seasons and the norm is for the winners' form to gradually deteriorate. The table provides the details of their careers as three-year-olds and beyond:

TWO-YEAR-OLD WINNERS AT 'ROYAL ASCOT' BETWEEEN 2003-2008				
HORSE	WINS WHEN AGED 3-y-o+	RUNS WHEN AGED 3-y-o+	HIGHEST WINNING GRADE	DISTANCE
SILCAS GIFT	1	5	GROUP 3	7f
THREE VALLEYS	0	6	-	-
ATTRACTION	5	11	GROUP 1	8f
JEWEL IN THE SAND	1	4	CLASS 3	6f
ICEMAN	0	5	-	-
CHAMPLAIN	0	2	-	-
DUTCH ART	0	6	-	-

HENRYTHENAVIGATOR	4	7	GROUP 1	8f
DAMSON	0	3	-	-
CUIS GHAIRE	0	3	-	-
MAZE	0	12	-	-
FREE AGENT	0	5	-	-
WINKER WATSON	0	7	-	-
BLUE DAKOTA	0	2	-	-
HELLVELYN	1	3	LISTED	5f
DRAWNFROMTHEPAST	0	10	-	-
PEARL OF LOVE	0	6	-	-
RUSSIAN VALOUR	0	4	-	-
WHAZZAT	0	6	-	-
ART CONNOISSEUR	1	6	GROUP 1	6f
SANDER CAMILLO	0	4	-	-
ELLETELLE	1	5	LISTED	6f
ELHAMRI	2	26	CLASS 2	5f
NIJOOM DUBAI	0	6	-	-
TOTALS	**16**	**154**		

Only eight of the twenty-four managed to win a race after their two-year-old season and between them they recorded just sixteen wins from a total of one hundred and fifty-four outings (10%) – a very disappointing return in light of what they achieved at Royal Ascot as juveniles. Only three of them went on to win at the very top level in a Group One race and crucially not one of them recorded a win at a distance beyond eight furlongs.

By contrast have a look at the table below which is a list of all the horses that made their two-year-old debuts after Royal Ascot (between 2003 and 2008) and won either a Group or Listed race over eight furlongs or further on one of their first three runs. The table details their careers as three-year-olds and beyond:

HORSE	WINS WHEN AGED 3-y-o+	RUNS WHEN AGED 3-y-o+	HIGHEST WINNING GRADE	DISTANCE
ANTON CHEKHOV	1	8	GROUP 2	11f
MIKADO	2	10	LISTED	10f
YEHUDI	0	1	-	-
AZAMOUR	4	10	GROUP 1	12f
ALLEXINA	2	11	LISTED	12f

SEPTIMUS	6	10	GROUP 1	14f
AYAM ZAMAN	0	2	-	-
MOTIVATOR	2	5	GROUP 1	12f
AMERICAN POST	3	5	GROUP 1	8f
UNDER THE RAINBOW	0	24	-	-
KITE WOOD	2	5	GROUP 3	13f
AUTHORIZED	3	5	GROUP 1	12f
BOCA DANCER	0	2	-	-
ENTICEMENT	1	4	LISTED	10f
ALBERT HALL	0	2	-	-
ALLESSANDRO VOLTA	1	7	GROUP 3	12f
PASSAGE OF TIME	2	9	GROUP 3	10f
TOTALS	**29**	**120**		

Only five of the seventeen failed to win after their two-year-old season. The other twelve won twenty-nine races between them and five of them succeeded at Group One level. The figures would have been significantly better if they had not been skewed by the dismal record of Under The Rainbow who ran twenty-four times without success. The others produced an outstanding average winning strike rate of thirty percent. Importantly, most of their subsequent successes came in races of ten furlongs or more and many of them appeared to improve as they stretched out over longer distances. The tables confirm the fact that early season two-year-olds are far less likely to progress over subsequent seasons than those that debut over longer distances in the second half of the year and this is an important consideration for anyone seeking to identify those three-year-olds that are likely to improve as they mature.

The disparity between the levels of improvement shown by the two different groups of horses can largely be explained by their breeding and conformation. In contrast to the early season sprinters that are often strong and compact, horses that are bred for longer distances are usually lengthier and more angular in appearance and are generally less furnished as two-year-olds than their sprinting counterparts. They tend to improve as they get older simply because they become bigger and stronger as they mature and fill their frames. If they are lightly raced as two-year-olds they will also usually show some initial improvement as they gain valuable experience of racing and more especially as they stretch out over the longer trips that they are bred for.

It is always worth noting the month in which a two-year-old was born because it can have a bearing on how it performs during its debut season and beyond. Because a horse's official birthday is on the first of January each year (i:e a two-year-old becomes a three-year-old on that date) those two-year-olds that are born in the early days of January will have a significant physical advantage over many of their peer group, the majority of whom will have been born several months later. Those extra few months can make a big difference at that age because the older horses are both physically and mentally more mature. I always look out for two-year-olds that are born in either late April or May because there is a good chance that they will improve more than their older counterparts as the season progresses and they are likely to do better as three-year-olds.

A good example of this is provided by Love Lockdown (trained in Ireland by Ger Lyons) who travelled over to contest a six furlong Group 3 race staged at Kempton on 5 September 2009. Have a look at the following table which shows the finishing positions of the runners, their previous best speed figures and their dates of birth:

TOTEPOOL SIRENIA STAKES (GROUP 3)				
Kempton (AW)				
FINISHING ORDER	HORSE	DATE OF BIRTH FIGURE	BEST TOPSPEED	SP
1	LOVE LOCKDOWN	10/05/07	91	7/2
2	IVER BRIDGE LAD	10/02/07	92	7/1
3	MONSIEUR CHEVALIER	23/01/07	105	13/8
4	IN SOME RESPECT	09/03/07	95	7/2
5	RED AVALANCHE	09/03/07	92	16/1
6	CHAPERNO	26/01/07	88	12/1
7	ANGEL'S PURSUIT	15/03/07	77	16/1

Strictly on the form Monsieur Chevalier looked to be a worthy favourite. However, although he had run well enough on his first try over six furlongs last time out at York (when he clocked a speed figure of 101 and his joint highest RPR of 108) he had nevertheless suffered only his second defeat in eight outings and I was pretty sure that five furlongs was his trip. Significantly he was an early foal, having been born on 23 January 2007, and he had undoubtedly enjoyed an advantage over his peers in the first few months of the season. He had made a winning debut on 9 April 2009 and proceeded to win four races on the bounce. Although he was subsequently defeated at Royal Ascot he went on to win his next two races and his overall form was excellent. However, there were good grounds for believing that Love Lockdown could improve sufficiently to beat him. Despite having been an unusually late foal (he was born on 10 May 2009) he had performed with great credit early on in his career and belied his immaturity. Notably he had managed to clock a speed figure of 90 back on the 14th of June in a six furlong contest at Cork and it was likely that he would be able to improve significantly on that now that he had had a further three months in which to strengthen and mature. After almost two months off the track he had run in a five furlong Listed race at York on 19 August 2009 and had put in an eye-catching performance. It was evident that the five furlongs on fast ground was too sharp for him that day but he did well to finish third, having stayed on well to be nearest at the finish. He clocked a personal best speed figure of 91 that day and it was likely that he could improve on that now that he was returning to six furlongs.

Looking at the speed figures achieved by the runners I was confident that Love Lockdown had probably improved enough to beat all of them bar Monsieur Chevalier. I also believed that he had a genuine chance of beating Monsieur Chevalier as he was in receipt of three pounds from that horse and he appeared to be the better suited of the pair to six furlongs. Furthermore, Monsieur Chevalier appeared to have already peaked, whereas Love Lockdown was still maturing and improving. I backed him each-way at 15/2 because I was convinced that he would finish second at least but those odds did not last long in the face of heavy support that drove his odds down to 7/2 before the off. He actually exceeded my expectations and only had to be pushed out to win comfortably by one and a half lengths from Iver Bridge Lad (there was a further neck back to Monsieur Chevalier in third). There was no doubt that he was improving as he matured and his connections were certainly wise to the fact!

Speed figures are an excellent tool for identifying the best two-year-olds as soon as they make their debuts. Any two-year-old that clocks a Topspeed figure of 80 or more first time out is very likely to prove to be at least of Listed class and a significant proportion of them will be Group class. Very few horses are able to overcome their lack of experience to run so quickly on their debuts and those that do are worth monitoring closely. I have devised six rules to highlight debutants that are likely to make up into Group One winners and I will back those of them that I consider to be exceptional, for either the Derby or the Oaks, ante-post. The rules are as follows:

1. The horse must record a Topspeed figure of 80 or more on its debut.
2. The horse must win on its debut.
3. Its debut must come in July or later.
4. Its debut must be over seven furlongs or further.
5. Its debut must be in a Class 4 race or higher.
6. The debut race must have been in Great Britain or Ireland.

Rules three and four reflect the fact that horses that debut before July over sprint distances are very unlikely to develop into contenders for the Classics in June the following year. During the 2008 season the rules isolated the following two-year-olds and most of them went on to enjoy success at a high level:

HORSE	DEBUT TS	DEBUT CLASS	DEBUT DISTANCE	HIGHEST CLASS OF RACE THEY WENT ON TO WIN
GOLDEN STREAM	90	4	7f	LISTED
JUKEBOX JURY	82	2	7f	GROUP 1
BURGUNDY ICE	83	4	7f	HANDICAP, CLASS 4
FATHER TIME	86	4	8f	GROUP 2
PRINCE SIEGFRIED	90	4	7f	LISTED
YOUR OLD PAL	100	4	8f	LISTED
SARISKA	85	4	7f	GROUP 1 (OAKS)
RAINBOW VIEW	88	4	7f	GROUP 1
REDWOOD	81	4	8f	LISTED
BEAUTY O'GWAUN	82	2	7f	GROUP 3
WINGWALKER	85	4	7f	STAKES, CLASS 3
CHIEF LONE EAGLE	88	2	7f	-
ZACINTO	95	4	7f	GROUP 2
SECRECY	85	3	7f	HANDICAP, CLASS 2
LASSARINA	81	2	7f	-

As you can see only two of the qualifiers failed to win after their impressive debuts and the majority turned out to be either top class or just below that level.

Godolphin subsequently bought two of the qualifiers – Prince Siegfried and Secrecy and although they both appeared to be potential Group One winners I downgraded my interest in them after they switched yards. In my opinion Godolphin horses have a tendency to underperform in the first half of the season and I put that down to the yard's habit of wintering their best horses in Dubai. In my opinion, having to switch between the radically different climates of the UK and Dubai sets their horses back and the majority of them are rarely at the peak of their form in May and June. It is surely no coincidence that the stable invariably do particularly well in the last two or three months of the season. Until such time as they rethink their strategy of sending horses to Dubai I will not consider any of their runners for the Classics in May or June.

Although Secrecy has only won a handicap to date and has been gelded I feel that he could progress significantly during 2010. He has been kept to a mile or less so far but is in my opinion crying out for ten furlongs or further and if he is upped in trip I am sure that he will do very well.

When deciding which of the qualifiers to back ante-post for the Classics I pay particular attention to what their connections say after the race, their breeding, their conformation and to whom they are trained by. I did not want to back Rainbow View because she was too small and to me she looked like a two-year-old who would struggle to maintain the same level of form the following season. There was sure to be one or two horses with more scope that would improve past her. I was not convinced by Your Old Pal either because connections expressed surprise at his debut win. In my opinion trainers know when they have a top class animal in their care and they usually anticipate a debut victory. I felt that his high speed figure may have been exaggerated by the soft ground that he had encountered on his debut at Newbury.

The two that I considered backing were Zacinto and Sariska. They were both trained by Classic winning trainers and were held in high regard. However, I was concerned that Zacinto's breeding meant that he might lack the necessary stamina to win the Derby. His sire and dam sire indices were just 9.1f and 7.8f and his dam Ithaca had appeared not to stay beyond one mile. Over the last seven years the average sire and dam sire indices of the Derby winners have been 10.3f and 10.3f and the averages for the Oaks winners have been 9.9f and 11.5f so the evidence suggested that Zacinto was unlikely to win the Derby. That left Sariska who had the ideal profile. Her sire and dam sire indices were 7.7f and 10.5f and although the sire index was low the dam side of her breeding was stamina laden. Her dam Maycock's Bay had won over fourteen furlongs and that mare's only other foal Gull Wing had also won over fourteen furlongs. I did not doubt that she would stay and when I read the comment made by her trainer Michael Bell after her debut win I felt sure that she was potentially special: 'She's a very very nice filly and the best in the yard.' After reading such an unequivocal statement I was more than happy to back her at 33/1 for the Oaks.

All of the qualifiers from the 2009 season are shown below:

HORSE	DEBUT TS	SIRE INDEX	DAM SIRE INDEX	TRAINER	HIGHEST WINNING CLASS
NAJD	84	7.6f	8.7f	S BIN SUROOR	CLASS 4
EMULOUS	80	9.1f	7.8f	D WELD	CLASS 2
CRYSTAL GAL	90	11.2f	9.1f	K PRENDERGAST	CLASS 2
SILVER GRECIAN	85	9.1f	8.1f	J RYAN	GROUP 2
PRIZEFIGHTING	80	11.4f	7.6f	J GOSDEN	CLASS 4
ELUSIVE PIMPERNEL	90	7.8f	11.3f	J DUNLOP	GROUP 3
ST NICHOLAS ABBEY	88	11.6f	10.1f	A O'BRIEN	GROUP 1
BLACK SPIRIT	90	10.4f	9.3f	C COX	CLASS 4
VALE OF YORK	90	7.6f	10.4f	S BIN SUROOR	GROUP 1
PASSION FOR GOLD	90	10.0f	9.6f	S BIN SUROOR	GROUP 1
AL ZIR	83	10.0f	?	S BIN SUROOR	CLASS 2
EOLITH	80	?	10.1f	W KNIGHT	CLASS 3
MODEYRA	84	8.6f	10.7f	S BIN SUROOR	CLASS 4
AZMEEL	81	?	8.7f	J GOSDEN	LISTED

For the reasons that I have already expressed I was happy to pass on backing any of the Godolphin runners ante-post but I expect all of them to do well in the second half of the season, particularly Modeyra and Najd. Silver Grecian is too small and compact for my liking so I have passed on him. He looks to be a two-year-old and how many horses bought at the 'breeze ups' go on to win a Classic? Emulous does not have the stamina in her breeding to win the Oaks. Her dam did not stay beyond eight furlongs and her two other foals have not won beyond six furlongs. She may however be a contender for one of the 1,000 Guineas races. I backed Crystal Gal for the Irish Oaks (for which she holds an entry) as she is well bred and is held in high regard by her trainer Kevin Prendergast. Unfortunately, she has disappointed twice since her debut at the Curragh but I have not given up all hope just yet as she was unsuited by the slow pace in both of those races and I am sure that she will only really come into her own over ten furlongs and beyond. My one doubt is whether the 90 speed figure she clocked first time out was accurate because after the race her trainer stated that: 'They walked in the race and it wasn't a proper test.' Given that the race was on heavy ground it could be that all of the races that day were slowly run and that her figure may have been magnified as a consequence.

I have not backed Prizefighting because he has no big race entries but he looks a promising colt in the making. John Gosden's number one contender is probably Azmeel who is entered in the Derby but his breeding on the dam side is a little inconclusive. I have not backed either Black Knight or Eolith mainly because their yards do not win many big races and I feel that they will fall short of being top class. Of the two, Eolith would be the one to follow.

St Nicholas Abbey is bred to excel at beyond ten furlongs and he is under the expert care of Aidan O'Brien who has won numerous Classics. After his debut win O'Brien said the following about his charge: 'He's exciting ... he's a fast ground horse, he's a very good mover and floats on the ground.' When O'Brien declares himself to be 'excited' about a horse you should sit up and take notice because he has had so many champions under his care over the years. The fact that St Nicholas Abbey was able to record such a good speed figure despite evidently being much better suited to quicker conditions also spoke volumes and I felt sure that he was a live Derby contender. He was born in April and was still rather unfurnished so I suspected that he would improve on what he had achieved so far. I backed him at 25/1 and 20/1 and those odds have now shrunk to just 9/4 following his magnificent victory in the Racing Post Trophy. He is indeed a very exciting prospect and I am just keeping my fingers crossed that he gets to Epsom in one piece and that he stays the trip!

Elusive Pimpernel impressed me when he won on his debut at Newmarket because he finished the seven furlong contest very powerfully indeed and it took an age for his jockey to pull him up. He is a big powerful colt and is likely to get better with time. Although his sire stamina index is a bit low, the dam side has plenty of stamina on it and his dam's only other foal has won over ten furlongs. He is in the hands of John Dunlop who is no stranger to winning a Classic and Dunlop stated that he 'could not be more delighted with him' after his debut success. I backed him for both the 2000 Guineas and the Derby at 25/1 and 20/1 and I was pleased when he went on to win next time out in a Group Three contest at York and then ran well to finish a good second to St Nicholas Abbey in the Group One, Racing Post Trophy at Doncaster.

There were four horses that fitted all of my qualifying rules other than winning a class four race or above. They were Elspeth's Boy, Siyaadah, Layline and Workforce. Of those I was particularly taken by Workforce and I have recently decided to back him for both the 2000 Guineas and the Derby. He won a class five, seven furlong maiden at Goodwood on his only run to date and he could not have been more impressive. Described as a big, strong colt he managed to quicken up off a fast pace and stormed clear of his rivals in the final furlong. It took his jockey an age to pull him up and he clearly had plenty more to give. Ryan Moore stated that this well bred colt 'felt nice' and in my opinion he is likely to stay twelve furlongs (the stoutly bred dam Soviet Moon's only other foal placed over fourteen furlongs).

It was possible to draw an interesting comparison between the performance of Workforce and that of the third horse Exceedthewildman. Both of them were held up in the rear in the early stages with Workforce the furthest back of the two. They both made their move over two furlongs out and finished the race strongly. Exceedthewildman, who had had the benefit of a previous race, 'stayed on well' in the closing stages but he was absolutely swamped by Workforce who powered seven lengths clear of him. Assuming that Workforce started his run a length behind Exceedthewildman he could be rated at least eight lengths superior to that rival, but the likelihood is that he had more in hand than the winning margin suggested. Exceedthewildman was subsequently officially rated 74. Working to two and a half pounds per length it is reasonable to project that Workforce achieved a rating of 94+ on his debut, which almost tallies with the Topspeed figure of 90 he clocked. Any horse that can achieve such a rating on its debut is likely to be top class and the fact that he was able to quicken off a strong pace (albeit against pretty moderate opponents) suggests that he is. However, I have been a little baffled by the fact that he currently has no big race entries and I just hope that he takes part in the races that I have backed him for.

Incidentally, I should point out that the great Sea The Stars clocked a Topspeed figure of 87 on his debut in a class two, seven furlong maiden at the Curragh in July. Unfortunately, he did not fully register on my radar because he came fourth in what was an unusually competitive maiden. The three horses that beat him were Driving Snow, Black Bear Island and Freemantle, all of whom were subsequently rated in excess of one hundred and were very good horses in their own right.

As I said earlier I do not place many bets on two-year-old races. Apart from looking for the future Classic winners among the first time out winners I only really become interested in a two-year-old when it first qualifies for a handicap rating. I will then check through its form to assess whether or not it has, in my opinion, been underrated. Ideally, by the end of its first season it will only have had three or four runs and will have the profile of a potential improver. I particularly like the late developing types that have the scope to strengthen and mature over the winter months and that are likely to do better as they stretch out over longer distances. However, any horse that has achieved a Topspeed figure that is higher than its initial handicap rating is of interest to me, particularly if it achieved the figure at a distance that is shorter than its breeding suggests it should be suited to. Such horses have demonstrated that they have the speed to be competitive off their handicap mark at a distance short of their best and when they step up in trip they are unlikely to be found wanting for pace in handicap company off their initial rating. As well as using speed figures I also attempt to give my own ratings to horses that have finished strongly in slowly run races in order to determine whether they are well-handicapped using a method that is discussed elsewhere in the book.

Horses that have not come to my attention by the time they first receive a handicap rating often do so after their first or second run in a handicap race. Horses having their fourth or fifth runs need to be carefully assessed for any signs that they are well treated. At this stage it is particularly important to spot when a horse appears to run well despite being disadvantaged by a pace or draw bias, or by the distance or going. If it has, there is every chance that it has been leniently treated by the handicapper. If a horse has raced five times without indicating that it is well-handicapped the likelihood of it being well treated begins to diminish and the more it runs without achieving anything noteworthy the less likely it is to be ahead of the Handicapper. Of course it may well become well treated once its rating is dropped to a more suitable level, but I would have little interest in it because I want to be on horses that are progressive rather than potentially regressive.

Chapter Six

Extracts from the Journal

When I saw the result of the Cowthorpe Median Auction Maiden Stakes (run at Catterick on 28 october 2008) I quickly realised that it merited further investigation. It was a run of the mill auction maiden for two-year-olds that had been won by a horse with a selling plater's rating of 57 and although this type of race does not normally feature too many future winners I had reason to believe that this one might be an exception. The more I looked into it the more convinced I became that I had made a lucrative discovery. The result is reproduced below:

COWTHORPE MEDIAN AUCTION MAIDEN STAKES (CLASS 6)
6F GOOD/SOFT CATTERICK 28/10/2008

HORSE	DIST	DRAW	COMMENT	OR	TS
REAL DIAMOND	-	1	made all: kept on strongly: cheekily	57	71
FIFTH AMENDMENT	½	2	chsd ldrs: kpt on wl fnl f	-	74
ZEGNA	1¼	4	trkd ldrs: t.k.h: hrd rdn 1f out: kpt on	-	70
GRISSOM	2¼	3	chsd ldrs: one pce fnl 2f	62	63
LEGAL LEGACY	nk	9	mid-div: outpcd 4f out: styd on fnl 2f	-	62
KIAMA BAY	1	10	sn in rr: kpt on fnl 2f: nvr nrr	-	58
MR FREDDY	shd	12	mid-div: outpcd 4f out	-	58
TOP FLIGHT SPLASH	1¼	11	mid-div: outpcd 4f out	-	49
MISS XU XIA	2¾	6	prom: outpcd 3f out: wknd 2f out	38	40
VALID POINT	1¼	5	s.i.s: always rr	-	40
AVITUS	hd	7	s.i.s: sn behind	-	40
ADDISON DE WITT	14	8	s.i.s: sn behind	-	-

What made this race stand out was the fact that the winner had clocked a Topspeed figure of 71 despite officially being rated only 57 and importantly, the fourteen pound discrepancy between the two figures looked believable. Only two of the other horses had raced enough times to qualify for an official handicap rating and it appeared that they had run to form. Grissom had an official mark of 62 and had earned a Topspeed figure of 63 in the race and Miss Xu Xia had an official mark of 38 and had earned a Topspeed figure of 40. Furthermore, the Topspeed figures awarded to the other five winners at the meeting also appeared, despite my initial scepticism, to be believable. Have a look at the figures awarded to all of the winners at the meeting:

HORSE	DISTANCE	OR	TS	DIFFERENCE
REAL DIAMOND	6f	57	71	+14
COVERT MISSION	12f	50	58	+8
HARLECH CASTLE	6f	75	75	-
SHOTLEY MAC	7f	70	59	-11
MISTER PETE	12f	60	33	-27
JOYEAUX	5f	61	71	+10

The large negative figures attached to Shotley Mac and Mister Pete can be ignored as they were simply the winners of two slowly run races. As you can see, three horses were awarded Topspeed figures considerably in excess of their official ratings. It is not common to see three winners at a single meeting awarded figures so much higher than their official ratings and differences of +14, +8 and +10 would normally suggest that Topspeed had misjudged the going allowance and that all the winners at the meeting had been overrated. When I conclude that a meeting has been overrated I revise the figures downwards by whatever I consider to be appropriate. In this case, for the following reasons, I decided that the figures were believable and that no amendment was warranted.

REAL DIAMOND The apparent improvement made by this filly could be explained by a combination of factors. She was still relatively lightly raced and was open to improvement as she matured mentally and strengthened physically, particularly as she had been spoiling her chance in previous races by taking a keen hold. Horses that take a keen hold can prove suited to taking the lead in races and from the best draw in stall one she had been ideally berthed to attack and make all along the far rail. She wasn't pressed for the lead and, as so often happens when a horse is unchallenged, she galloped on resolutely in the closing stages to win a shade 'cheekily'. The fact that both Grissom and Miss Xu Xia clocked Topspeed figures similar to their official ratings supported the view that Real Diamond had improved.

COVERT MISSION This five-year-old mare had been very lightly raced on the turf. She had started her career as a four-year-old by competing in four NH bumper races. She was then switched to the Flat and after running in three turf maiden races she was given an official handicap rating of 59. After two disappointing runs in handicaps she was switched to the all-weather but she fared no better and after four runs on Polytrack her official rating had tumbled to 50. I took the view that she was relatively unexposed on the turf and that because she had been rated 59 prior to switching to the all-weather her speed figure of 58 was believable. This assessment was supported not only by the fact that she had won by two and a quarter lengths but also by the fact that the first three home pulled six lengths clear of the other eleven runners. If the winner of a handicap records a Topspeed figure that is ten or more pounds higher than its official rating you should expect the rest of the field to have been more strung out than usual. If the majority of the runners are bunched up behind the winner the validity of the high rating would be questionable. As things transpired, I did not have to wait long for confirmation that my assessment was probably correct because Covert Mission ran again only five days after her Catterick victory. On 3 November 2008 she was returned to the all-weather to contest a fourteen furlong handicap at Wolverhampton under a six pound penalty that took her official rating up to 56. She finished second, beaten only by a neck, but probably would have won if she had not hung right in the final furlong before being switched left. Thirteen runners had contested the race and the fact that there was a distance of three and a quarter lengths back to the third horse strongly suggested that a mark of 56 was merited and that if anything a slightly higher mark was appropriate.

HARLECH CASTLE This gelding had already clocked Topspeed figures of 75 and 80 earlier in the season so a repeat figure of 75 was clearly within his capabilities.

JOYEAUX This fully exposed mare's figure of 71 (+10), although somewhat of a surprise was also believable. To begin with, the winning margin of two lengths (in a 5f race) suggested that it was a good performance. Secondly, it was only eight runs ago that she had been officially rated 70 and although her rating had dropped to 55 following some poor performances she had returned to form when finishing second and third on her last two outings. She had, in the past, clocked Topspeed figures of 74 (on good/soft ground) and 73, so had shown herself capable of producing a figure of 71 when things fell into place. On this occasion she had the plum draw in stall one and also had her ideal underfoot conditions. Furthermore, the race panned out perfectly for her when a gap appeared against the far rail affording her a clear run to reel back the leader who had gone off at a strong pace.

Once I had decided that the speed figure achieved by Real Diamond was believable it was then a matter of waiting to see how the Handicapper reacted to the race and what ratings he allotted to the runners. I anticipated that he would underestimate the race and that most of the runners would be well-handicapped as a result. The Handicapper was faced with a difficult decision because he had already allotted the comparatively exposed Real Diamond a rating of 57. From a handicapping rather than a speed figure perspective she did not look like a horse that merited a rating of 71. Working to three pounds per length she was demonstrably seven pounds superior to Grissom (officially rated 62) and 25lbs superior to Miss Xu Xia (officially rated 38) and could therefore be rated somewhere between 69 and 63. The likelihood that the race would be underrated was supported by the *Racing Post* analyst who opined: 'Her trainer does well with this type and she can now expect a mark of around 60 when moving back into a handicap.' When the new/revised ratings were published, they were not as generous as the *Racing Post* analyst had estimated, but they were by my reckoning too low, and most of the runners were therefore well-handicapped. Real Diamond had been given a revised mark of 66 – an average of the 69 and 63 ratings suggested by the above pounds per length calculations. The table below shows the ratings allotted by the Handicapper and how they compared to each runner's Topspeed rating.

HORSE	NEW/REVISED OFFICIAL RATING ON NEXT RUN	TOPSPEED ACHIEVED ON 28/10/08
REAL DIAMOND	66	71
FIFTH AMENDMENT	-	74
ZEGNA *	78	70
GRISSOM	62	63
LEGAL LEGACY*	61	62
KIAMA BAY*	57	58
MR FREDDY*	61	58

TOP FLIGHT SPLASH*	49	49
MISS XU XIA	38	40
VALID POINT	-	40
AVITUS*	50	40
ADDISON DE WITT*	49	-

Both Fifth Amendment and Valid Point had not yet run enough times to qualify for an official rating but by coincidence seven of the twelve runners (those marked with an asterisk above) were having their third run on 28 October 2008. As a consequence they were allotted official ratings following the Catterick race and began their handicap careers on lenient looking marks. One or two pounds may not seem a lot but for a variety of reasons most of the runners were also open to considerable improvement.

The three that were of particular interest to me were Legal Legacy, Kiama Bay and Mr Freddy because they had not only been disadvantaged by being drawn out wide in stalls nine, ten and twelve respectively, but also by Catterick's sharp six furlongs which was an inadequate test of stamina for them. Their respective sire and dam sire indices were 9.6f & 9.2f, 8.7f & 9.8f and 8.7f & 7.7f so it was no surprise that all three found themselves outpaced towards the back of the field before staying on in the closing stages. Although Mr Freddy had less stamina on the dam sire side than the other two, his dam Bubble N Squeak stayed twelve furlongs and one of her three progeny stayed ten furlongs so I had little doubt that he would need at least a mile to show his best form. The fact that they had been disadvantaged by the conditions of the race suggested they would prove to be better than their speed figures indicated when they were stepped up in trip and, if so, they were thrown in off their lowly handicap marks. I noted that Kiama Bay had cost his connections 40,000 euros to purchase and was therefore likely to prove better than a selling plater.

Top Flight Splash could also be rated several pounds better than her speed figure because she too had been inconvenienced by being drawn out wide (in stall eleven). Unlike the other three, however, she appeared to have the speed to cope with six furlongs because she had been able to take a prominent early position in the Catterick race and her sire Bertolini had a stamina index of 6.6f.

I did not have to wait long before the form started to be franked and to begin profiting from my research. Before the end of the 2008 turf season only Grissom ran again. I was not particularly interested in Grissom because the Catterick run had been his fifth outing and he had done little more than match his official rating. He had been well drawn in stall three that day and although his sire's stamina index (9.1f) suggested he may improve for a step up in trip in due course, he appeared to be handicapped in line with the ability he had shown over sprint distances. I did not back him on 1 November 2008 when he contested a seven furlong nursery handicap run on heavy ground at Ayr. He finished third that day after his stamina seemingly gave out in the final furlong. I also declined to back him six days later when he reappeared at Musselburgh in a five furlong handicap run on soft ground and scooted home to win by over three lengths at the generous odds of 20/1. However, the result strengthened my belief that most of the horses that had competed in the Catterick race were well-handicapped.

Five days later Top Flight Splash ran in a six furlong handicap at Southwell off her mark of 49 and I was happy to take the chance that she would adapt adequately to the fibresand surface given that she was available at the generous odds of 16/1. I surmised that her prominent style of racing would allow her to avoid the worst of the kickback and as it turned out she made most of the running under the reliable Dale Gibson and won fairly comfortably by one and a half lengths. Significantly, she clocked a Topspeed figure of 54 in the process which provided further proof that her Catterick performance had been underrated. Following her victory her official rating was raised to 55 and she ceased to be of further interest to me now that she was handicapped in line with the ability she had shown.

Only two of the other runners raced again during 2008. Sir Mark Prescott's Valid Point competed in two more six furlong maiden races but was comprehensively beaten in both. This was no surprise as he was clearly crying out for a longer trip judging by the fact that he was reported to have been 'outpaced' in his races and that his sire and damsire indices were 9.1f and 9.9f. In fact it was not until he was stepped up to ten furlongs for the first time in August 2009 that he was able to shed his maiden tag and he then (as is so typical of Sir Mark's charges) went on to win a succession of races over the following few months.

The other horse to run again was Miss Xu Xia. She competed in an all-weather maiden on 7 November 2008 but was comprehensively outclassed. She then ran in a Southwell (AW) handicap off a handicap rating of 45 and finished fifth of nine runners (beaten 5½ lengths). In view of the fact that her best speed figure was the 40 she had clocked in the Catterick race she was of no interest to me that day. Unfortunately, she was also of no interest to me on her next outing on 18 November 2008 when she surprisingly managed to win a Southwell seller at 33/1, beating horses rated 74 and 63 in the process. However, she only clocked a modest Topspeed figure of 39 that day and had not necessarily improved. It seemed probable that she had simply beaten some out of form and overrated rivals who were also perhaps unsuited to the idiosyncratic Fibresand surface. Following her victory the Handicapper raised her mark to 54 but I felt that was probably an overreaction given that her career best speed figures were 40 and 39. Predictably she went on to be beaten in two subsequent handicap races by fourteen lengths and thirteen lengths.

I had to endure the frustration of waiting until the start of the 2009 Flat season before any of the other horses returned to the track. The first of them to reappear was Mr Freddy. He began his three-year-old campaign on an official rating of 61 and he made his seasonal debut in a 0-75 nine furlong handicap at Epsom on 22 April 2008. Although his Catterick speed figure had only been 58 I was sure he would prove better than that because he had been poorly drawn that day and I anticipated that he would improve significantly for being stepped up in trip. However, I decided not to back him on his reappearance. Not only was it his first run of the season but Richard Fahey's runners are normally well supported if they are ready to win and the fact that he drifted slightly in the pre-race market was off-putting. I suspected that he would probably need the run in order to bring him to peak fitness and I was relieved when he finished a respectable sixth of the eighteen runners. Unfortunately he put in a noteworthy performance and this would have ramifications in terms of his future odds. After being held up towards the rear in the first part of the race he kept on well to close on the leaders in the final couple of furlongs, clocking another speed figure of 58 in the process and the *Racing Post* analyst was subsequently to note that: 'Mr Freddy caught the eye with the way he kept on and will surely win a race or two this season.'

He next ran on 4 May 2009 in a 0-70 eight furlong handicap at Newcastle on good to soft ground. I felt that he would be hard to beat and I was happy to accept the rather skinny odds of 9/4. Although Mr Freddy ran well and looked like he might win when striking the front inside the final furlong he was caught near the line by Tiger Reigns. My expectation that

Mr Freddy would improve was vindicated by the fact that the first two pulled five lengths clear of the third horse and that he clocked a speed figure of 65. With hindsight I was guilty of underestimating Tiger Reigns before the race due to being blinkered by the strength of my conviction for Mr Freddy. When I looked at Tiger Reigns' form again it was easy to see why he had been a serious contender. As a two-year-old he had run twice in seven furlong maidens and finished third on each occasion. He did not run again until reappearing on 1 April 2009 in a six furlong Catterick maiden. Despite the fast ground, running wide round the bend and perhaps needing what was his first run of the season, he managed to stay on well to win by three quarters of a length. Although his Topspeed figure of 51 (which bettered his previous best of 49) did nothing to indicate that he was well-handicapped when running in the Newcastle race on a mark of 68 it was significant that the stamina indices of his sire and dam sire were 10.4f and 11.1f respectively and it was pretty obvious (if only I had noticed) that he was likely to improve significantly for the step up from six furlongs on fast ground to eight furlongs on good to soft. As it transpired, from a handicapping point of view, Mr Freddy had stood little chance against Tiger Reigns at Newcastle because the latter went on to win a further three races and to achieve an official rating of 93.

Following that run the Handicapper reacted by raising Mr Freddy seven pounds to a mark of 67. I considered that to be harsh so I declined to back him at the prohibitive odds of 13/8 when he next ran on 27 May 2009 in a Beverley handicap. He did manage to win (just!) when getting up in the final stride to force a dead heat with Aldaado. Mr Freddy clocked a speed figure of 75 in the Beverley contest but I concluded that the race had been overrated given that the 54 rated fourth, Vita Mia, had been awarded a figure of 58, particularly as her previous best figure had been a lowly 39. Furthermore, a strong draw bias in favour of high numbers was in evidence that day and I felt that Mr Freddy among others had benefitted from it. I decided that a figure of 70 or 71 was more appropriate and as the Handicapper reacted to the dead heat by raising Mr Freddy to 71 I concluded that he was handicapped in line with his ability and was therefore of no further interest to me. At the time of writing, he has run a further three times, finishing second once and third twice, clocking speed figures of 68, 68 and 70.

The next horse out that season was Avitus who reappeared on 25 April 2009 in a maiden race. As it was a non-handicap the gelding was of no interest to me from a betting point of view. Stepped up to ten furlongs for the first time he ran with credit to finish third of seven but only clocked a modest speed figure of 43 - a slight improvement on the 40 he achieved at Catterick. Following that run his official rating was raised from 50 to 60 and unless he was able to find significant improvement for one reason or another I felt that the ten pound rise had left him poorly handicapped. I did not back him on his next run which was in a nine furlong Redcar handicap contested by only five horses. He managed to come second at 16/1 but his finishing position could be attributed to the fact that he was gifted the early lead in a very slowly run race. His speed figure of 18 spoke volumes about the quality of the form and I felt sure that if the early pace had been stronger he would have been beaten more comprehensively. I did not back him when he competed in a further two handicap races and the fact that he was well beaten in both seemed to confirm that his official rating of 60 was too high.

Legal Legacy made his reappearance in a six furlong handicap at Thirsk on 2 May 2009. He and Kiama Bay were the two Catterick qualifiers that I was most excited about because I was sure that they would prove to be particularly well-handicapped on marks of 60 and 57 respectively. I knew that they would benefit from a step up in trip and that they had been poorly drawn in the race at Catterick and in view of the fact that the form had begun to be franked they looked sure-fire future winners. I felt that the Thirsk race was intended to be no more than a pipe opener for Legal Legacy as I considered that six furlongs on fast ground was likely to be too short a trip for the horse and I was put off by the fact that his jockey Dale Gibson had a poor strike rate for the Dods yard. However, for a while I thought that I may have misread things after Legal Legacy's price initially contracted from 7/1 into 5/1 but it subsequently drifted alarmingly out to 8/1 and my confidence was restored. In the event he dwelt at the start and was then outpaced before keeping on in the final two furlongs to finish six lengths behind the winner in fourth place. I was reassured that he would show considerable improvement when stepped up in trip and with his future odds in mind, I was relieved that he had not finished closer to the winner.

He next ran on 19 May 2009 and I was encouraged to see that he had been dropped in class to a 0-65 handicap over seven furlongs at Musselburgh and that he had the decent enough draw of stall seven of eleven (high numbers are favoured). The excellent stable jockey Philip Makin had been booked to ride and although I would have preferred the horse to have been running over a stiffer seven furlongs than

Musselburgh's I felt that he was well enough handicapped to ge
with it on this occasion. I was sure that the horse was ready to win so I
decided to get on early at the slightly disappointing price of 7/2. Before
the off he was backed into 9/4 from 7/2 but then drifted out to 3/1 in
the face of strong support for the John Quinn trained Solis who went off
as the 5/2 favourite. As the race unfolded I thought I was in trouble two
furlongs out when Island Chief, who had been allowed his own way at
the head of affairs, suddenly stormed into a clear lead. However, much
to my relief, once Legal Legacy was switched to the outside he powered
up the middle of the course to nail Island Chief on the line, with Solis
one and a half lengths back in third. There was a massive eight lengths
back to the fourth placed runner. I was impressed by the way in which
he had managed to overcome what had looked a certain losing position
and I felt that he was worth following again. The handicapper reacted
by raising his rating to 65 but he had clocked a speed figure of 66 in the
Musselburgh race and with further improvement still likely, he remained
well-handicapped.

He next ran in another seven furlong handicap at Musselburgh on 6
June 2009. This time the ground was good rather than good to firm but
I thought that this would probably benefit the horse by making the race
more of a test of stamina. I backed him at 2/1 with some trepidation
(considering that Island Chief was once more in opposition on the same
weight terms as last time) but his many other supporters were happy
to back him into evens before the off. I was made to sweat once again
when the lightly weighted Northern Flyer quickened into a decent lead
two furlongs out, but once again Legal Legacy produced enough speed
to wear the front runner down and mug him on the line. Island Chief,
who I had considered to be the main danger, finished six lengths back in
third, after being carried wide by another runner when negotiating one
of the sharp turns.

Legal Legacy clocked a speed figure of 74 which confirmed that he was
still improving and although the Handicapper reacted by pushing him
up to 70 it was clear that he remained ahead of the assessor. I was happy
to back him again on 26 June 2009 when he was upped in class to a 0-80
handicap over seven furlongs at Doncaster (good ground). This time he
was backed from 7/2 into 5/2 and having clearly appreciated the more
galloping nature of Doncaster's straight course he showed a nice turn
of foot to win by two and a half lengths, recording an improved speed
figure of 80 in the process. The Handicapper countered the improvement

that Legal Legacy had shown by raising his mark to 80 and I should with hindsight have ceased supporting the horse. However, I was persuaded by the way that he quickened up in the Doncaster race that he was still a few pounds ahead of the Handicapper and I backed him at 3/1 when he next ran in a seven furlong handicap at Carlisle on 3 August 2009, despite the fact that he was drawn out wide in stall one of eight. He finished a game second but I decided after the race that I would not back him again. At the time of writing he has run one more time and finished a respectable fourth in a Newmarket handicap.

Kiama Bay began his seasonal campaign on 4 May 2009 when running in a seven and a half furlong handicap at Beverley on good to firm ground. I decided that I would not back him unless a significant market move spoke in his favour. The booking of Jamie Moriarty to ride did not catch the eye and John Quinn's runners often benefit from their seasonal debuts. In the pre-race market he drifted from 15/2 out to 9/1 so I declined to get involved and I was relieved to watch him stay on steadily from the rear into seventh place, some seven lengths behind the winner. I considered that it was a decent run given that a further step up in distance was likely to suit and I was pleased that he had not run too eye-catching a race. One bonus of his low-key performance was that the Handicapper lowered his official rating by one pound to 56.

He appeared next on 17 June 2009 at Hamilton in a 0-60 handicap run over eight and a half furlongs on good ground. I was delighted to find that he had been drawn in stall twelve of thirteen because a high draw is a definite advantage in races run over this course and distance and also that an excellent apprentice, the late Jamie Kyne, had been booked to ride (his 5lb claim ensured that the horse was even better handicapped). With the slightly softer underfoot conditions and the extra furlong likely to be in Kiama Bay's favour I felt confident that the horse would win, particularly now that he was likely to be spot on fitness wise. I was relieved to get on at 7/1 (which I considered to be an excellent price) because a gamble began a couple of minutes before the off and his odds quickly tumbled down to 4/1. Despite still portraying signs of greenness when wandering about under pressure the race went pretty much to plan and he won comfortably enough in the end by one and a half lengths with the rest of the field well strung out behind.

I had been fortunate to get 7/1 because the bookmakers' generosity was largely the result of a substantial gamble going astray on Dreamonandon who started the 100/30 favourite. Dreamonandon had had five previous runs and had been well beaten on each occasion. However, his official rating had slid down to 60 from an initial 65 and he had previously clocked a speed figure of 61 so he was potentially well-handicapped too. However, that figure had been achieved in a ten furlong race and he had already run twice over eight furlongs with less success. I could see no reason why he should improve in this race, particularly as he had the big disadvantage of being drawn widest of all in stall one. Despite the confidence behind him he never got into the race from his wide position (due in part to losing ground round the turns) and his many supporters were probably bemused to witness him trail in sixteen lengths behind Kiama Bay. Unfortunately, Kiama Bay did not run again that season and I suspect that he may have suffered some sort of injury. It remains to be seen whether he fulfils his potential.

Fifth Amendment proved to be a major disappointment as a three-year-old. He began his 2009 campaign by running in a maiden which qualified him for an official rating. The handicapper gave him an initial mark of 69 which looked lenient on the evidence of the 74 speed figure he earned at Catterick despite the fact that he had been favoured by racing up with the pace that day and had also been well drawn. Somewhat surprisingly Fifth Amendment's next two outings were also in maiden races and it was disappointing that the best speed figure he earned in his first three runs of the new season was a lowly 50. I had not backed him in any of his races because I was waiting for him to run in a handicap but my interest in him came to an abrupt end when he was dropped into a selling race at Carlisle on 4 July 2009. I concluded from the regressive nature of his form and also from his engagements that he had not trained on as a three-year-old and it came as no surprise that he was comprehensively beaten in the seller by twenty-eight lengths and also that he went on to finish last in two subsequent handicap races.

The last horse from the Catterick race to make its seasonal reappearance was Real Diamond. On 26 May 2009 she began by running in a six furlong handicap at Redcar on good to firm ground. Considering that she had clocked a speed figure of 71 at Catterick her revised official rating of 66 suggested that she was well-handicapped. I was, however, mindful that she had been flattered to some extent in that race because she was gifted an easy lead and also had the best draw in stall one. I had no interest in backing her at Redcar because her trainer Alan Dickman's charges invariably need their first run of the season and I believed that neither Redcar's straight six furlongs nor the prevailing fast ground would be to her liking. The fact that she was in need of the outing was highlighted when she drifted out from 11/1 to 16/1 before the race and I was not surprised that she weakened tamely in the final two furlongs after initially showing early speed to lead the field.

Her next run was on 8 July 2009 and on this occasion she was definitely of interest. She had been returned to the scene of her previous victory – Catterick's turning six furlongs – and the ground was once again on the easy side of good. I had no doubt that she was well-handicapped (particularly as she had been dropped a pound following her Redcar run) and the fact that the excellent 5lb claimer Jamie Kyne had been booked to ride was an added bonus. My only concern was that she was drawn in stall five (in an eight runner race) but having checked for other front runners drawn on her inside I felt that she possessed enough early speed to get across to the rail. I was confident that connections expected better things of Real Diamond on this occasion and I anticipated that there would be a market move at some stage. I backed her at 10/1 and her price subsequently contracted to 7/1 before the off.

When the stalls opened she did not get the best of breaks and found herself in competition for the early lead with Rossett Rose who had grabbed the inside rail. At that stage I was apprehensive, but Real Diamond shook off the attentions of Rossett Rose as they exited the bend into the straight and once she moved over to the inside rail she galloped on strongly and was never in any danger of being caught. She won by two and a quarter lengths and clocked a speed figure of 66 in the process. The Handicapper reacted by raising her mark to seventy which I considered to be an accurate reflection of her ability and she ceased to be of any further interest to me.

My belief that the Catterick maiden run on 28 October 2008 was likely to produce plenty of future winners proved well founded. I placed a total of eight bets on horses that had run in the race and six of them won, returning a profit of forty points. Ironically, I would have made a greater profit if I had bet blindly on all of the subsequent runners, bearing in mind that I declined to back Grissom and Miss Xu Xia at 20/1 and 33/1. However, I remained philosophical about those disappointments because I am convinced that to make a profit over the long term it is necessary to pick your bets carefully, rather than adopting a scattergun approach. Knowing when to stop backing a horse is just as important as knowing when to back it if you wish to maintain a healthy strike rate and avoid wasting profits. The unusually high strike rate of seventy five per cent that I achieved when betting on the Catterick qualifiers was down to the fact that (with the exception of Legal Legacy) I stopped backing them as soon as their official ratings reflected the improvement they had shown. The more times a horse runs the more exposed it becomes and once it has raced several times over its optimum trip and ground its scope for further progression diminishes sharply. In these circumstances the Handicapper normally gets the measure of the horse in question and unless it proves that it is still ahead of the assessor by clocking a Topspeed figure in excess of its revised official rating it ceases to be of interest to me. Furthermore, as a rule it is more profitable to anticipate the improvement a horse is about to make, as opposed to backing them after they have shown their hand.

LARGEM When I discovered that this three-year-old gelding had been given an opening handicap rating of 53 I could hardly believe my luck because I believed that a mark in the 60s would have been more appropriate. Largem had only had three outings and was presumably a big backward type who had needed time. His one and only outing as a two-year-old had been in an 8f Southwell (AW) maiden. He was unfancied that day and went off at odds of 33/1 and he ran as though in need of both the outing and the experience when finishing seventh, after weakening two furlongs out. He did not race again until 2009 when making a belated seasonal debut on the 30th of July in an 8f Nottingham maiden run on heavy ground. Interestingly he was backed from 25/1 in to 16/1 but that support proved to be wide of the mark when he again weakened two furlongs out, having probably found his lack of fitness and the bottomless ground too much to overcome. On 24 August 2009 he stepped up significantly in trip to 12f when he competed in a Kempton (AW) maiden. He was drawn near the outside on this right-handed track in stall two of eight and despite being heavily disadvantaged by racing wide throughout and also losing ground on the bend three furlongs out he plugged on to finish a respectable fifth, 13 lengths behind the 75 rated winner Bagber and only 1½ lengths behind the 72 rated Pyrus Time. This apparent improvement was confirmed by a Topspeed rating of 60, but as he had been disadvantaged by racing wide and failing to handle one of the bends there seemed little doubt that he was capable of a higher mark than that, particularly as he had only had three runs and was open to further improvement. When I discovered that the Handicapper had erred by giving him an opening rating of just 53 I was confident that he would represent a good thing next time he ran in a handicap.

I did not have to wait long because he reappeared on 11 September 2009 in a 12f (0-55) handicap at Wolverhampton (AW). I was anticipating a major gamble but it did not materialise and I began to question whether his trainer John Jenkins shared my view that his gelding was 'thrown in' on his lowly rating. I backed the horse at the opening price of 14/1 but he drifted out slightly to 16/1 before the off. Soon after the race started my confidence evaporated when I saw that Largem's jockey Simon Whitworth had opted to hold the gelding up at the rear because the early pace set by Saute was pedestrian. If it turned into a sprint for home, as seemed likely, I doubted that Largem would have the speed to make up the ground he had forfeited to the leaders. However, I need not have worried. The gelding had so much in hand of his rivals that, despite Whitworth waiting to make his move until there were just two furlongs remaining, he was able to scoot round the outside of the field and stay on well up the straight to win by one and a half lengths from the well backed Jachol. The fact that he clocked a speed figure of just 22 showed how slow the pace had been and to come from the rear in that fashion proved that he had been a well-handicapped horse. The *Racing Post* analyst wrote: 'Largem had shown ability in maidens but turned in a much improved effort on this handicap debut. He probably deserves extra credit being dropped out last in a race run at just an ordinary gallop and making his ground widest of all and this scopey sort is the type to make further progress.' Whilst I agreed with the gist of the analyst's comment I didn't agree that he had necessarily put in a much improved performance because according to the speed figures his Kempton run was arguable just as good, if not better, and it should be remembered that he had been opposed by much better horses on that occasion. After the Wolverhampton race his trainer John Jenkins was quoted as saying: 'He ran well at Kempton, he was racing wide all the way but he stayed on well. At the bottom of the handicap he had to have some sort of chance.'

CLASSIC CONTOURS This John Quinn trained gelding's sire's stamina index was 12.1f and his dam sire's index was 9.5f so he had been bred with middle distance races in mind and it was pretty obvious from the outset of his career that stamina would, in time, prove to be his forte. I am particularly interested in this type of horse because if they are campaigned astutely as two-year-olds they often begin their three-year-old careers on potentially lenient official handicap ratings. They are unlikely to be suited to five or six furlongs races because they do not possess the inherent speed to keep up with rivals that are often both more precocious and more speedily bred. Even seven furlongs often proves inadequate, particularly on fast ground, or on sharp tracks and it is not until this type of horse encounters eight furlongs or a testing seven furlongs as a two-year-old that they are able to be competitive with horses of a similar class to themselves. Often this type of horse will need time to mature and strengthen and as there are very few two-year-old races run over further than a mile it makes sense that connections should be patient with them in their first season and instead target a successful three-year-old campaign. I like to see this type of horse given three runs over inadequate trips as juveniles in the hope that they begin their three-year-old careers on lenient handicap ratings.

Classic Contours was trained as a two-year-old by Alan Swinbank. During his debut season he was restricted to just four races over either six or seven furlongs. In his first two runs he was beaten ten lengths and eleven lengths and clocked modest speed figures of 34 and 15. He then ran in a maiden race over Catterick's sharp seven furlongs on fast ground and it was a bit of a surprise that he was able to finish a good second of six runners (having stayed on well in the closing stages) and to clock a much improved speed figure of 64. After this third run the Handicapper allotted him a lenient looking rating of 66 and he was duly added to my list of horses to follow. I was sure that he could win off that rating when he was stepped up in distance.

On his fourth and final outing as a two-year-old he competed in his first handicap race but once again he was kept to the inadequate distance of seven furlongs and once again he was found wanting for a change of pace. He kept on in the final furlong to finish sixth and once again clocked a speed figure of 64.

By the time he returned to the track as a three-year-old at Musselburgh on 3 April 2009 he had switched stables and was under the care of John Quinn. Although I was pleased to see that his official rating had been lowered by three pounds to 63 I had no interest in him that day because he was once again racing over seven furlongs and there was no way that he would be competitive over a sharp seven furlongs on fast ground in his three-year-old season. Sure enough he finished a well beaten eighth of ten runners, fourteen lengths behind the winner. Following that performance his mark was not surprisingly lowered to just 61 by the

Handicapper and he was beginning to look very well treated. He next ran on 23 April 2009 in a ten furlong Beverley handicap. In view of his stout breeding I felt that even ten furlongs might prove to be short of his best trip. However, despite the fact that he also did not have the best of draws in stall four of thirteen, I decided to back him at 16/1 because I felt that those odds more than compensated me for the doubts that I had.

Before the race he drifted ominously out to 20/1 and I began to suspect the worst. Sure enough he never got into contention. Although he was not aided by his rider dropping his reins in the final furlong he stayed on well from the rear to finish fifth, eight lengths behind the winner. I had lost, but I took consolation from the fact that he had been beaten quite convincingly which would have ramifications for his odds next time out. I anticipated that he would be stepped up further in trip, because on the evidence of the Beverley run he needed at least twelve furlongs.

I did not have to wait too long before I recouped my losses with interest. Classic Contours ran again on 8 May 2009 in a Hamilton handicap and as I predicted he was upped in trip to twelve furlongs. The Handicapper had helped by dropping the gelding a further pound after his failure at Beverley and I was pleased to find that Jamie Kyne had been booked to take a further seven pounds off his mount's back. Now that the gelding finally had everything in his favour I felt very confident that he would win and considering that there were only nine runners I was pleased to get on in the morning at the generous looking odds of 6/1. I didn't experience an anxious moment during the race and Classic Contours ran out a comfortable enough winner, staying on well to win by two and a quarter lengths having been backed in to 4/1 before the off.

Six days later he ran again under a six pound penalty in a twelve furlong race at Beverley, but his latest speed figure had only been 58 and he was thus now on a mark two pounds above his highest speed rating. Given that he was available at odds of around 2/1 I decided not to back him. He did manage to win, but only just. After being trapped out wide for most of the contest he found enough to fend off the attentions of Tae Kwon Do and to his credit he showed plenty of courage to come out on top and clock a Topspeed figure of 49. Following this victory his official rating was raised to 70 and as he had not achieved a speed figure above 64 he was beginning to look rather exposed. He next appeared on 27 May 2009 in another three-year-old handicap over the same course and distance, but this time there were several other contenders that appeared to have started life in handicaps on favourable looking official ratings:

CLASSIC CONTOURS (J J Quinn) Najran (12.1f) – What's Up Kittycat (Tabasco Cat (9.5f)) OR 70

DATE	COURSE/DISTANCE	RACE TYPE	OUTCOME		SP	OR	TS
12/05/09	Bev 12GF	Handicap	1st	hd	13/8	66	49
08/05/09	Ham 12 GS	Handicap	1st	2L	4/1	60	58
23/04/09	Bev 10GF	Handicap	5th	8L	20/1	61	59
03/04/09	Mus 7GF	Handicap	8th	14L	9/1	63	43
04/09/08	Red 7GS	Handicap	6th	3L	14/1	66	64
05/08/08	Cat 7GF	Maiden	2nd	1L	50/1	-	64
20/07/08	Red 7Gd	Maiden	7th	11L	12/1	-	15
16/06/08	Crl 6 GF	Maiden	7th	10L	9/1	-	34

ANTIGUA SUNRISE (R Fahey) Noverre (7.9f) – Staff Approved (Teenoso (10.7f)) OR 69

DATE	COURSE/DISTANCE	RACE TYPE	OUTCOME		SP	OR	TS
15/05/09	Yor 12f	Handicap	1st	1L	6/1	67	72
23/04/09	Bev 10f	Handicap	3rd	5L	7/2	67	71
03/04/09	Mus 7f	Handicap	3rd	6L	11/2	67	67
18/10/08	Cat 7f	Handicap	2nd	½L	11/2	65	67
20/09/08	Cat 6f	Maiden	5th	10L	12/1	-	51
25/07/08	Thi 7f	Maiden	5th	7L	7/1	-	49
12/07/08	Yor 6f	Maiden	5th	4L	16/1	-	64

NORTHSIDE PRINCE (G A Swinbank) Desert Prince (9.1f) – Spartan Girl (Ela-Mana-Mou (12.3f)) OR 65

DATE	COURSE/DISTANCE	RACE TYPE	OUTCOME		SP	OR	TS
29/04/09	Pon 10Gd	Maiden	3rd	15L	80/1	-	64
11/10/08	Mus 7GS	Maiden	8th	11L	50/1	-	49
24/09/08	Red 7GS	Maiden	8th	11L	33/1	-	-

DAZINSKI (M H Tompkins) Sulamani (11.7f) – Shuheb (Nashwan (10.0f)) OR 69

DATE	COURSE/DISTANCE	RACE TYPE	OUTCOME		SP	OR	TS
19/09/08	Nmk 9GF	Handicap	5th	6L	11/2	72	52
29/08/08	Sal 8GF	Handicap	6th	5L	9/2	73	67
21/07/08	Yar 7GF	Maiden	1st	nk	3/1	-	51
28/06/08	Nmk 7Fm	Maiden	7th	8L	25/1	-	37

Antigua Sunrise was officially rated 69 and she was the only contender that was definitely well-handicapped having achieved speed figures of 72 and 71 on her last two starts. She was a three-year-old filly that clearly needed a decent test of stamina. A check on the progeny of her dam, Staff Approved, revealed that four of them had won over either ten or twelve furlongs so it was no surprise that she had shown some improvement since being stepped up to middle distances from seven furlongs or less. Northside Prince and Dazinski were lightly raced and their breeding suggested that they would improve for this step up in trip to twelve furlongs and, if they did, they were likely to prove to be well-handicapped as well, given that they had already clocked speed figures that nearly matched their current official ratings. Of the two, I favoured Northside Prince because he had already had an outing this season and he had had one less race. Furthermore, I felt that Dazinski's breeding suggested that even twelve furlongs might be short of his best. In comparison to the other three contenders Classic Contours was now looking a shade exposed on his revised mark of 70, as he had already scored twice over this distance and the best speed figure he had managed was 64.

Although it was a close call between Antigua Sunrise and Northside Prince I came down on the side of the former even though she was available at 5/2 as opposed to the 5/1 about Northside Prince. Antigua Sunrise had done particularly well to record a Topspeed figure of 64 on her racecourse debut over the inadequate trip of six furlongs and having shown her hand to some extent in that race it was a little surprising that she was able to start life in handicaps on the lenient looking mark of 65. The fact that she was gambled on from 10/1 in to 11/2 on her first run in a handicap was a measure of how well treated connections felt their filly to be because Catterick's sharp seven furlongs was clearly an inadequate trip for her. The gamble was very nearly landed but unfortunately for her supporters Antigua Sunrise got slightly outpaced four furlongs out when the pace quickened and despite finishing the race strongly she just failed to reel in Amber Sunset who managed to make all.

Her first run of the following season was once again over the inadequate trip of seven furlongs at Musselburgh and it was no surprise that she was beaten six lengths into third place. Interestingly, she managed to clock a respectable speed figure of 67 which matched her official rating. With that pipe opener behind her she then went to Beverley on 23 April 2009 where she was stepped up in trip to ten furlongs. I had fancied her to win on that occasion because she had had the best of the draw and I thought that she was sure to show improved form, however, she only managed to finish third after once again coming in for strong support. My initial reaction was that she had been a shade disappointing, but when

I saw that she had clocked an improved speed figure of 71 I concluded that she had simply come up against a decent opponent in the shape of the winner Topolski. The latter had clocked an impressive figure of 83, despite being rated only 68, and it was no surprise that he had gone on to win his next race on 30 April 2009 by six lengths. I backed her again when she was upped to twelve furlongs for the first time at York on 15 May 2009 and on that occasion she had obliged at 6/1. Her speed figure of 72 confirmed that she had improved and that she remained ahead of the Handicapper.

There was little doubt that she was the form pick for the race at Beverley but I have to admit that I should not have accepted odds of 5/2 about her. I had identified three other contenders in the race and 4/1 should have been the minimum price that I was prepared to accept. But like most punters I break my own rules! On this occasion I justified the bet by convincing myself that Antigua Sunrise was the best handicapped of them all and fortunately my indiscretion was rewarded when she stayed on strongly from an unpromising position to lead on the line. Classic Contours finished second and Northside Prince and Dazinski finished fourth and fifth respectively. Surprisingly, Northside Prince managed only a couple of placings during the rest of the season but that was perhaps due to the fact that connections erred by deciding to drop him back down in trip. Dazinski on the other hand went on to win two races once he was upped to sixteen furlongs and the huge improvement that this extended trip brought about was highlighted by speed figures of 86 and 88. His breeding had suggested that he needed two miles and that was emphatically proven to be the case. Classic Contours unsurprisingly failed to win another race as his revised mark of 71 accurately reflected his ability and he was always likely to be vulnerable to better handicapped horses.

LEARN FROM THE MASTER

The career of Point Of Light provides an excellent example of the skill so typically displayed by his trainer Sir Mark Prescott who is, in my opinion, the master at preparing his horses so that they begin their handicapping careers on favourable official ratings and then at taking full advantage of their ratings to win as many races as possible. Of course his skill is legendary and most of his unexposed runners go off at restrictive odds but, nevertheless, there are valuable lessons to be learned from analysing and understanding his tried and tested methodology.

POINT OF LIGHT (Sir Mark Prescott) Pivotal (7.7f) – Lighthouse (Warning(8.8f))							
DATE	DISTANCE	RACE TYPE	OUTCOME		SP	OR	TS
16/09/09	12f	HANDICAP	1st	2½L	4/5	80	47
12/08/09	11f	HANDICAP	1st	1¼L	2/5	72	86
10/08/09	12f	HANDICAP	1st	2L	8/13	66	69
06/08/09	12f	APP H'CAP	1st	1½L	4/5	72	76
31/07/09	10f	HANDICAP	1st	1L	7/4	60	61
25/07/09	10f	APP H'CAP	1st	1L	11/4	60	44
13/10/08	6f	MAIDEN	10th	14L	16/1	-	35
20/09/08	6f	MAIDEN	3rd	9L	10/3	-	53
13/09/08	6f	MAIDEN	8th	12L	16/1	-	43

As a two-year-old Point Of Light was given time to mature before making his debut on 13 September 2008 but he was then given three races in relatively quick succession to give him experience and to ensure that he qualified for an official handicap rating prior to the end of the season. Typically those three runs were over an inadequate trip and as a result Point Of Light was well beaten on each occasion. Having performed moderately in the three maiden races he was allotted a lowly official rating of 60 and unsurprisingly that was in no way representative of his true inherent ability. He was then gelded before being put away until the following season to allow him time to overcome the operation and to mature and strengthen.

Sir Mark is meticulous when preparing the campaign of a well-handicapped horse to ensure that he fully exploits the situation before the Handicapper can react. While the horse in question begins to reveal its latent talent, Sir Mark manages to stay one step ahead of the Handicapper by skilfully placing it in the right races and by running it several times in quick succession. To do this he has to make numerous race entries for the horse and this fact alone usually provides punters with an invaluable clue as to what is about to unravel. If one of his lightly raced horses does not have multiple entries it is probably not about to embark on a series of victories and you should exercise caution before backing it.

Point Of Light's first outing in the 2009 season provided other clues that he was about to win several races on the bounce. Firstly, he had been entered in a ten furlong handicap and given Sir Mark's well established modus operandi this four furlong increase in distance was likely to herald significant improvement. Secondly, it was an apprentice handicap. Importantly, horses that win these races do not attract a penalty and if they are returned to the racetrack before the Handicapper has time to raise their ratings they can run off the same mark they were on when they won the apprentice race. Sir Mark looks to exploit this rule to avoid penalties with the intention of maximising the chance of his horses following up one victory with another. It is always worth scrutinising the multiple entries he has made for a horse to see whether they include one or two apprentice events because if they do it is likely that the trainer believes the horse can embark on a trademark winning sequence.

Point Of Light duly won his first race of the season having been strong in the market and was returned at odds of 11/4. He was sure to come on for his first run of the season and it was interesting to note that the manner of his victory suggested that he would do better over a longer trip. The *Racing Post* analyst noted that: 'Having travelled well he took a while to hit top stride and on this evidence may well improve for another couple of furlongs.' No doubt Sir Mark was well aware that the gelding would do better over further but deliberately started him out over a slightly inadequate trip in the knowledge that he was well enough handicapped to overcome that particular obstacle. He did not want to reveal the gelding's hand until a bit later and he intended to ensure that the gelding would have further scope to improve and remain ahead of the Handicapper as he was stepped up in distance.

Point Of Light reappeared six days later at Bath in another ten furlong race, but this time it was a standard 0-80 handicap. He was able to race once more off his opening official rating of 60 and the outcome was very similar with him again having to work hard to win by just under a length. Six days later he was out again at Bath in another apprentice handicap and importantly he had been stepped up in trip by two furlongs to one and a half miles. He had to race under a six pound penalty for his last success and because his official rating had in the meantime been raised to 66 in response to his first win, he now had to overcome a twelve pound rise - effectively a revised mark of 72. I suspect that if he had competed in another ten furlong race he may have struggled to win but with the extra two furlongs bringing out further significant improvement he was able to score again, but this time in a more convincing manner for he only had to be pushed out in the final furlong to win by one and a half lengths, with a further eight lengths back to the third horse.

His continued improvement was highlighted by the fact that he clocked an impressive Topspeed figure of 76. He was turned out again four days later before the Handicapper had had the opportunity to raise his rating beyond 66. The gelding had not attracted a penalty for winning an apprentice race last time out and he was therefore able to race off his old mark of 66 – a mark six pounds below the rating he had won off at Bath last time out! It was no surprise when he won 'readily' by two lengths under the welter burden of ten stone. Despite his exertions he had not yet earned a rest and he was back on a racecourse two days later to compete in an eleven furlong handicap at Yarmouth. Having attracted a six pound penalty for his previous win he was now on a mark of 72 but this clearly held no fears for him as he had won off 72 already and had clocked a speed figure of 76. The Yarmouth race was a particularly poor event and was little better than a seller considering that the next highest rated horse was on the lowly mark of just 63. It was therefore a formality for the improving Point Of Light and he stayed on well in the final furlong to win by one and a half lengths. Significantly, he clocked a much improved Topspeed figure of 86 which demonstrated that he was capable of winning off a much higher mark than 72.

Sir Mark now relented and gave the gelding a much deserved break before he returned to the track just over a month later to compete in a twelve furlong handicap at Beverley. During his absence the Handicapper had reacted to his string of victories by raising his rating to 80, but on the evidence of his 86 Topspeed figure that rise was unlikely to stop him. Sure enough he won by a convincing two and a half lengths margin and took his tally to an impressive six wins in under two months.

His six wins earned his owners the rather modest sum of £23,000 and you could argue that his efforts didn't amount to much from a financial point of view, but that has to be balanced against the enjoyment his owners must have had from watching their pride and joy win six in a row. Some trainers like to target the better grade races and focus more on the potential financial returns but I am a big fan of Sir Mark's methodology. His strategy with horses that he considers will never reach Group class is to win as many races with them as possible and then sell them, often abroad or to National Hunt trainers. Once a horse has become fully exposed it is by definition hard to win with and once it has demonstrated that it cannot win from a career high mark it makes good economic sense to sell it whilst its recent good form makes it look an attractive purchase. The alternative is to keep the horse, but it is likely to struggle to win again until its official rating is reduced. However, unless the horse finishes unplaced on numerous occasions it is unlikely that the Handicapper will significantly drop its rating and, for that reason alone, keeping it in training becomes more uneconomical than ever.

The career of Valid Point is worth highlighting because it demonstrates that things do not always go to plan for Sir Mark. The Handicappers do have some discretion as to when they first allocate a rating to a horse and it is not necessarily after its first three runs, or after it has won a race. In this case they refused to give Valid Point an official mark until he had run no less than six times in maiden races because they did not feel that the horse had shown enough on the racetrack to warrant one! I suspect that Sir Mark was pulling what is left of his hair out in frustration at their unusual show of obstinacy. He had little choice but to keep returning Valid Point to the track deep into the winter months and it was not until he upped the horse to seven furlongs on 21 January 2009 that they relented (even though he was once again beaten out of sight by fifteen lengths). Perhaps the Handicappers are becoming a little tired of the Prescott modus operandi and have decided that his horses need to reveal a little more of their latent talent before they are given ratings in the future – we shall see.

VALID POINT (Sir Mark Prescott) Val Royal (8.9f) – Ricadonna (Kris (9.9f)) OR 83						
DATE	DISTANCE	RACE TYPE	OUTCOME		SP	OR	TS
24/09/09	10f	HANDICAP	1st	4l	4/6	73	68
20/09/09	11f	HANDICAP	1st	4l	6/5	67	72
03/09/09	9½f	HANDICAP	1st	1½l	8/11	57	68
30/08/09	10f	HANDICAP	1st	2l	4/5	51	59
26/08/09	10f	HANDICAP	1st	3l	7/2	46	57
18/08/09	8f	HANDICAP	4th	3l	17/2	45	40
21/01/09	7f	MAIDEN	6th	15l	33/1	-	-
07/01/09	6f	MAIDEN	6th	22l	33/1	-	6
22/12/08	6f	MAIDEN	9th	14l	66/1	-	21
11/12/08	6f	MAIDEN	8th	13l	33/1	-	27
28/10/08	6f	MAIDEN	10th	10l	16/1	-	40
21/10/08	6f	MAIDEN	9th	10l	20/1	-	26

Once the goal of achieving a lowly rating had finally been accomplished Valid Point was put away by his trainer and given a decent break of over two hundred days, during which time he was gelded. He returned to the track on 18 August 2009 in an eight furlong handicap at Brighton and ran off an official rating of just 45. He probably needed this first run and it was unlikely that Brighton's sharp eight furlongs would prove to be a sufficient test of stamina for the gelding so it was no surprise when he drifted in the market from 6/1 out to 17/2. He finished a promising fourth and in so doing caught the eye of the *Racing Post* analyst who wrote: 'He hit a flat spot at a crucial stage before staying on again, suggesting a stiffer test is required, and he looks one to take out of the race.' Eight days later he reappeared at Ayr in a ten furlongs handicap on soft ground. If he was able to cope with the underfoot conditions the greater test of stamina was sure to bring about significant improvement and the opening 9/2 looked generous. After being backed in to 7/2 he made all and having gone clear in the final furlong he was eased down in the last hundred yards. Despite taking it easy in the closing stages the gelding managed to clock a decent Topspeed figure of 57. Now that the bandwagon had begun to roll from the basement official rating of 45 there was not much chance of it being stopped and at the time of writing five consecutive victories had been racked up.

It is worth noting how Valid Point's improvement was highlighted by the ever increasing Topspeed figures that he was awarded and how they indicated that he would take each revised official rating in his stride. After he clocked a 57 on 26 August 2009 he next ran off a mark of just 51 so had at least six pounds in hand on that occasion. He then clocked a 59 and his next revised mark was 57 so once again he was ahead of the Handicapper. When winning off his 57 rating he clocked a 68 and this once again was higher than his next revised mark of 67. His subsequent win achieved a speed figure of 72 and although his next official rating was a slightly higher 73 he had drawn clear from two furlongs out that day and had been eased near the finish so it was obvious that he was better than the bare figure of 72.

Whenever you are weighing up the chance of any lightly raced horse that is about to have its first run in a handicap, or has already run in a handicap but is yet to win a race, it is always worth checking its entries for clues as to its chance. I use the facility on the *Racing Post* website to do this but it is possible to use the paper version, as long as you buy it on the days when the entries are published. Although there are no hard and fast rules it is a negative if any trainer enters a lightly raced horse for either a claimer or a seller during a five day period whilst at the same time also entering it for handicap races. Furthermore, I do not like to see an entry for a maiden race that is preceded by entries for handicaps because it suggests a lack of belief on the part of the trainer that the horse will win one of the handicap races! Entries such as these suggest that the trainer is not convinced that he has a well-handicapped horse on his hands. Although it may win one of the races that it has been entered for I make the assumption that the horse in question is unlikely to improve much beyond its current rating and is unlikely to win several races on the bounce.

THE PACE ANGLE

Have a look at the form of Waahej up to and including his debut win at odds of 22/1 on 25 September 2009.

WAAHEJ (P W Hiatt) Haafhd (8.8f) – Madam Ninette (Mark Of Esteem (8.6f))							
DATE	COURSE/ DISTANCE	RACE TYPE	OUTCOME		SP	OR	TS
25/09/09	Wol 9½f	Handicap	1st	hd	22/1	61	43
10/09/09	Kem 8f	Handicap	6th	13L	9/1	62	30
18/08/09	Not 8f	Handicap	3rd	2L	16/1	62	25
05/08/09	Bri 8f	Handicap	10th	23L	12/1	66	5
26/06/09	Nmk 8f	Handicap	5th	7L	12/1	68	56
19/06/09	Nmk 8f	Handicap	12th	11L	14/1	68	47
13/08/08	Sal 6f	Maiden	5th	5L	6/1	-	60
18/07/08	Not 6f	Maiden	6th	7	11/1	-	62
12/06/08	Nby 6f	Maiden	5th	8L	20/1	-	43

Once again we have the familiar pattern of a horse having had just the three runs as a juvenile over an inadequate trip in order to acquire a potentially favourable handicap rating. With that goal having been partly achieved Waahej was then put away for the winter and was presumably gelded at some stage during this period. I say 'partly achieved' because I doubt whether his then trainer, John Dunlop was particularly delighted with the gelding's opening rating of 68 on the balance of what he had achieved in his first three outings. Although he was likely to improve for being stepped up in distance he did not look to be 'thrown in' on his handicap debut on 19 June 2009 and it was not until his run at Nottingham on 18 August 2009 that it first came to my attention that he may be a horse to follow. Have a look at the result of the Nottingham race which is reproduced below:

DG TAXIS FIRST PAST THE POST APPRENTICE HANDICAP
Nottingham, 18/08/2009 (8f, good/firm)

HORSE	DIST	COMMENT	OR	TS
ZENNERMAN	-	Made all, stayed on	59	29
FOLLOW THE FLAG	½	Prominent, lost place 5f out, hdwy 1f out to chase winner, ran on	69	38
WAAHEJ	2	Held up, switched right over 1f out, ran on	62	25
BELLE NOVERRE	nk	Prominent, lost place after 1f, headway 4f out, chased winner 1f out	72	36
DANEHILLSUNDANCE	1½	Prominent, saddle slipped 6f out, lost place 3f out, stayed on final furlong	74	34
WEST END LAD	¾	Chased winner, ridden 3f out, no extra final furlong	75	33
INSIDE STORY	½	Prominent, ridden 2f out, no extra final furlong	66	23
FOL LIAM	15	Started slowly, held up, headway 2f out, weakened if out	65	-

In view of the fact that the winner Zennerman recorded a speed figure of just 29 it was obvious that this apprentice handicap had been run at a sedate early pace. Unsurprisingly, it was the horses that took a prominent position in the initial stages that were favoured by the way in which the race unfolded. Zennerman was gifted an easy lead and was able to make all without being seriously challenged at any stage. Although most of the other runners had held a prominent early position, when the pace picked up towards the end of the race they had lacked the necessary speed to make inroads on the leader. Waahej, on the other hand, had been held up in the rear for most of the race, but unlike the others, once he was belatedly switched right over one furlong out to make his run towards the outside of the field he ran on in eye-catching fashion and went past several rivals that were not weakening. Furthermore, he closed significantly on Zennerman despite the fact that the leader had kept plenty in reserve for his finishing effort as a consequence of setting such slow early fractions.

Waahej's performance suggested that he would benefit from a step up in trip following four runs over eight furlongs and if that brought about some improvement I felt confident that he could win a race because he was beginning to look well treated even in the context of his eight furlong form. His official rating had quickly dropped from 68 to 62 following only three runs and that looked to be generous given that he had excuses in all three of those outings. First time out as a three-year-old he would have been in need of the run. By the time of his second outing he had switched stables from John Dunlop's to Peter Hiatt's and may not yet have been fully settled into his new surroundings. In any event the Newmarket race proved to be totally unsatisfactory because Waahej was disadvantaged by racing with three other horses on the far side whilst the larger group of six finished six lengths ahead of them on the stands' side. Under the circumstances he may have performed better than it appeared when coming only a neck behind the 'winner' of the race that took place on the far side of the track. His third outing of the 2009 season was at Brighton and although he finished a disappointing last that performance could be ignored because he raced 'awkwardly' on the idiosyncratic track's undulations and some horses just cannot act there.

Following these three excusable runs Waahej was dropped a total of six pounds by the Handicapper and bearing in mind that he had clocked Topspeed figures of 62 and 60 as a two-year-old (when racing over the inadequate trip of six furlongs) it was likely that he would be capable of winning off his revised official rating of 62. When he next appeared in a Kempton (AW) handicap over eight furlongs on 10 September 2009 I decided to back him. He was potentially well drawn in stall eleven of eleven but I was concerned that if he was held up as usual a high draw could turn out to be a disadvantage as he would probably have to switch wide in the straight and come around the other runners in order to obtain a clear run. Furthermore, this was an apprentice race and Waahej's rider was relatively inexperienced – a fact that would magnify the difficulties that he could encounter if trapped behind a wall of runners turning into the home straight. More often than not inexperienced pilots lack the guile and the confidence needed to extricate themselves from difficult positions. I also decided to take a bit of a gamble with regard to the distance of the race. I was pretty sure that Waahej needed nine or ten furlongs to be seen at his best but I decided that my doubts about the race conditions were adequately compensated for by the available odds of 12/1. I gambled that the early pace would be strong enough to bring Waahej's anticipated stamina into play and to also cause the field to become strung out, thereby reducing the likelihood that the gelding would encounter traffic problems.

Soon after the race started I was rubbing my hands with glee because Uncle Brit, lit up by being blinkered for the first time, set off at a furious pace and soon had most of the other runners on the stretch. However, although the fast pace set the race up beautifully for those that were held up in the early stages, Waahej never looked liked being one of the beneficiaries! He made moderate late headway from the rear to finish sixth, beaten by a resounding thirteen lengths. The *Racing Post* analyst reported that: 'Waahej made a satisfactory all-weather debut and would be interesting at around ten furlongs.' I made a note not to back the gelding again unless he was stepped up in trip.

Two weeks later Waahej reappeared in a nine and a half furlong handicap at Wolverhampton – a track that suits hold up horses with a turn of foot. He had been dropped a further two pounds in the ratings to a mark of 60; he was well drawn in stall two and had one of the best all-weather jockeys in the business on board – Chris Catlin. Everything seemed in place for a big run and I was quite surprised to find that he was available at the massive price of 25/1. Although there were several other lightly raced types in the race that were genuine contenders there was no doubt in my mind that Waahej was overpriced. The other runners are detailed below:

WOLVERHAMPTON (AW) 25/09/2009						
'William Hill – Quote Bonus25 Handicap' 9½f						
HORSE	SIRE INDEX	RUNS	BEST TS	OR	DRAW	CONCLUSION (SP)
WAAHEJ	8.8f	8 (0)*	62	60	2	Contender (22/1)
INSOLENCE	7.9f	4 (2)*	71	70	5	Contender (9/2)
TOO TALL	8.7f	7 (0)*	67	68	6	Contender (4/1 Fav)
STARLA DANCER	8.0f	8 (2)*	64	70	3	Not well-handicapped
BURNS NIGHT	8.8f	7 (1)*	77	75	7	Regressing
NAVAJO NATION	8.4f	7 (4)*	67	68	8	Exposed at the trip
DIAMOND TWISTER	10.0f	21 (9)*	78	66	4	Exposed /Regressing
WEST WITH THE WIND	8.2f	8 (0)*	70	72	9	Contender (13/2)

(*The figures in brackets are the number of runs over 9f or further)

As you can see only four horses were technically well-handicapped on the basis of having achieved a Topspeed figure higher than their current official rating and they were Waahej, Insolence, Burns Night and Diamond Twister. However, the last two appeared to be regressing and could be eliminated – particularly Diamond Twister who was fully exposed at the trip and had only managed one win in twenty-one starts. Starla Dancer did not look well enough handicapped to figure here and Navajo Nation did not look well enough treated either because he was exposed at the trip and his high draw was likely to cost him a pound or two. I rated West With The Wind the least likely of the contenders to win. Although he was unexposed at the trip he had the worst of the draw and did not look as well-handicapped as some of the others. I rated Too Tall the most likely danger. I felt that he might be the one to benefit most from the step up in distance and, if so, he would improve past the lightly raced Insolence who had proven that he was well-handicapped at present but had already run twice at the trip. I decided to combine Waahej and Too Tall in a reverse forecast.

Before the race I was unimpressed to discover that Catlin was putting up a pound overweight but in the end it made no difference. The jockey rode a canny race and crucially switched right when rounding the home turn to bring the gelding with a winning run down the centre of the track and the pairing held on by a diminishing head from the Sir Michael Stoute trained Insolence (who may have been unlucky not to win having been taken very wide on the final turn) with Too Tall further back in third. Had the verdict gone to Insolence by a nostril or a head I may have been tempted to send Catlin some dietary advice but fortunately the overweight made no difference. Although pleased with the win I had some regrets that I had missed out on a course straight forecast that paid £118 to a £1 stake and perhaps, with hindsight, I should have combined more of the contenders in forecasts with Waahej.

UNEXPECTED IMPROVEMENT

Horses will sometimes suddenly become well-handicapped on the evidence of a single speed figure. Take a look at the first seven races in the career of the Henry Cecil trained Cloudy Start:

CLOUDY START (H R A Cecil) Oasis Dream (7.2f) – Set Fair (Alleged (11.6))							
DATE	COURSE/ DISTANCE	RACE TYPE	OUTCOME		SP	OR	TS
25/09/09	Wol 9½f	Handicap	1st	hd	22/1	61	43
05/06/09	Eps 7Gd	Handicap	1st	½L	10/1	88	93
20/04/09	Yar 7GF	Conditions	3rd	7L	6/1	88	73
17/04/09	Nby 7GS	Handicap	9th	8L	11/2	88	56
04/10/08	Red 7Gd	Maiden	1st	6L	8/11	86	91
18/09/08	Yar 8Gd	Maiden	2nd	1½L	5/6	-	59
02/08/08	Goo 7GF	Maiden	3rd	2L	13/2	-	77
09/07/08	Nmk 7Sft	Maiden	7th	1½L	12/1	-	75

After three runs in maidens Cloudy Start was given an official rating of 86. At that stage it was hard to know whether 86 was an attractive mark or not because the colt had seemingly shown his hand to the Handicapper. If he had taken after his sire Oasis Dream it was likely that seven or eight furlongs would prove to be his forte and this was supported by the fact that he had shown no sign of being outpaced in the early stages of his first three outings in which he either 'tracked the leaders' or was 'with the leaders'. As he appeared to have been competing over his optimum trip from the outset and had finished a second and a third on his previous two runs it was hard to argue with the Handicapper's initial assessment of the colt's form (particularly as his best Topspeed figure to that point had been 77) and for that reason he was of no particular interest to me. However, that changed after the next and final outing of his two-year-old campaign. Rather than going straight into a nursery handicap Cloudy Start ran in another maiden, this time at Redcar over seven furlongs. He won the race easily by six lengths, having only to be pushed out in the final furlong, and although he beat an ordinary looking bunch to win at odds of 8/11 the true merit of his performance was highlighted by the fact that he clocked an above average Topspeed figure of 91. Bearing in mind that he was not fully extended in the race it was pretty obvious that he was somewhat better than the bare 91 indicated. I was surprised to find that the Handicapper reacted by raising Cloudy Start's official rating by only two pounds to 88. That looked to be overly generous and the colt was added to my list of horses to follow. I subsequently discovered that the two horses that he had finished only one and a half lengths behind at Goodwood (Jukebox Jury and Full Toss) finished the 2008 season rated 112 and 100 respectively and this provided me with further evidence that Cloudy Start was well-handicapped.

He did not race again as a two-year-old and I had to wait until 17 April 2009 before he returned to the track. His seasonal debut came in a seven furlong handicap at Newbury and it looked quite a competitive race with fifteen other runners, many of which were from the top yards. I doubted that Cloudy Start would be fully fit and I was unsure whether he would be suited to the good to soft ground but Henry Cecil is more than capable of having his horses ready to win at the first time of asking. However, my decision not to back Cloudy Start was simplified by the fact that he was likely to race on the wide outside from stall one. With the stalls placed in the centre of the straight course stall one was likely to be a big disadvantage, particularly if the early pace was set by one of the horses drawn high. If the runners were to come down the centre and take on the usual arrow head formation Cloudy Start would struggle to get into the race from his wide position.

He opened at the skinny odds of 4/1 but drifted out to 11/2 and with the market vibes speaking against him I was more than happy not to get involved. As it turned out the early pace was set by Makaamen from stall fifteen and he was pressed for the early lead by Babycat who started from stall fourteen. With the race developing away from Cloudy Start he was always going to struggle and it was no surprise to see him drop away rather tamely in the final furlong to be beaten by eight lengths in ninth place. I was pleased with the end result because I knew the run could be ignored and it meant that Cloudy Start was sure to be sent off at decent odds next time he ran.

I had a simpler decision to make on his next outing, which came in a conditions race at Yarmouth on 20 April 2009. This time it was likely that he would be outclassed by some better rivals and he was also disadvantaged by taking on older horses at this early stage of the season. I do not like betting on three-year-olds when they are taking on older horses before June because I think that they are disadvantaged by their immaturity. Furthermore, Cloudy Start was up against the consistent and classy five-year-old Mia's Boy, who was officially rated 101 and there seemed little chance that he would beat that rival. Because of this I was confident that Cloudy Start would get beaten and I again declined to bet on him. Under the circumstances he ran a respectable race to finish third, some seven lengths behind Mutheeb and Mia's Boy. I had hoped that the Handicapper would drop him a pound or two following these two defeats but unfortunately he remained on a mark of 88.

He next ran on 5 June 2009 in a seven furlong handicap at Epsom on good ground. It was another big field of fifteen runners, but now that he had had two runs he was sure to be at peak fitness and I felt that conditions were in his favour, particularly as the sharp track would suit his prominent style of racing. I was delighted to find that he opened at odds of 12/1 and I had no reason not to take what I considered to be a generous price. Before the off he was backed in to 10/1 and the support proved to be justified. In the race he chased the leaders before being driven to the front inside the final furlong and he then ran on well to win by a cheeky half length. He clocked a Topspeed figure of 93 which confirmed that a mark of 88 had been too lenient. The Handicapper responded by raising him to 93 and I thought that he could win again off that mark but my belief was not put to the test because his next outing was in a conditions race for three-year-olds at Kempton. He was of no interest to me on that occasion because once again he looked to be outclassed by rivals rated 111, 106 and 100. Surprisingly, he made all to win in emphatic style by four lengths at odds of 5/1. However, the apparent merit of that performance was undermined by a Topspeed figure of only 90 which suggested that he had enjoyed the run of the race out in front and that he may not have improved as much as the bare form indicated. Following that victory his rating was hoisted to 108 but predictably that proved too much for the colt and at the time of writing he has failed to win another race.

Another example of a horse that suddenly became well-handicapped on the basis of an improved Topspeed figure is provided by Fastnet Storm.

FASTNET STORM (T P Tate) Rock of Gibraltar (8.8f) – Dreams (Rainbow Quest (11.1f))							
DATE	COURSE/ DISTANCE	RACE TYPE	OUTCOME		SP	OR	TS
21/06/09	Pon 10GF	Handicap	1st	1L	11/4	84	95
02/06/09	Rip 10GF	Handicap	1st	3L	4/1	78	87
13/05/09	Yor 10GF	Handicap	8th	3½L	50/1	79	70
27/04/09	Ncs 8GF	Handicap	7th	29L	3/1	79	14
20/10/08	Pon 8GS	Handicap	1st	shd	11/1	75	81
19/09/08	Nmk 9GF	Handicap	2nd	¼l	5/1	72	65
14/08/08	Bev 7Sft	Handicap	5th	5L	9/2	75	65
25/07/08	Nmk 7GF	Handicap	5th	4L	7/2	76	59
24/06/08	Bev 7GF	Maiden	1st	nk	9/4	-	42
31/05/08	Don 6Gd	Maiden	7th	9L	100/1	-	46

This gelding first came to my attention after winning a Beverley maiden on only his second start. Following an unremarkable debut in a six furlong maiden at Doncaster in which he finished a well beaten seventh (having been sent off at 100/1) he was surprisingly heavily supported to win a seven furlong race at Beverley next time out. This support suggested that the gelding was well regarded by connections and he did not let them down by battling on well to repel the challengers in the closing stages, albeit after benefitting from taking the lead in a slowly run race. The *Racing Post* analyst reported that the gelding was a 'grand looker' and that 'he stuck to his task in fine style when tackled and kept on well to the line.' His breeding suggested that he would not be seen to best advantage until he was stepped up in trip to middle distances during his three-year-old campaign so I decided to keep an eye on him as he appealed as the type with scope to improve over time and importantly he had already demonstrated that he had a good attitude.

After his maiden victory he was given an initial handicap rating of 76. It was hard to know whether that was a lenient mark because he had enjoyed the run of the race when winning at Beverley and had up to that point only clocked modest speed figures of 46 and 42. However, I suspected that he would be capable of winning off that sort of rating once he was stepped up in trip. On his third outing he ran at Newmarket in a handicap over seven furlongs. Although he was again well supported (from 5/1 into 7/2) I was not tempted to back him because his breeding suggested that seven furlongs was short of his best and he was likely to be caught out by some faster rivals. He tried to make all but went off at too fast a pace and once headed he appeared to weaken away in the closing stages.

Different tactics were employed when he next ran at Beverley in another seven furlong handicap on 14 August 2008. Once again he came in for support but I declined to back him on account of the trip and also because he was unproven on soft ground. Rather than attempting to make all he was held up in midfield in the early stages, but these tactics placed less emphasis on his stamina and they never looked like coming off. In a race that appeared to favour those that raced towards the head of affairs Fastnet Storm simply did not have the speed needed to make up the ground that he had conceded to the winner Musical Maze, who made virtually all. Following these two defeats Fastnet Storm's handicap rating was reduced to 72 but there was still no hard evidence to prove that he was now on a winning mark because the best speed figure he had achieved was just 65.

Although the gelding had let down his supporters since winning his maiden I decided that I would back him when he next ran on 19 September 2008. On this occasion he was set to compete in a nine furlong handicap at Newmarket on fast ground and now that he had been dropped a few pounds in the ratings and was running over what I considered to be a suitable trip for the first time I considered that he would be hard to beat. Once again he came in for support before the race and was sent off at 5/1. Predictably, he reverted to front running tactics on this occasion and they nearly worked, but unfortunately

Oasis Knight proved just too good and beat him by a neck in a driving finish. The fact that they finished four lengths clear of the rest of the field seemed to suggest that they were both well-handicapped. However, the modest speed figure of 65 indicated that Fastnet Storm's jockey had probably got away with setting some sensible early fractions and that the gelding had been favoured by the way the race was run. On his final outing as a two-year-old he dropped back in distance to eight furlongs when running in a handicap at Pontefract. I decided not to back him as he had been raised three pounds by the Handicapper following his narrow defeat at Newmarket and he was disadvantaged by being drawn widest of all out in stall 17. Furthermore, I did not feel that the drop back to eight furlongs was in his favour. Unfortunately for me he pinged out of the gates, crossed over to the rail and proceeded to make all to win by a short head at the rewarding odds of 11/1.

Although I was irritated to have missed out on a winner my interest in Fastnet Storm was only reaffirmed by this performance. I considered that the Handicapper had underestimated the gelding when he raised his rating to 79 because he had clocked a much improved speed figure of 81 and he had managed that in spite of his wide draw. I concluded that, as with front runners in general, he was likely to be at his best on a turning track and I was still convinced that he would do even better when stepped up in trip. Following his Pontefract victory the gelding was then put away until the next Flat season.

The likelihood that he was well-handicapped was advertised when he was strongly supported on his seasonal reappearance at Newcastle on 27 April 2009 in an eight furlong handicap. Now that he was a three-year-old, eight furlongs was sure to be short of his best trip and I was surprised that he was backed in to 3/1 before the off. He never looked like rewarding his supporters and finished well beaten. No doubt they had expected that the gelding would be able to bounce out from his poor draw in stall two of eight and tack over to the nearside rail, but he lacked the speed to get past Johnmanderville who broke quickly from stall four and made all. When the rail bias is in evidence at Newcastle it is one of the strongest there is and unless a horse races hard up against the rail it is very unlikely to win a handicap. Fastnet Storm could not get next to the rail and having raced away from the favoured strip it was no surprise to see him weaken tamely two furlongs out, particularly as he was not at peak fitness on his seasonal debut. He was well beaten and I was pleased that he had appeared to run poorly because his odds were sure to be decent next time out and I hoped that the Handicapper might drop him a pound or two in the meantime. Unfortunately, his official rating remained the same, but his poor performance certainly did wonders for his odds next time out!

He was upped in trip to ten furlongs when he next appeared on 13 May 2009 in a competitive looking York handicap and I could not believe it when I saw that he was available at 50/1. I knew that he was well-handicapped and that he would relish this longer trip and now that he was fitter following his excusable Newcastle defeat I felt sure that 50/1 was a ridiculously generous price. I thought that if he could bounce out from stall ten of sixteen and grab the inside rail he would go very close and at least finish in the first four so I backed him each-way. Unfortunately, things did not go to plan. Alan Munro decided not to take the lead and his efforts to restrain the gelding behind the leaders were resented by his mount which pulled for its head and wasted valuable energy in the process. Despite this, Fastnet Storm took the lead two furlongs out and for a moment looked all over the winner. However, his headstrong antics in the early part of the race caught up with him and my enthusiastic shouts died away as he began to tire entering the final furlong. At that stage he still looked sure to finish in the first four but was unfortunately hampered in the closing stages and lost several positions before finishing eighth just over three lengths behind the winner. I was disappointed after the race that things had not panned out better because it is not often that I genuinely feel my selection will win or go very close at odds of 50/1 and it was some time before I ceased hurling profanities (aimed at Fastnet Storm's connections) at my TV!

Surprisingly, the Handicapper responded to that good run by reducing the gelding's rating by one pound to 78. He next appeared in another ten furlong handicap on 2 June 2009 at Ripon and it looked to be a much easier assignment. This time he only faced seven opponents and he had been dropped down a grade to a 0-80 race. Furthermore, there did not appear to be much early pace in the race and I anticipated that he would either take the lead or be second soon after the start. This was important because a prominent early position is a big advantage in races run over Ripon's round course. It is vital to take a position against the inside rail and stay there for as long as possible. Not only do horses save ground round the bend but there is also a strong draw bias on the straight part of the course in favour of those that race hard up against the far rail. This in turn makes it very hard for horses to come from behind unless they are lucky and gaps appear for them against the rail. If they have to switch out towards the centre of the track to make their challenge they are normally doomed. Everything looked in place for Fastnet Storm on this occasion and I was surprised to be able to get on at 5/1. Those odds didn't last long and he was backed into 4/1 before the off.

The race went to plan and he ran out a ready three length winner after enjoying the run of the race. In the process he clocked a new best Topspeed figure of 87. Although the Handicapper upped his official rating by six pounds to 84 he still looked to be well-handicapped when he returned to a racetrack on 21 June 2009. On that occasion he ran in a ten furlong handicap at Pontefract (the scene of a previous victory) and I anticipated that his front running style would be perfectly suited to this turning track. Although he was drawn widest of all out in stall eight there was little other pace in the race and it appeared likely that he would be able to bounce out and grab the inside rail. I got on at 7/2 and he was well supported before the off into 11/4. He broke smartly, got over to the rail and made all to win by a length. Once again he appeared to have improved and the merit of his performance was highlighted by a speed figure of 95.

He appeared to be better than his revised official rating of 87 so I backed him again when he next ran at Goodwood on 30 July 2009. However, on this occasion he got caught up in a protracted duel for the lead with Geneva Geyser and weakened tamely two furlongs out. I reckoned that that defeat was excusable so I backed him again when he ran at Chester on 21 August 2009. On that occasion he was well drawn in stall three and I envisaged that he would be able to get to the favoured inside rail by taking an early lead and I felt sure that he would be well suited to the Chester turns. However, connections strangely adopted different tactics and were content to track the pace on this occasion before challenging two furlongs out. The plan almost worked but he was caught on the line and went down by a short head. I was disappointed that he had not attempted to lead but I suppose that connections were mindful of getting caught up in another speed duel after the Goodwood debacle. Following those two defeats I did not back him again. I concluded that his recent runs suggested that he would not win again unless everything fell into place for him with regard to the draw, the type of track and the number of other front runners in the field. Although his speed figure of 95 meant that he was technically still well-handicapped on a mark of 87 I concluded that that figure had flattered him and I did not want to be guilty of going to the well once too often!

Have a look at the form of Bahraj before this two-year-old filly contested a seven furlong nursery handicap at Catterick on 6 October 2009. Bahraj was well bred, as is typical of all Sheikh Hamdan Al Maktoum owned horses, and it is not often that a horse of this type proves to be no better than a 61 rated handicapper – the sort of mark usually held by selling platers. As a rule fillies and mares are better suited to long distance races rather than sprints and Bahraj's breeding suggested that she would be best served by seven or eight furlongs as a two-year-old and then by middle distances once she had reached maturity.

BAHRAJ (M Johnston) Key of Luck (9.2f) – Alattrah (Shadeed (7.7f)) OR 61							
DATE	COURSE/ DISTANCE	RACE TYPE	OUTCOME		SP	OR	TS
13/08/09	Bev 5Gd	Maiden	4th	4L	11/2	-	60
30/07/09	Mus 5Gd	Maiden	6th	8L	Evs	-	9
13/07/09	Ayr 6GF	Maiden	4th	3L	6/1	-	36

With that in mind I was interested to see that to date she had been kept to either five or six furlongs. Her performances were a little misleading because in all three outings she had shown good early speed to lead until at least halfway and this may have given punters the impression that she was a sprinter in the making. However, her breeding suggested otherwise and I reckoned that she was probably a lot better than she had been able to show. Although she had the speed to be able to lead against the low class opposition that she had competed against, she was notably small in size, and the fact that she had 'weakened' once headed in both of her five furlong races made me suspect that she had been too weak at that stage of her development to sustain her speed for five furlongs. It was interesting that on her first run (which was over six furlongs) she had not weakened but had kept on at the same pace to finish only three lengths behind the winner. The *Racing Post* analyst reported that she had 'blown hard' after that race so it was safe to assume that when fully fit Bahraj would stay at least six furlongs. I reckoned that she had 'weakened' only because she had gone off too fast.

Despite the fact Bahraj had been running over too short a trip she had still managed to clock a Topspeed figure of 60 on her most recent outing and it was pretty obvious that her initial official rating of just 61 would prove to be lenient if she was able to show any sort of improvement over longer trips. I noted with interest that she had been given a fifty-four day break since her last run because such breaks often benefit horses that lack physical strength. She had had plenty of time to get over her earlier exertions and it was probable that she may have grown and strengthened somewhat during this period. Not only was she was likely to be fresh and well but her trainer was in excellent form and he was also, by some way, the top trainer at Catterick, where his two-year-olds had won no less than eighteen of fifty-nine races (31%). I liked the fact that Francis Norton (who I consider to be the strongest of the lightweight jockeys) had been booked to ride, even though he had to put up two pounds of overweight to ride at eight stone, three pounds. He had a decent strike rate for the yard and his booking, together with the other factors mentioned above suggested the filly was primed to run a big race. The one slight negative was that she was drawn in stall seven of twelve, which can be a disadvantage on this turning course and distance but in view of the fact that she had shown the speed to lead in her last two races over five furlongs I suspected that she would bounce out of the stalls, go clear of her rivals and then tack over to the inside rail. She was available at odds of 6/1 and I was pleased to be able to back her at what I considered to be a generous price. The race went to plan; Norton jumped her out quickly, tacked over to the inside rail and then proceeded to make all on the filly. She kept on well at the finish to win by just under a length, with a further three lengths back to the third horse, and never really looked to be in danger of defeat.

WELL-HANDICAPPED STAYERS

One look at Teeky's breeding was enough to predict that the filly was unlikely to achieve much until raced over at least twelve furlongs and it was probable that she would be best suited by further. It was therefore no surprise to me that she failed to make much of an impact in her two races as a two-year-old over the inadequate trips of seven and eight furlongs even though she came in for market support on both occasions.

DATE	COURSE/ DISTANCE	RACE TYPE	OUTCOME		SP	OR	TS
30/10/09	Nmk 12Gd	Handicap	1st	3L	9/2	76	54
05/09/09	Kem 16St	Handicap	5th	10L	6/1	78	67
19/08/09	Kem 11St	Handicap	2nd	2½L	2/1	76	81

TEEKY (J H M Gosden) Daylami (11.4f) – Las Flores (Sadler's Wells (11.3f)) **OR 82**

31/07/09	Nmk 12Gd	Handicap	1st	6L	9/2	68	82
11/06/09	Not 10Gd	Handicap	7th	6L	8/1	69	64
03/04/09	Bat 10GF	Maiden	2nd	3L	9/2	-	71
24/10/08	Don 8Gd	Maiden	5th	5L	6/1	-	42
21/07/08	Yar 7GF	Maiden	5th	8L	3/1	-	24

She again came in for some support when she was upped to ten furlongs on her seasonal reappearance at Bath 3 April 2009 and considering that she may have been in need of the outing she ran well to finish second. However, the race reader reported that she had 'plugged on' in the final furlong and this comment confirmed that she lacked the pace to be effective at ten furlongs. Although she was clearly crying out for further, she nevertheless managed to clock a Topspeed figure of 71 and when the Handicapper erred by allocating her a lenient opening rating of 69 she went onto my list of horses to follow.

Two months went by before she reappeared at Nottingham on 11 June 2009 and I was disappointed to see that she was running in another ten furlong race. The fact that she had been kept to ten furlongs and was also coming back from a two month absence made me suspect that she had met with a setback in training and that this run over an inadequate trip was designed to ready her for a more suitable race in the future. I therefore decided not to back her but I watched her performance with interest. Although she finished a modest seventh and was six lengths behind the winner she ran another race full of promise. After taking a prominent early position she soon fell back through the field. When her rider switched her to the far rail in the home straight she stayed on in good style and I felt that it was not a bad effort under the circumstances. The Handicapper responded by dropping Teeky's rating by one pound which was an added bonus.

I had to wait over a month and a half before seeing Teeky on a racecourse again and she was evidently not the easiest of horses to train. On 31 July 2009 she was entered in a twelve furlong handicap at Newmarket and had been eased in grade slightly from a 0-75 race at Nottingham to a 0-68. Not only was she the highest rated horse in the race but she was also effectively three pounds well in on her ten furlong form from Bath. With today's extra two furlongs likely to bring about significant improvement I was confident that she was handicapped to win on this occasion. I backed her at 7/1 in the morning which proved to be a good move because her odds contracted to 9/2 before the off. I never had a moment's anxiety during the race because she travelled conspicuously well throughout and when asked to go on she readily quickened and pulled six lengths clear of her toiling rivals. She clocked an impressive speed figure of 82 and I was surprised that the Handicapper reacted to this performance by increasing her rating by only eight pounds to 76.

She next ran on 19 August 2009 but this time she was switched to Kempton's all-weather surface and surprisingly she had been dropped down in distance to eleven furlongs. I was not convinced that the combination of a sharper track, faster surface and a drop in distance would suit her and I felt that these factors, combined with her eight pound rise in the ratings, meant that she was poor value at odds of around 2/1. Even though I felt sure that she was still well-handicapped I declined to back her at those odds and I was relieved when she finished second after appearing to have been unsuited by the sharp turns. The *Racing Post* analyst reported that: 'She was under pressure some way out and although she eventually found her stride and stayed on for second, she was never going to trouble the easy winner. She will need at least twelve furlongs on this surface.'

Teeky returned to the same venue on 5 September 2009 but this time she had been entered in a sixteen furlong handicap. Unfortunately, she had been raised two pounds for coming second last time out but I felt that two miles would be right up her street and I was confident that she could win again off a mark of 78. I backed her at 4/1 but she subsequently drifted ominously out to 6/1. In the race she proved to be a disappointment, getting readily left behind when the pace quickened three furlongs out and never getting back into contention. It was possible that she had not stayed the trip, but I felt her performance had been too bad to be true. Despite being undeniably well-handicapped she had now been unable to take advantage of her lenient official rating on two occasions and I began to suspect that she was simply unable to reproduce her best form on a Polytrack surface. I decided that I would not back her again unless she was running on turf.

Teeky finally ran again some seven weeks later in a twelve furlong handicap for fillies at Newmarket. Although her previous victory had been on the July course it was likely that the Rowley Mile course would suit her just as well, particularly as the ground was once again 'good'. She was running off a mark of 76 and was clearly well treated having clocked a speed figure of 82 when winning with ease on the July course. Having had a seven week break I anticipated that she would be fresh and well on her return and with conditions in her favour I thought that she would be hard to beat so I was happy to back her at 4/1. She defied some weakness in the market to win with authority by three lengths under Jimmy Fortune who sensibly had her well placed near the front of the field in a race in which the early pace was modest. When her rider asked her to take the lead entering the final furlong she stayed on powerfully and drew right away from her rivals, confirming that she had had pounds in hand of them. Her trainer John Gosden reported after the race that: 'We ran her on the all-weather last time out but she doesn't like it and we have had to wait seven weeks for this race. Luckily it has paid off and there is one more race for her – a listed race at Fontainebleau. After that she will retire to the paddocks.'

It is always worth keeping an eye on any young and unexposed three-year-old that has unusually high sire and damsire indices. Most of them will not fulfil their potential until they are allowed to race over distances of more than two miles because they are usually too slow to win over ten furlongs or less. When they eventually progress to trips of two miles or beyond they should improve and if so they may become well-handicapped as a result. Patience is often required though, because inevitably such horses race many times over shorter distances before they are finally allowed to compete in contests over their optimum distance.

Have a look at the career record of Bernie The Bolt before he won a Cesarewitch trial over eighteen furlongs at Newmarket on 19 September 2009. The first thing to note is the unusual sire stamina index of 16.0f because it is very rare to come across one so high. From the outset of this gelding's career it was obvious that he would need marathon distances in order to show his best form and his first four outings in maiden races only reinforced that assumption.

BERNIE THE BOLT (A M Balding) Milan (16.0f) – Chaparral Lady (Broken Hearted (10.1f)) OR 83						
DATE	DISTANCE/ GOING	RACE TYPE	RESULT/ RAN	COMMENT	OR	TS
21/08/09	14f GF	H'cap	3rd of 13	held up; kept on well	80	87
07/08/09	14f GS	Maid	1st of 4	trckd ldrs; led 1f out; kpt on	75	46
10/07/09	16f Gd	H'cap	3rd of 8	held up; hdwy 2 out; nvr nrr	74	52
12/06/09	14f Gd	H'cap	3rd of 11	rear; hdwy 4f out	75	73
25/05/09	12f Gd	Maid	3rd of 13	held up; hdwy 3f out	-	63
11/05/09	10f GF	Maid	5th of 12	held up; styd on steadily	-	56
20/11/08	8f St	Maid	10th of 12	in touch; outpaced 3f out	-	49
05/11/08	8f Hy	Maid	10th of 17	chasd ldrs; weakened 2f out	-	21

In three of the four he was either outpaced or stayed on steadily from the rear and he was clearly crying out for further. Interestingly, the Handicapper declined to give the gelding an official rating after his third run and presumably felt that he was a fair bit better than he had shown. Following his third run he was stepped up to twelve furlongs for the first time and once again made belated headway from the rear to finish third. The Handicapper then relented and allotted Bernie The Bolt an opening mark of 75. I suspect that he was still not entirely happy with what he had seen to date because 75 seemed a little harsh on the evidence of the bare form, the best of which had merited a Topspeed figure of only 63 and a best RPR figure (not shown) of 71.

His first run in a handicap coincided with a further step up in trip to fourteen furlongs. I did not back him because I considered that he needed further still. Nevertheless, he showed some improvement on the clock when finishing third, recording a personal best figure of 73. He was dropped one pound in the ratings following that solid performance and I felt that he could win off his new mark.

On 10 July 2009 he contested a sixteen furlong handicap at Ascot. Having recorded a Topspeed figure only one pound below his official rating last time out I reckoned that with further improvement likely as a result of having another two furlongs to race over, he was well enough handicapped to win. However, the fact that he had stepped up in class from grade five to grade three had resulted in him being five pounds out of the handicap and consequently he was in effect racing off a mark of 79. I reluctantly decided not to back him as I felt that the extra five pounds might prove decisive. In the event he came a promising third despite having been completely unsuited by the way in which the race unfolded. Once again he was held up in the rear, but on this occasion the early pace was pedestrian. The early leader Alanbrooke was gifted an uncontested lead in a slowly run race and it was no surprise when he proceeded to make all in ready fashion, beating Sweetheart (who had also raced prominently throughout) by five lengths. Bernie The Bolt finished a further three lengths back in third having been unable to muster sufficient speed to challenge the leaders in what turned out to be a sprint to the finish. Furthermore, he had been disadvantaged by having to come wide on the final turn and considering that he had been five pounds wrong at the weights it was a decent enough performance. His lowly speed figure of 52 reflected the fact that the early pace had been too slow for him and I felt that had it been much stronger he would have finished a good deal closer.

I didn't back him at odds of 13/8 when he dropped back to fourteen furlongs on his next outing, which came in a four runner Lingfield maiden on good to soft ground. I felt that both the drop in distance and the small field were against the gelding and I was quite surprised when he managed to win by three lengths, particularly as the pace was once again slow. The *Racing Post* analyst made the following comment: 'An uncompetitive maiden in which Bernie The Bolt displayed a more willing attitude than his main rival. He looks a dour stayer, so the easy ground probably suited, and he gradually responded to pressure in the straight.'

I was disappointed that he was kept to fourteen furlongs on his next outing, which came in a class two handicap at York on 21 August 2009 and I once again declined to back him. The going was good to firm and I felt that the quicker ground would result in the gelding finding fourteen furlongs to be an insufficient test of stamina. He surprised me a little by finishing third but he was helped by the fact that the early pace was strong. Once again he was held up before keeping on well up the straight. He finished only one length behind the leader and almost turned the form around with the second placed horse Alanbrooke (who had beaten him by eight lengths at Ascot), despite being only three pounds better off with that rival. Significantly he clocked a personal best speed figure of 87 and even though Topspeed may have slightly overrated the race I was confident that he was a well-handicapped horse despite being raised to a mark of 83. I reckoned that when he was upped in trip he would prove hard to beat, with the proviso that he encountered a decent early pace.

My long wait to back the gelding finally came to an end on 19 September 2009 when he contested the aforementioned Cesarewitch trial which was run over eighteen furlongs. After analysing the race in the morning I was pretty confident that Bernie The Bolt would win and I thought I knew which of the others would finish second. As you can see from the profiles of the contestants (outlined below) six of the ten runners were fully exposed having had sixteen or more outings. Interestingly, the three least exposed of the runners (Alanbrooke, Bernie The Bolt and Saga De Tercey) had had no more than two attempts at sixteen furlongs or beyond despite possessing the three highest average sire and damsire indices. With further improvement likely now that they were attempting eighteen furlongs for the first time they appeared to be well-handicapped in relation to the opposition.

INVESTEC CESAREWITCH TRIAL HERITAGE HANDICAP
(Newmarket 2m 2f)

HORSE	RUNS	RUNS AT 16f OR MORE	SIRE INDEX	DAMSIRE INDEX	SPEED POINTS
ALANBROOKE	11	2	12.4f	11.7f	6
BERNIE THE BOLT	8	1	16.0f	10.1f	0
EPSOM SALTS	24	3	9.0f	9.2f	0
DOUBLE BANDED	24	6	8.6f	10.6f	0
RAGAMUFFIN MAN	12	2	10.9f	11.3f	12
INCHPAST	45	24	8.9f	11.1f	0
BADDAM	45	28	8.5f	12.3f	3
SAGA DE TERCEY	6	2	14.5f	9.9f	6
ALEATRICIS	16	1	9.8f	10.0f	2
INCHNADAMPH	43	19	8.9f	10.3f	0

The speed point chart predicted that the early pace would be sound because there were three horses that had led in at least one of their recent races and Ragamuffin Man was an out-and-out front runner. I knew that a strong early pace would play to the strengths of Bernie The Bolt by placing an emphasis on stamina and so too would the galloping nature of the Newmarket track. Unfortunately, Bernie The Bolt was four pounds out of the handicap so was effectively running off a mark of 87 but I was not unduly concerned because he had clocked a speed figure of 87 last time out when racing over the inadequate trip of fourteen furlongs and I knew that he would improve significantly now that he had everything in his favour. In fact he was four pounds worse off with Alanbrooke compared to when he finished a head behind that opponent at York last time out, but he was staying on much the better of the two that day and I was confident that he would turn the form around over this longer trip.

I did not fear any of the exposed runners because I was sure that Bernie The Bolt was ahead of the Handicapper. The one possible danger, apart from Alanbrooke, was Saga De Tercey. This four-year-old gelding had won a National Hunt flat race over seventeen furlongs first time out on 22 March 2009, prior to being switched to the Flat. There seemed little doubt therefore, that staying was his game and he was likely to relish the step up to eighteen furlongs. Although he had been a model of consistency having won three and come second twice in five appearances I felt that he had perhaps shown the Handicapper a little too much and doubted whether he remained as well-handicapped as the other two contenders. The best speed figure that he had achieved to date was a lowly 73 and as you can see from his Topspeed figures in the table below, on the occasions of his last two victories he had benefitted from either leading, or racing prominently, in slowly run races.

DATE	DIST/ GOING	RACE TYPE	RESULT/ RAN	COMMENT	OR	TS

SAGA DE TERCEY (G A Swinbank) Sagacity (14.5f) – Fanciulla Del West (Manila (9.9f)) OR 87						
DATE	DIST/ GOING	RACE TYPE	RESULT/ RAN	COMMENT	OR	TS
28/8/09	16 Gd	H'cap	1st of 8	trckd ldr: rdn to lead 2f out; kpt on	82	27
21/8/09	16 GF	H'cap	2nd of 15	trckd ldrs; led 3f out; hdd fnl f	83	69
04/8/09	14 Gd	H'cap	1st of 8	set slow pace; hdd fnl f; rallied	78	34
26/7/09	11 Gd	H'cap	2nd of 8	chased ldr; kept on fnl f	78	73
21/4/09	12 GF	Maid	1st of 9	trckd ldrs; styd on to lead finish	-	-

On the two occasions when the pace had been reasonable he had been defeated. Furthermore, he had had four races in just over a month which is a lot for a stayer to endure and there was the possibility that he may not have fully recovered. By comparison both Alanbrooke and Bernie The Bolt had recently proven that they were ahead of the Handicapper. Alanbrooke had clocked a speed figure of 101 at York on 21 August 2009 and was currently officially rated 96 whilst Bernie The Bolt had clocked 87 and was currently rated 83. I concluded that Bernie The Bolt was the likely winner so I backed him to win at 9/1. I also combined him in a straight forecast with Alanbrooke, who in my opinion was clearly best of the rest.

The race went to plan with Ragamuffin Man setting a decent early gallop and ensuring that it was a good test of stamina. Despite the good early pace Saga De Tercey pulled hard towards the rear of the field and clearly resented his rider's attempt to hold him up for the first time. Unsurprisingly his antics took their toll and he weakened tamely three furlongs from the finish. Alanbrooke took the lead over four furlongs out and was travelling well but Bernie The Bolt had also begun to cruise into contention from the rear and when his rider finally asked him for an effort inside the final furlong he powered clear of Alanbrooke to win by over four lengths. There was a massive thirteen lengths back to the third horse - the fully exposed Epsom Salts. The forecast paid £14.66 but would have been quite a bit more if Bernie The Bolt had not been heavily backed in to 9/2 before the off. The *Racing Post* analyst summed the result up as follows: 'Bernie The Bolt, who was 4lb out of the handicap but well supported, finished a head behind Alanbrooke at York last time, but in a race run at a decent gallop sitting further back in the pack helped Bernie The Bolt conserve energy for the finish and reverse the form in no uncertain manner. They are clearly both progressive stayers ahead of the Handicapper and can win again.'

SELLERS AND CLAIMERS

Although selling and claiming races attract the worst type of horse it is still worth reviewing the results of these races carefully to see whether any of the runners have put in an improved performance. If they have they often provide decent betting opportunities because their efforts go relatively unnoticed. Sellers and claimers normally bring horses of widely different abilities together on similar weight terms and it is easy to draw the wrong conclusions from the results. Horses rated 50 or less frequently beat, or finish close behind opponents that are officially rated stones ahead of them and it is easy to fall into the trap of concluding that they must have improved. In most cases this is not true. The higher rated horses are usually regressive (normally due to having developed an infirmity) and they are no longer capable of running to a level of form that reflects their official ratings. It can be hard to gauge just how much one runner has deteriorated and how much another might have improved and the form is often confusing and hard to unravel. Furthermore, in any type of race that bring horses of widely different abilities together on similar weight terms, strange results tend to occur whenever there is a slow pace for the majority of the contest. When this happens most of the runners remain tightly bunched heading into the final few furlongs and the ensuing sprint for the finishing line is a test of pure speed rather than the ability of a horse to sustain its speed over the full distance. Under such circumstances the official differences between the abilities of the runners is seldom mirrored by their finishing positions and the traditional pounds per length calculations are worthless. I have learned over the years that it is best to ignore what appears to be an improved performance in this type of race unless it is backed up by a speed figure that confirms beyond doubt that it was meritorious. Have a look at the example of Little Sark:

LITTLE SARK (P D Evans) Singspiel (10.5f) – Notequeen (Turfkonig (GER)) OR53							
DATE	COURSE/ DISTANCE	RACE TYPE	OUTCOME		SP	OR	TS
08/10/09	Kem 12St	Claimer	4th	6L	18/1	50	57
23/09/09	Kem 12St	Claimer	7th	8L	33/1	50	41
04/08/09	Chp 12Hy	Handicap	10th	56L	12/1	51	-
15/07/09	Lin 16GF	Handicap	7th	40L	6/1	54	-
01/07/09	Chp 12GF	Handicap	3rd	3L	20/1	53	43
19/06/09	Red 10GF	Handicap	6th	10L	20/1	56	24
20/05/09	Lin 11Gd	Maiden	8th	15L	25/1	-	48
05/05/09	Chp 10GF	Maiden	8th	12L	80/1	-	35
22/03/08	Don 10Gd	Maiden	9th	16L	100/1	-	4

Little Sark was clearly a gelding of limited ability. He was still a maiden after nine outings and up until his run on 8 October 2009 his best speed figure had been a poor 48. Although his official rating had steadily declined down to 50 from an opening 56 there was nothing to suggest that he was well-handicapped. The closest he had ever finished behind the winner was three lengths and the fact that he had been returned at big prices on all but one occasion spoke volumes about his form and level of ability. In fairness, two of his runs could be ignored because he failed to stay two miles on 15 July 2009 and he was evidently unsuited by the heavy ground on 4 August 2009.

So what was one to make of the much improved Topspeed figure of 57 which he had clocked last time out? On the face of it the figure did not appear to be a fluke and in fact it probably underestimated the merit of his performance because he had not enjoyed the run of the race. He received the comment 'chased leaders, ridden to chase leading pair over 3f out, hampered from over 2f out until switched right over 1f out, plugged on same pace.' In view of the fact that he had been continuously hampered for over a furlong in the later stages of the race he could probably be rated at least a couple of pounds better than his finishing position which would have put him on 59 or higher. Close scrutiny of the race (reproduced below) led me to conclude that there was no element of fluke involved and that the speed figure of 57 was believable. Significantly Little Sark was the only runner to achieve a speed figure that was higher than its official rating. The three highest rated runners finished first, second and third in the correct order which lent credibility to the form and it was reassuring that these three did not clock speed figures that matched or bettered their official ratings because I do not expect the better horses in sellers and claimers to run to their handicap marks.

TURF TV BETTING SHOP SERVICE CLAIMING STAKES
Kempton (AW) 12f (Polytrack) 08/10/09

HORSE	WEIGHT	BEATEN LENGTHS	OR	TS
BANDAMA	9-10	-	85	71
QUINCE	9-6	1¾	68	64
GHUFA	9-8	3¾	65	60
LITTLE SARK	9-5	½	50	57
IFFY	8-12	1½	60	52
NEW ENGLAND	9-5	3½	59	48
KILMEENA MAGIC	8-10	17	45	16
FELICIA	9-0	2	45	15
GASAT	9-5	19	60	-
LORD ORPEN	8-10	17	38	-

I concluded that the gelding had probably improved for the switch to Kempton's Polytrack surface because I noted that on his first try on the artificial surface on 23 September 2009 he had also performed with credit when meeting significantly superior horses on disadvantageous weight terms (although this was not reflected by his speed figure that day due to the race being slowly run in the early stages).

I anticipated that Little Sark's astute trainer David Evans would return the gelding to handicap company next time out and that the surface would once again be Polytrack. Thankfully he reappeared at Kempton on 14 October 2009 in a 0-50 handicap over twelve furlongs. Evans had managed to get the gelding into this race before his new mark of 56 was due to take effect and to my mind he looked thrown in against a very ordinary bunch of platers. Given that he was obviously well-handicapped I was surprised to get on at 6/1 and although he initially drifted out to 13/2 those prices did not last long before he was backed in to 9/2 before the off. The support was justified, but only just! The long time leader It's Josr kicked into a commanding three length lead off the final turn and looked all over the winner before tiring rapidly approaching the line, allowing Little Sark to snatch victory away from him in the final strides. Tivers Song was only a further head behind having been a little unfortunate in running. The fact that Little Sark had improved was confirmed by the clock which showed that he had once again recorded a speed figure of 57.

WELL-HANDICAPPED TWO-YEAR-OLDS

Occasionally the Handicapper makes a rick when assessing a two-year-old before it runs in a nursery handicap for the first time and if you can identify a horse that has been significantly underrated it is usually worth betting on. Have a look at the form of Layali Al Andalus before he first ran in an eight furlong nursery at Newcastle on 31 August 2009.

LAYALI AL ANDALUS (M Johnston) Halling (10.4f) – Lafitem (Robellino 10.2f)) **OR 88**							
DATE	COURSE/ DISTANCE	RACE TYPE	OUTCOME		SP	OR	TS
27/06/09	Don 7GF	Maiden	1st	7L	EVS	-	94
03/06/09	Ayr 6GF	Maiden	2nd	1½L	6/1	-	62

This colt's breeding strongly suggested that he would prove to be best over middle distances as a three-year-old (particularly as he was out of a mare that got ten furlongs well) so it was likely that the step up from seven furlongs to a mile would bring about some improvement on what he had achieved so far. On his debut he found Ayr's easy six furlongs to be an inadequate test of stamina but performed with credit by coming second and recording a reasonable speed figure of 62. The race reader signalled that there was plenty more to come from the colt when he wrote: 'kept on final furlong, improve.'

On his next run he was upped to seven furlongs and he showed his appreciation for the extra distance when winning emphatically by seven lengths, having been strong in the pre-race market. He took the lead three furlongs out and although he briefly had to be ridden by his jockey approaching the final furlong he responded in the manner of a good horse by quickening clear to win 'easily', giving the impression that he had more to give if needed. The *Racing Post* analyst reported that: 'He looked magnificent beforehand ... and has ample physical scope for improvement.' The colt earned an impressive Topspeed figure of 94, but the ease of his victory suggested that he was capable of a much higher rating. Importantly, the fact that he had come under some pressure in the race gave substance to the rating and indicated that he had not achieved an inflated figure on the back of having been allowed to do his own thing out in front for most of the race. When pressured he had responded and he was clearly no quitter.

How the Handicapper decided that the colt's first two runs merited an official rating of only 88 shall remain a mystery. I reckoned that a mark of

88 meant that Layali Al Andalus had at least twelve pounds in hand and his connections must have been rubbing their hands with glee when the figure of 88 was published. I was not surprised when they declared him to run in the aforementioned Newcastle nursery on 31 August 2009, even though a check of his entries had revealed that he had several alternative engagements in Group races. With the step up to eight furlongs sure to suit and with the benefit of a low draw in stall two of eleven (the stalls were positioned on the far side) Layali Al Andalus looked to be a near certainty. I envisaged that he would bounce out and proceed to make all against the far rail and I have seldom felt more confident about the chance of a horse in a handicap race. His forecast odds of 7/2 were always unlikely to be available in reality and I was more than happy to back him at 7/4. Things went much as I had anticipated; he made all against the rail and was ridden clear over one furlong out. After the race Mark Johnston stated that: 'Layali Al Andalus was going to go for the Chesham but was injured. When we saw his rating we thought we'd take in a nursery, but he'll step up in grade now and the Royal Lodge is a likely race for him ... but I don't think I would want to drop him back to seven furlongs.'

It was somewhat surprising, therefore, that the colt's next engagement was a seven furlong Group Two race at Doncaster! Johnston should have heeded his own advice because Layali Al Andalus found the drop back in trip combined with the significant rise in class far too much for him and he finished a disappointing fifth, over nine lengths behind the winner. However, he went on to prove that he is a Group class horse next time out at the Curragh on 27 September 2009. Having reverted to eight furlongs on slower ground he produced an excellent performance to come second by three quarters of a length to the current Derby favourite St Nicholas Abbey.

The example of Layali Al Andalus demonstrates just how difficult it is for a horse to successfully step back in distance from a trip that it has won over, particularly if raised in class at the same time. More often than not they lack the necessary speed to be competitive.

Some trainers pass over the opportunity to win a handicap with a well treated horse but I did not expect the shrewd Mark Johnston to make this mistake. If one of your horses is gifted a lenient rating why not exploit it first before moving on to bigger and better things? If a trainer opts to raise such a horse in class to Group company and bypass the handicap route, it had better win or place because if it runs well it can kiss goodbye to its lenient official rating. Take a look at the two-year-old filly Clarietta:

CLARIETTA (J L Dunlop) Shamardal – Claxon (Caerleon (10.7f)) **OR 97**							
DATE	COURSE/ DISTANCE	RACE TYPE	OUTCOME		SP	OR	TS
11/09/09	Don 8GF	Group 2	5th	4L	9/1	85	91
07/08/09	Nmk 7GS	Handicap	1st	1L	9/4	77	81
16/07/09	Don 7GS	Maiden	1st	2½L	7/2	-	78
23/06/09	Nby 7GF	Maiden	7th	8L	12/1	-	42

Following her victory in a maiden on only her second start she was given an opening official rating of 77. Given that she was open to improvement she was obviously well-handicapped on the basis of her Topspeed figure of 78. It was no surprise that she was heavily supported in the morning before her handicap debut on 7 August 2009. The race was worth over £5,000 to the winner and she won in convincing style, posting an improved speed figure of 81 in the process. The Handicapper responded by raising her rating to 85 but I was pretty sure that she was better than that and her breeding suggested that a step up in trip would bring about further improvement. I anticipated that she would be able to win a decent handicap or two before going on to better things, but surprisingly, her connections decided to raise her sharply in class to Group 2 level and to bypass the handicap route. Although she ran with credit on 11 September 2009 she came up short in the much higher grade, finishing fifth of seven (for which her connections received the modest sum of just over £2,000 in prize money). Her improved speed figure of 91 confirmed that she had been well-handicapped on a mark of 85 but inevitably the Handicapper attached a pump to her rating and inflated it to 97! It will be interesting to see how she fares from now on, but I suspect that she may be caught in the twilight zone between not being good enough for Pattern races and being too high in the ratings to win one of the better handicaps.

Perversely, although the gamble of placing a well-handicapped horse in Group class backfired on Clarietta's connections it worked handsomely for the Richard Hannon team in the very same race. They had also entered a well-handicapped filly in the shape of Pollenator who, after four runs, had an official rating of just 83. However, she managed to win the race and although her rating was subsequently hoisted to 105 she collected £45,000 in prize money and also secured the sought after 'black type' that will enhance her paddock value. Although it worked for Richard Hannon on this occasion I don't like to see trainers taking a gamble with the rating of a well-handicapped horse in this way.

Even though you may have identified that the Handicapper has made a rick when assessing a two-year-old before it runs in a nursery handicap for the first time, you still have to decide whether it has enough in hand to be capable of overcoming any bias that it may be confronted with. This is not easy to do and there is often a balance to be drawn between the reduced likelihood of it winning as a consequence of the bias and the probability that it will be returned at significantly bigger odds than it would have been otherwise. The example of Bonheurs Art is a good one to demonstrate this particular problem.

BONHEURS ART (B W Hills) Acclamation (6.7f) – Anneliina (Cadeaux Genereux (7.8f)) OR 69							
DATE	COURSE/ DISTANCE	RACE TYPE	OUTCOME		SP	OR	TS
29/08/09	Nmk 6Gd	Maiden	5th	5½L	9/2	-	49
10/08/09	Wdr 6GF	Maiden	2nd	¾L	11/4	-	79
29/07/09	Goo 6Gd	Maiden	4th	7½L	12/1	-	56

When I came across the form of this filly prior to her nursery debut in a six furlong race at Windsor on 19 October 2009 I had absolutely no doubt that the handicapper had made a rick. The fact that she had clocked a Topspeed figure of 79 on only her second start suggested that she was thrown into this contest off an official rating of only 69 and a little research into her form seemed to prove this. On her last start she was fifth in a Newmarket maiden run over six furlongs and the sixth horse there, Guest Book, had since landed a Chepstow maiden and finished second off a mark of 79 in an Ascot nursery. The fourth horse at Newmarket was Saboteur, a colt that had subsequently attracted a rating of 84 and had recently won a maiden at Nottingham by seven lengths.

In my opinion, Bonheurs Art had at least ten pounds in hand and would have been a shoo-in if it were not for the fact that she was drawn widest of all out in stall one of fourteen. Stall one is usually the kiss of death on the straight course at Windsor when the ground is good or faster, and now that the straight course was back to its full width (rather than the strip next to the stands' side having been dolled off) the bias was likely to be significant. However, I was mindful that on the previous Monday, when the going was good to soft, all the races ended over on the far rail so it was possible that stall one might prove to be an advantage if there was some give in the ground. On a cloudy day much depended on whether any rain would fall at the track and I decided that I would wait and see what happened in the first two races on the card (which were over five and six furlongs) before deciding whether to back the filly.

No further rain fell at the course and it came as no surprise when the action in the first two races unfolded down the stands' side. Although it can be hard to judge a draw bias from the results of a maiden and a claimer (because the different abilities of the contestants are not levelled by weight in the same way that they are in handicaps) on this occasion I considered that the evidence from the first two races was compelling. The first two to finish in the opening sixteen runner maiden were drawn eleven and fifteen and in the following fifteen runner claimer the first five home were drawn fourteen, ten, twelve, four and fifteen. Significantly the two horses in the claimer that raced on the outside of the field finished twelfth and thirteenth. One of those (Keep Dancing) was joint third favourite in the betting and her trainer Andrew Balding had said that he expected the filly to run well when interviewed prior to the race.

I had little doubt that should Bonheurs Art be trapped out wide for most of the race she would probably lose, even with ten pounds in hand. However, when her odds drifted out to 7/2 I decided to back her. I reasoned that if she could get across from her wide pitch she would almost certainly win and decided that 7/2 took account of the risk involved and just about represented value. Unfortunately, my gamble did not pay off. Once again the runners came over to the stands rail but Bonheurs Art's jockey did not to try to get the lead and tack over, or take a pull and move across behind the other runners. The filly raced wide for most of the contest but still managed to hit the front with just under two furlongs to go. At that stage I felt that Michael Hills should have moved across to the rail but he elected to stay well away from it and inevitably the filly was caught near the finish by the exposed Coolree Star who came through against the rail having been switched over from stall five. From my point of view it goes against the grain to back horses that are badly drawn and I certainly would not countenance backing exposed horses (that have nothing in hand of the Handicapper) to overcome strong biases. However, as I have already alluded to, there is a balance to be drawn between the reduced likelihood of a well-handicapped horse winning in the face of a bias and the probability that it will be returned at significantly bigger odds than it would have been otherwise. Whether I got that balance right on this occasion is debatable!

THE IMPACT OF GROUND CONDITIONS ON PERFORMANCE

Certain horses are poorly handicapped when encountering one type of underfoot conditions, but well-handicapped when encountering another. If for example a horse proves to be particularly well suited to either soft ground or Fibresand it may be as much as ten pounds better whenever it encounters such a surface compared to its form on fast ground. It is worth monitoring this type of horse closely to see whether they become well treated by the Handicapper following a sequence of runs on going they dislike because if they do they will usually be worth betting on the next time they encounter their ideal conditions. Amethyst Dawn provides a good illustration of this type of horse.

DATE	COURSE/ DISTANCE	RACE TYPE	OUTCOME		SP	OR	TS
27/04/09	Ncs 8GF	Handicap	5th	14L	4/1	72	46
15/04/09	Bev 10GF	Handicap	7th	9L	7/1	75	48
24/10/08	Don 8Gd	Handicap	13th	10L	12/1	77	63
10/09/08	Don 7Sft	Handicap	5th	6L	9/1	77	70
23/08/08	Bev 7Sft	Maiden	1st	1L	10/3	-	76
25/07/08	Yor 7GF	Maiden	3rd	1L	16/1	-	57
17/07/08	Don 7Gd	Maiden	8th	5L	33/1	-	55

AMETHYST DAWN (T D Easterby) Act One (11.7f) – Al Aube (Selkirk (8.9f)) **OR 61**

The above form summary only shows the filly's first seven runs. It was after her unplaced effort at Newcastle on 27 April 2009 that I added her to my list of horses to follow. On her third start she had won quite impressively on soft ground at Beverley, making virtually all and producing a good turn of foot to quicken away in the final two furlongs. She clocked a speed figure of 76 that day so her initial mark of 77 looked justified. Her first run in a handicap came on 10 September 2008 and she performed with credit, finishing fifth of sixteen, particularly as she did best of those that had raced prominently in the early stages and she had stuck on well towards the finish, displaying a likeable attitude in the process. Although clearly at home on a soft surface there was little to suggest that she was well-handicapped at that stage. However, her next three runs came on good ground or faster and it soon became obvious that she was not the same filly when she encountered those conditions. Following the run at Newcastle her official rating dropped a further three pounds to 69 and her new rating was seven pounds below the Topspeed figure of 76 that she had clocked on soft ground at Beverley. I considered that her poor recent form could be excused on account of the fast ground and it was clear to me that whenever she next encountered soft ground she would be a well-handicapped horse.

Amazingly she raced a further nine times before she finally encountered soft ground again, just before the end of the Flat season on 4 November 2009. In between time her rating had justifiably tumbled down to 61 because she had been unable to reproduce anything like her best form on the fast ground that she had had to endure. She had had one run on good to soft ground at Newcastle on 7 September 2009 but that had been over twelve furlongs. Before that race it had been pretty obvious from her form that a stiff twelve furlongs was beyond her and she had unsurprisingly weakened in the final furlong having looked the likely winner three furlongs out.

On 4 November 2009 she reverted to eight furlongs and finally had the soft ground that she revels in. Now that she was running over the right trip and had the genuinely soft ground she needed I reckoned that she had as much as fourteen pounds in hand of the opposition, none of whom had previously won on soft ground. Furthermore, her front running style was likely to be an advantage because it is harder for horses that are held up to make headway on soft ground and given that she was proven to stay further than eight furlongs there was little chance of her tiring significantly in the closing stages. I was delighted to back her at 13/2 because I thought that she was so well-handicapped that her true chance of winning was 2/1 or less. I had had to wait an awful long time to capitalize on the homework I had done at the start of the season but it was worth it. Amethyst Dawn travelled conspicuously well in second place for most of the contest and when her rider asked her for an effort two furlongs out she quickly shot clear of her toiling rivals before being allowed to coast home to a comfortable two and a half lengths victory. The manner of her win confirmed that she had had pounds in hand of her rivals, as her previous speed figure of 76 suggested she would.

Chapter Seven

Odds and Ends

STAY AHEAD OF THE CROWD

It is an enduring truth that you need to be among the first to spot the over-lays and to take advantage before the odds shorten and the value evaporates. You must identify the latent talent in horses before the crowd does because as soon as everybody realizes that a horse is better than its rating it will be sent off at restrictive odds; the crowd likes nothing better than a handicap good thing. Although I do not have the statistics to prove it, I believe that the market is now so well-informed that market moves have become more significant. When a horse drifts alarmingly it is more of a negative than it used to be and I like to see at least a small contraction in the odds about my selection, whether that be in the morning or just before the race. I expect my selections to contract in the market because if I have correctly assessed that they are well-handicapped it is likely that the leniency of the Handicapper will not have been lost on their connections. When I am convinced that a horse is well-handicapped I will back it as early as possible to secure the likely best price but if I am less certain I will wait for confirmation from the market that the horse is fancied before committing myself. If the horse drifts significantly I will either pass on the race or reduce my stake.

These days there is not much mileage in opposing the market and it is more important than ever to pre-empt it. This point was succinctly put by Dave Nevison in his book *No Easy Money* when he wrote: 'The market is different from pre-Betfair days. It is now an amalgam of the best racing brains in the country and it is more accurate than ever before. There isn't much profit to be made from following the crowd but if the crowd forms the [accurate] market, then instead of being against the crowd, I have to try to be ahead of it.'

A good recent illustration of the need to be ahead of the crowd is provided by the bets I placed on the three-year-old Rock A Doodle Do. This colt had all the hallmarks of a well-handicapped horse that I look for when he ran at Lingfield on 12 January 2010, but as you can see the fact that he was well-handicapped had not been advertised by what he had achieved on the racecourse, or on the clock.

ROCK A DOODLE DO (27Apr07) (W Jarvis) Oratorio (9.5f) – Nousaiyra (Be My Guest (10.1f))								
DATE	COURSE/ DISTANCE	RACE TYPE	OUTCOME		SP	OR	TS	RPR
23/01/10	Lin 10St	Handicap	1st	3L	2/5f	61	77	76
18/01/10	Wol 9St	Handicap	1st	2½L	6/5f	55	65	65
12/01/10	Lin 8St	Handicap	2nd	1¼L	6/1	55	39	59
12/10/09	Wdr 6GS	Maiden	12th	18L	50/1	-	-	27
01/10/09	Nmk 6GF	Maiden	7th	10L	12/1	-	24	51
01/06/09	Lei 6GF	Maiden	8th	16L	9/1	-	22	38

It needed a subjective interpretation of his profile to determine that he was significantly better than his initial official rating, but all the evidence was there for those prepared to do the necessary research.

Rock A Doodle Do had been quite an expensive purchase for his connections at 42,000 euros and his price reflected that he was well bred, being by the Eclipse winner Oratorio. He was a relatively late foal, having been born on 27 April 2007, so he was likely to improve on what he achieved as a two-year-old. The stamina indices of both his sire and damsire suggested that he would get at least ten furlongs and probably further so it was clear that he had been unsuited to the distance of the six furlong maiden races that he had run in prior to making his handicap debut. Unsurprisingly he had been outpaced and out of his depth.

Another piece of the jigsaw was put in place by Steve Taplin's book on two-year-olds which included the following encouraging quote from Rock A Doodle Do's trainer William Jarvis: 'Yes I like him and he'll be fine. A strong, neat colt, that goes well.' All the evidence suggested that he would prove to be significantly better than his opening rating of 55 and now that he was stepping up to the more suitable distance of eight furlongs for the first time I expected him to prove it. I got on early at 8/1 because I suspected that if my assessment of his ability was correct he was sure to be strongly supported and he was. He was subsequently backed in the morning in to as low as 7/2 but later drifted out on course and was returned at 6/1.

There was no doubt that he should have won the race but he was given a poor ride and finished second. Despite having broken well and gained a good position in mid-division, his over confident jockey Jim Crowley appeared happy to allow him to be shuffled back to last place, despite the fact that the early pace was pedestrian. The pace was still modest as the field approached the final bend and it was no surprise when the leader Ostentation was able to suddenly kick into a clear lead next to the far rail. Crowley was forced to make his belated move out wide on the bend, but once in the clear the partnership stormed up the straight to narrow the gap on the leader from six lengths down to just over one. Needless to say I was unimpressed with the ride the colt had received but I have come to expect bad luck in running at what is my least favourite racecourse. The pedestrian pace was reflected in Rock A Doodle Do's low speed figure of 39 and I had no doubt that his chance had been compromised by how the race unfolded and by the ride he had been given. It is another enduring truth that, irrespective of how well-handicapped your selection is it can always get beaten by bad luck or incompetence!

Of course, by the time he next ran six days later every man and his dog knew that he was a handicap good thing. I had gone from being ahead of the crowd to a reluctant member of the crowd, but I was determined to recoup my losses. I took 11/8 only because I was convinced that he would win, particularly as he was stepping up in trip to nine and a half furlongs. He was subsequently backed in to 6/5 and ran out a comfortable winner, clocking a speed figure of 65. Five days later he was turned out again under a six pound penalty that took his mark up to 65 and he won easily by four lengths, despite having been hampered several times during the race, and clocked an impressive Topspeed figure of 77. That speed figure proved he had been at least twenty-two pounds ahead of the Handicapper when he had raced off 55 at Lingfield only eleven days earlier. I did not back him at odds of 2/5 but some would argue that he had been value even at that prohibitive price.

I know from experience that, over the long-term, I do not make any impression on the layers by betting on horses at short prices. In order to make a long-term profit I have to spot the well-handicapped types before the competition do and they must win before their improvement becomes apparent.

THE RIGHT TYPE OF HORSE

When you have identified an unexposed horse that you think possesses latent ability it is important to consider whether your assessment is reinforced by the factors that allude to the likely quality of the animal in question. If it has already clocked a speed figure in excess of its official rating you know that it is well-handicapped but if it has not, as in the case of Rock A Doodle Do, it is imperative to assess the quality of the individual and to use that assessment to project what it is likely to be capable of.

The main clues as to the likely quality of a horse are provided by its breeding and by its purchase price, if applicable. Very cheap horses generally turn out to be moderate and you should downgrade your expectations of them. A low price usually reflects their plain looks or unfashionable breeding, but it might also indicate that they are either small, light framed, or that they have conformation faults that will prove a hindrance to them. Market rates vary from year to year so it is impracticable to put a figure on what constitutes a cheap purchase. You should try to get a handle on the going rates each year so that you have an idea of the sort of prices being paid for the better quality individuals. Whether the purchase price of a horse will be reflected in its performances on the track is never certain, but it pays to side with the more expensive ones.

Of course not every horse has a purchase price because many are home bred and put into training by their owner/breeders. These are usually quality animals, particularly those belonging to the top owners and they tend to be under the care of the more successful trainers. You will not find too many selling platers among this sort and the majority will be capable of a rating of at least 70 but probably a good deal higher.

As I mentioned in an earlier chapter I have no interest in precocious two-year-olds that debut early in the season because they seldom make up into decent progressive three-year-olds. Horses that are out early over five furlongs and obtain a handicap rating before July are to be avoided, particularly those that go on to race many times in their first year. As a rule I want to be on horses that debut after June and have no more than four races as two-year-olds because they are far more likely than their precocious counterparts to be progressive in their second season and beyond.

When it comes to assessing a horse's potential its breeding is a major factor to consider and it is important to know which sires are producing the best horses and which of the newer ones look to have a bright future, particularly when deciding which of the two-year-olds are likely to make up into genuine contenders for the Classics. The following chart lists the top twenty sires in 2009 based on the amount of prize money won by their offspring and they are listed in descending order. I have calculated the strike rates of their progeny on soft/heavy ground and on good/good to firm to highlight those that do better on either soft or fast:

SIRE	WINS TO RUNS PERCENTAGES	SOFT/HEAVY	GOOD/GOOD TO FIRM
DANEHILL DANCER	11%	16%	11%
CAPE CROSS	13%	8%	13%
MONTJEU	13%	13%	12%
GALILEO	17%	18%	14%
OASIS DREAM	14%	11%	16%
PIVOTAL	16%	18%	14%
SADLER'S WELLS	14%	13%	16%
DANSILI	10%	10%	10%
SHAMARDAL	17%	24%	12%
DALAKHANI	16%	17%	20%
HAWK WING	9%	11%	7%
HIGH CHAPARRAL	13%	12%	11%
INVINCIBLE SPIRIT	11%	9%	11%
ROCK OF GIBRALTAR	11%	12%	12%
EXCEED AND EXCEL	11%	7%	12%
GIANT'S CAUSEWAY	13%	11%	10%
SINGSPIEL	12%	8%	12%
BAHAMIAN BOUNTY	12%	10%	10%
NAYEF	12%	18%	10%
SELKIRK	12%	11%	12%

You can access this information and much more through either the *Racing Post* website, or *Raceform Interactive*. Whenever you are contemplating whether an unexposed horse might be well-handicapped one of the first things you should do is closely examine the statistics pertaining to its sire, damsire and dam for clues as to its likely quality and preferences.

TEMPERAMENT

One of the things most likely to stop a horse fulfilling its potential is a suspect temperament and I usually avoid any unexposed horse that has shown signs of waywardness on more than one occasion. Most horses making their debuts will display signs of greenness and they can generally be forgiven, but I don't like to see problems continuing beyond a horse's second outing.

Horses that repeatedly fail to settle and are constantly pulling for their heads are to be avoided, particularly if they have pulled despite the fact that the early pace was strong. By taking a keen hold they waste valuable energy and they invariably weaken in the closing stages of a race. This appears to be a trait that trainers find hard to iron out and it is likely to reappear whenever the horse in question encounters a slow early pace.

I also avoid horses that have repeated problems with the starting stalls. Those that are reluctant to be loaded or become restless in the stalls; that rear, duck down or repeatedly break slowly are less likely to fulfil their potential than their more relaxed opponents. You can forgive a one-off performance but a repeated misdemeanour tends to become habitual and it is best to downgrade the culprit's chance of realizing its potential.

Other types to avoid are those that show signs of reluctance when they come under pressure. Some horses will throw their heads up in the air or swish their tails. Others will attempt to duck in behind other runners and then resist their rider's attempts to pull them back out. Some will fold tamely having been scared by the slightest bit of interference or refuse to go through narrow gaps despite appearing to be going well at the time. These are signs that the horse might be a quitter and although I am prepared to put an isolated incident down to greenness any repeat offence is less forgivable.

AVOID HORSES THAT ARE ONE-PACED

Some horses are simply incapable of increasing their speed at the business end of a race and they rarely win as a consequence. Unless they are able to outstay their rivals either in strongly run races, or in races on soft or heavy ground, or over long distances they invariably get out-speeded in the final furlong. They always struggle to make an impact in any race that is slowly run because when the pace inevitably quickens in the final couple of furlongs they get left behind. One-paced horses should be avoided.

It is important not to confuse this type of horse with those that have been outpaced in a race simply because they were outclassed or because the distance of the race was too short for them on account of their breeding. The ones to look out for are those that have run in low class races and have attracted the comment 'plugged on' or 'one pace', particularly if they held a prominent position in the race before being outpaced by faster rivals. These negative comments are especially telling if the race was run on fast ground or if the pace of the race was slow or moderate. Horses may appear to plug on in heavy ground simply because the conditions are preventing them from running any faster.

Beware of any relatively cheap purchase that makes its debut over a trip of nine furlongs or more. The chances are the horse in question has shown no speed whatsoever on the gallops at home and it is likely to be woefully one-paced on the racecourse.

APPRENTICE JOCKEYS

I always keep an eye on any new apprentice jockey and if I believe that he or she is unusually talented I monitor their subsequent rides closely. I am happy whenever one of the horses on my list is to be ridden by a decent claiming apprentice because in my opinion his or her allowance magnifies the number of pounds in hand the horse in question has over its rivals. I particularly like the five-pound claimers because they have a certain amount of experience and can usually ride quite competently. Quite often they are worth one or two pounds of their allowance and that can be very useful to the chance of a horse in a handicap. The very best of the seven pound claimers can be worth a similar amount and once again their allowance can prove to be significant.

Apprentices are regularly put up on horses that have next to no chance of winning just to give them more riding experience, but when they are put up on horses with a genuine chance they do very well and under certain circumstances they do better than the fully-fledged jockeys.

The table below details how the three categories of claiming riders and the jockeys fare when they ride either the favourite, or joint favourite in a handicap race. The statistics were produced using *Raceform Interactive*'s database search facility. Before conducting the search I reasoned that apprentice allowances would be more beneficial in long distance races than in sprints because they theoretically equate to more lengths as distances increase. A seven pound allowance equates to seven lengths over two miles, whereas over five furlongs it equates to two lengths. I reckoned that the five length difference between the two would mean they had more time to overcome any errors they made during a race.

HOW APPRENTICES AND JOCKEYS FARE ON HANDICAP FAVOURITES								
	7LB CLAIMERS		5LB CLAIMERS		3LB CLAIMERS		JOCKEYS	
DISTANCE	STRIKE RATE	PROFIT/ LOSS	STRIKE RATE	PROFIT/ LOSS	STRIKE RATE	PROFIT/ LOSS	STRIKE RATE	PROFIT/ LOSS
5f	22%	-£18	32%	+£57	28%	+£22	23%	-£279
6f	21%	-£19	30%	+£62	26%	+£13	25%	-£174
7f	20%	-£4	18%	-£78	22%	-£10	23%	-£410
8f	14%	-£42	22%	-£59	22%	-£36	25%	-£199
9f	25%	-£2	31%	+£11	24%	+£6	26%	-£73
10f	23%	-£18	24%	-£12	30%	+£29	26%	-£108
12f	16%	-£42	22%	-£27	21%	-£26	26%	-£258
14f	33%	+£4.7	23%	-£11	18%	-£30	32%	+£40
16f	29%	+£0.2	33%	+£10	23%	-£7	30%	+£15
AVERAGES	23%	-£140	26%	-£47	24%	-£40	26%	£-888

The chart shows that seven pound claimers do fare better in the long distance races as I anticipated and relative to the other types of rider they struggle in races up to one mile because things often happen too quickly for them. However, it appears that as apprentices gain experience and get used to making the split second decisions that have to be taken in sprint races their strike rate improves dramatically. As you can see the 5lb and 3lb claimers have a remarkably high strike rate in five and six furlong races and have actually produced a significant level stake profit over the last seven years. The five pound claimers have an overall strike rate of twenty-six per cent when riding a favourite in a handicap and that exactly matches that of the fully-fledged jockeys. I suspect that the best of the claimers have slightly higher strike rates than the averages so it is definitely worth investigating their mounts closely.

Chapter Eight

Summing Up

If you are serious about making a success of your betting you should pay to access the wealth of information on the *Racing Post* website rather than rely on the paper version. In order to make money from betting you must either have information that is not being used by the crowd or you must become better than the crowd at interpreting and using the information that is public knowledge. The website affords you an edge over those who rely on the paper because it contains far more information. If you can afford to subscribe to *Raceform Interactive* you should because it also contains information that is not available to the majority of other punters. Furthermore, it has an excellent function that allows you to keep lists of horses to follow and highlights when they appear among the declarations. Lists can become a bit unwieldy after a while and it helps to be prompted when one of your horses is due to run.

I subscribe to the *Weekender* which comes out every Wednesday. This is the day when I do the majority of my research. The format of the results section is ideal for analyzing the previous week's form as it enables you to get a feel for each meeting in its entirety, rather than looking at the result of a single race in isolation. You can discern what the weather was like at each meeting and decide what impact that might have had and it is easier to detect whether any pace or draw biases were in play when looking at a meeting as a whole. It also makes it easier to check for any errors in the compilation of the Topspeed figures.

When I identify horses that appear to have done something out of the ordinary, or have performed better than the bare form suggests I then refer to the *Racing Post* website and to other sources of information such as Steve Taplin's book on two-year-olds, or previous interviews with trainers that I have filed away. Basically I want to find as much information as I can about the horse in question before I decide whether to add it to my list of horses to follow. That will always include a check of all its previous runs and of the *Racing Post* analysts' comments pertaining to them, which provide valuable insights and clues. It will also include a check and assessment of their breeding and their purchase price; their date of birth, any past quotes from their connections and any future entries that they might hold. I will also check to see how some of the horses that they have raced against have performed both before and since for clues as to what sort of handicap mark they might be capable of winning off. If all this information encourages me to think that the horse in question is well-handicapped and that it seems unlikely to be undone by its temperament I will add it to my list of horses to follow.

Once a horse of the right type has been identified it is then a question of monitoring how it is subsequently campaigned and deciding when and when not to back it. I like to have an opinion regarding its probable trip and going preferences so that I have a feel for when the time is right to strike. The horse's entries and the jockey booking often provide pointers as to when its connections are anticipating a win and I expect to see a market move speaking in favour of the horse at some stage during the day.

When I believe that I have identified a genuinely well-handicapped horse I do not concern myself unduly with the opposition. However, I will make a quick assessment of the other runners in order to see how many other potentially well-handicapped horses there are in the race. That includes exposed horses that are below a previous winning handicap mark (especially if they come in for significant market support during the morning), or unexposed runners that could be better than they have shown but have not done enough to earn a place on my list. If there are only one or two other potentially well-handicapped horses I will consider combining them in forecasts with the horse on my list. A check of the other runners also gives me an idea of the minimum price that I should accept about my selection. Much depends on just how well-handicapped I think my horse is, but obviously the more potentially well treated horses there are in opposition the bigger the price I want.

Each morning I check through the form of every three-year-old that is making its handicap debut that afternoon to ensure that I have not overlooked a horse that may have been given a lenient opening rating. Horses that do nothing out of the ordinary in their first three runs may not have come to my attention and sometimes it is only when I see their opening official rating that it becomes apparent that they may be well-handicapped. The aforementioned Rock A Doodle Do is an example of this type of horse. He had done nothing on his first three runs to merit attention and it was only the fact that he had been given an opening rating of 55 that made him stand out. Had he been given a rating in the seventies I doubt whether I would have considered him to be well-handicapped.

I recognize that my methodology will not suit the majority of punters because there are many days when there are no bets and when the days stretch into a week or more the lack of action can be frustrating. Discipline is required if you are to avoid the temptation of dabbling in other races and undoing your good work. Phil Bull once said: 'You cannot construct good bets, you have to wait for them to come along.' That simple sentence holds the key to success. The accuracy of the modern market and the wealth of information available to punters are such that you are unlikely to succeed by sitting down each morning with the aim of finding the winners of whatever races you choose to analyse. 'Constructing' bets in that way will not afford you an edge over the opposition and more often than not you will back the wrong type of horse at the wrong price. If you can discipline yourself to back only the right type of horse at the right time you will greatly improve your chance of succeeding at this difficult game.

Remember that if you manage to find an edge over the opposition you should not make the mistake of assuming that you have everything under control. I will sign off with some words of wisdom from my favourite author, Andrew Beyer: 'If the most astute of handicappers becomes complacent for a long enough time, he will wake up one day to find that his once-successful methods don't work anymore. So even after a horse-player has struggled for years and finally learned how to beat the races, he had better not pause for too long to rest on his laurels. The game will keep slowly changing, and the winning player must keep on observing, adapting his methods, and changing with it.'

Appendix A

Draw Figures

In the following draw tables I have used win ratios to quantify the extent of a bias where it exists. In theory each stall should record a figure of 1.0 because the percentage of winners exiting from each stall should equal the percentage of runners and any variant suggests that a bias might exist. A figure of 2.0 next to a stall number means that the stall has housed twice as many winners than it should, whereas a figure of 0.5 means that it has housed half the number of winners that it should have and so on.

Although the figures incorporate the results of handicap races from the last six seasons there are nevertheless some that are based on limited evidence. Certain tracks stage less racing than others and in some cases there is little point in producing draw figures for each stall because they are unlikely to be reliable. Therefore, where the figures are based on limited evidence I have only produced average figures which relate to small groups of stalls rather than individual ones.

As a rule, the higher the stall number the less reliable the figure will be because the higher the number, the fewer races the respective figure is calculated from. As a result you should not rely too heavily on the inflated figures that are sometimes attached to the highest numbered stalls because they may not accurately reflect the bias.

If the stalls position is described as LOW stall one in the chart refers to stall number one in the race, but if the stalls position is described as HIGH stall one refers to the highest numbered stall in the race and stall two refers to the second highest and so on. This is to reflect the fact that the stalls can be placed on either side of the track and that the position of the stalls can have a significant impact on the figures and how they should be calculated.

ASCOT

DISTANCE 5f	DISTANCE 6f	DISTANCE 7f	DISTANCE 8f
STALLS LOW	STALLS LOW	STALLS LOW	STALLS LOW

Stall	5f	6f	7f	8f
1	1.0	1.0	1.0	1.8
2				
3				
4				
5				
6				
7	1.2	1.2		
8			1.9	0.0
9				
10				
11				
12				
13	0.0	0.8		
14				
15			0.0	1.6
16				
17				
18				
19	1.5	0.7		
20				
21				
22			0.0	0.0
23				
24				
25				
26				
27				
28				

DUE TO THE RECENT REDEVELOPMENT OF THE COURSE THE FIGURES ARE BASED ON VERY LIMITED EVIDENCE

AYR

DISTANCE 5f STALLS HIGH		DISTANCE 6f STALLS HIGH		DISTANCE 7f STALLS LOW		DISTANCE 8f STALLS LOW		DISTANCE 9f STALLS LOW	
1		1		1		1		1	
2		2		2		2		2	
3	1.7	3	1.3	3	1.3	3	1.4	3	1.1
4		4		4		4		4	
5		5		5		5		5	
6		6		6		6		6	
7		7		7		7		7	
8	0.5	8	0.8	8		8		8	
9		9		9	0.8	9	0.8	9	1.0
10		10		10		10		10	
11		11		11		11		11	
12		12		12		12		12	
13	0.8	13	0.8	13		13		13	
14		14		14		14		14	
15		15		15	0.8	15		15	
16		16		16		16	0.4	16	0.4
17		17		17		17		17	
18	0.3	18		18		18		18	
19		19	0.0			19		19	
20		20							
21		21							
22		22							
23	0.0	23							
24									
25									

BATH

DISTANCE 5f		DISTANCE 5f 161y		DISTANCE 8f		DISTANCE 10f	
STALLS LOW		STALLS LOW		STALLS LOW		STALLS LOW	
1		1	1.7	1	0.5	1	0.3
2		2	1.0	2	1.5 **1.1**	2	0.9
3	**0.5**	3	1.4 **1.1**	3	1.1	3	1.6 **1.0**
4		4	1.1	4	1.3	4	1.3
5		5	0.3	5	1.1	5	0.9
6		6	0.3	6	0.5 **1.0**	6	1.8
7		7	1.1	7	0.5	7	1.2
8	**1.2**	8	0.8 **0.8**	8	1.9	8	1.8 **1.3**
9		9	1.0	9	2.1	9	1.5
10		10	1.0	10	1.3 **1.3**	10	0.3
11		11	1.8	11	0.8	11	1.2
12		12	0.8	12	0.8	12	0.7
13	**1.5**	13	0.6	13	0.3	13	0.4 **0.8**
14		14	2.4 **1.1**	14	1.1 **0.7**	14	0.5
15		15	0.8	15	0.8	15	0.7
16		16	0.0	16	0.9	16	0.0
17	**0.9**	17	0.0			17	1.8 **0.6**
18						18	0.0
19						19	0.0

BEVERLEY

DISTANCE 5f		DISTANCE 7f 100y		DISTANCE 8f 100y		DISTANCE 9f 207y	
STALLS	HIGH	STALLS	HIGH	STALLS	HIGH	STALLS	HIGH
1 — 2.2		1 — 1.7		1 —		1 — 1.5	
2 — 1.3		2 — 1.0	1.5	2 —	0.7	2 — 1.2	1.2
3 — 2.8	1.7	3 — 1.7		3 —		3 — 1.5	
4 — 1.9		4 — 1.4		4 —		4 — 0.6	
5 — 0.3		5 — 0.7		5 —		5 — 0.9	
6 — 1.3		6 — 1.0	1.2	6 —	1.1	6 — 0.6	1.0
7 — 1.9	0.9	7 — 2.4		7 —		7 — 0.9	
8 — 0.3		8 — 0.7		8 —		8 — 1.5	
9 — 0.9		9 — 0.7		9 —		9 — 1.2	
10 — 0.3		10 — 0.7	0.5	10 —	1.5	10 — 0.6	1.0
11 — 0.6		11 — 0.4		11 —		11 — 1.4	
12 — 0.0		12 — 0.0		12 —		12 — 0.9	
13 — 0.3	0.5	13 — 0.0		13 —		13 — 0.6	
14 — 0.3		14 — 0.8	0.5	14 —		14 — 0.0	0.3
15 — 1.2		15 — 1.1		15 —	0.7	15 — 0.0	
16 — 1.1		16 — 0.0		16 —		16 — 0.0	
17 — 0.7				17 —			
18 — 0.0	0.6						
19 — 0.0							
20 — 0.0							

BRIGHTON

DISTANCE 5f (GOOD, GOOD TO FIRM) STALLS LOW		DISTANCE 5f (GOOD TO SOFT, SOFT) STALLS LOW		DISTANCE 6f (GOOD, GOOD TO FIRM) STALLS LOW		DISTANCE 7f (GOOD, GOOD TO FIRM) STALLS LOW		DISTANCE 8f (GOOD, GOOD TO FIRM) STALLS LOW	
1 0.3		1		1 2.3		1 0.9		1 0.7	
2 1.3	0.8	2	0.0	2 1.4	1.3	2 0.5	1.0	2 1.2	0.8
3 0.5		3		3 0.7		3 1.1		3 0.7	
4 1.0		4		4 0.7		4 1.4		4 0.8	
5 1.9		5		5 0.3		5 2.2		5 0.7	
6 1.5	1.5	6	0.7	6 0.3	0.8	6 0.8	1.1	6 1.4	1.1
7 1.3		7		7 1.5		7 0.3		7 1.9	
8 1.3		8		8 1.4		8 0.9		8 0.5	
9 0.0		9		9 1.1		9 0.9		9 1.2	
10 1.0	0.7	10	1.8	10 0.4	0.7	10 1.1	1.1	10 1.4	1.0
11 0.4		11		11 0.8		11 1.3		11 0.7	
12 2.0		12		12 0.0		12 1.5		12 0.3	
13 0.7		13		13 0.7		13 1.0		13 1.6	
14 2.0	0.8	14	1.6	14 1.7	1.3	14 0.0		14 1.0	1.1
15 0.0		15		15 2.6		15 1.0	0.7	15 0.5	
16 0.0		16		16 0.0		16 0.0		16 1.3	
		BASED ON				17 0.0			
		LIMITED				18 4.0			
		EVIDENCE							

• When the going is softer than good it is normal for most of the runners to come over to the stands' rail in the straight and the high numbers usually fare best as a result.

CARLISLE

DISTANCE 5f			DISTANCE 5f 207y			DISTANCE 6f 206y			DISTANCE 7f 214y			DISTANCE 9f 61y		
STALLS	HIGH		STALLS	HIGH		STALLS	HIGH		STALLS	HIGH		STALLS	HIGH	
1	2.6		1	2.3		1	0.8		1	0.9		1		
2	1.0		2	0.4		2	1.9		2	0.9		2		1.4
3	0.5	1.0	3	1.5	1.1	3	0.8	1.1	3	1.9	1.0	3		
4	1.0		4	1.1		4	1.2		4	0.6		4		
5	0.5		5	0.4		5	0.8		5	0.9		5		
6	0.5		6	1.1		6	1.2		6	0.6		6		0.7
7	0.0		7	0.0		7	0.8		7	0.9		7		
8	1.6		8	1.1	1.0	8	1.6	0.9	8	0.3		8		
9	0.5	1.1	9	1.5		9	0.8		9	0.6	0.8	9		
10	2.1		10	1.1		10	0.4		10	1.2		10		
11	0.7		11	0.8		11	1.3		11	1.1		11		0.9
12	1.7		12	0.4		12	1.1		12	0.8		12		
13	1.0		13	0.0	0.7	13	0.9	0.9	13	1.3		13		
14	1.2		14	1.0		14	0.0		14	2.0		BASED ON		
15	0.0	0.7	15	1.2		15	0.0		15	0.6	1.4	LIMITED		
16	0.0		16	2.5					16	2.2		EVIDENCE		
17	0.0		17	0.0					17	1.4				
18	0.0		18	4.0	2.1				18	0.0				
			19	0.0										
			20	0.0										

CATTERICK

DISTANCE 5f (GOOD, GOOD TO FIRM) STALLS LOW			DISTANCE 5f (GOOD TO SOFT, SOFT) STALLS LOW			DISTANCE 6f (GOOD, GOOD TO FIRM) STALLS LOW			DISTANCE 6f (GOOD TO SOFT, SOFT) STALLS LOW			DISTANCE 7f (GOOD, GOOD TO FIRM) STALLS LOW		
1	1.3		1	3.0		1	1.6		1	1.4		1	1.5	
2	1.2		2	0.0		2	2.2		2	0.6		2	1.2	
3	2.0	1.5	3	0.0	0.8	3	0.6	1.5	3	0.0	0.7	3	0.4	0.9
4	1.8		4	1.1		4	1.6		4	0.7		4	1.0	
5	1.3		5	0.0		5	1.5		5	0.7		5	0.2	
6	1.9		6	1.0		6	0.3		6	0.0		6	1.9	
7	0.6		7	2.2		7	0.6		7	1.3		7	1.6	
8	0.6	0.8	8	2.4	1.3	8	1.4	0.5	8	0.7	1.3	8	0.7	1.2
9	0.6		9	0.0		9	0.0		9	1.6		9	0.8	
10	0.0		10	1.1		10	0.0		10	2.8		10	0.9	
11	1.9		11	0.0		11	0.9		11	0.9		11	1.3	
12	0.0		12	1.6		12	0.7	0.8	12	2.5	1.2	12	0.9	
13	0.8		13	1.3	0.8	13	0.0		13	0.0		13	1.2	1.1
14	0.0	0.7	14	1.5		14	2.6		14	0.0		14	1.2	
15	0.6		15	0.0								15	0.5	
16	0.0		16	0.0								16	0.0	
17	0.0											17	0.0	0.0
												18	0.0	

CHEPSTOW

DISTANCE 5f STALLS HIGH		DISTANCE 6f STALLS HIGH			DISTANCE 7f STALLS HIGH			DISTANCE 8f STALLS HIGH			DISTANCE 10f STALLS LOW		
1		1	0.8		1	0.5		1	1.3		1	0.0	
2		2	0.4		2	2.4		2	0.8		2	1.2	0.9
3	1.0	3	2.4	1.4	3	0.9	1.2	3	0.8	0.9	3	0.9	
4		4	2.0		4	0.9		4	0.8		4	1.6	
5		5	1.6		5	1.4		5	0.8		5	1.9	
6		6	0.8		6	0.9		6	1.0		6	1.6	1.5
7		7	1.6		7	1.9		7	1.0		7	1.6	
8	1.2	8	1.6	1.0	8	1.4	1.1	8	0.8	1.0	8	1.1	
9		9	0.4		9	0.5		9	1.0		9	0.9	
10		10	0.8		10	0.5		10	1.3		10	1.4	0.8
11		11	0.4		11	0.6		11	1.1		11	0.6	
12		12	0.5		12	0.0		12	1.2		12	0.0	
13	0.6	13	0.5	0.5	13	1.9	0.6	13	1.0	1.2	13	0.7	
14		14	0.5		14	0.0		14	1.2		14	0.0	0.6
15		15	0.7		15	0.8		15	1.7		15	0.8	
16		16	0.9		16	2.3		16	0.0		16	0.9	
17		17	0.0		17	1.4		17	0.0				
18	2.0	18	2.2	0.7	18	0.0	0.9	18	2.2	0.8			
19		19	0.0		19	0.0		19	0.0				
20		20	0.0		20	0.0		20	3.0				
LIMITED EVIDENCE													

CHESTER

DISTANCE 5f (GOOD, GOOD TO FIRM)			DISTANCE 6f (GOOD, GOOD TO FIRM)			DISTANCE 7f			DISTANCE 7f 122y			DISTANCE 10f		
STALLS	LOW		STALLS	LOW		STALLS	LOW		STALLS	LOW		STALLS	LOW	
1	4.2		1			1	0.5		1	0.9		1	0.6	
2	2.0		2			2	1.5	1.7	2	1.3		2	1.8	1.0
3	1.0	1.9	3		1.2	3	1.5		3	0.4	1.1	3	1.2	
4	1.4		4			4	3.3		4	0.8		4	0.3	
5	1.0		5			5	1.5		5	0.5		5	0.3	
6	0.7		6			6	1.0	1.2	6	2.5		6	2.3	1.2
7	0.7		7			7	1.0		7	0.8		7	0.9	
8	0.7	0.4	8		1.1	8	1.1		8	0.9		8	1.5	
9	0.0		9			9	0.0		9	0.9	1.1	9	0.7	
10	0.0		10			10	0.0	0.2	10	2.0		10	0.5	0.8
11	0.0		11			11	0.8		11	0.6		11	1.7	
12	0.0		12			12	0.0		12	1.4		12	0.6	
13	0.0	0.0	13		0.0	13	0.0		13	1.9		13	0.8	
14	0.0		14			14	0.0	0.0	14	0.0		14	0.0	0.4
15	0.0		15			15	0.0		15	0.0	0.6	15	0.0	
16	0.0		16			16	0.0		16	0.0		16	0.0	
									17	0.0				
									18	0.0				

DONCASTER

DISTANCE 5f			DISTANCE 6f			DISTANCE 7f			DISTANCE 8f (Straight)			DISTANCE 10f		
STALLS HIGH			STALLS HIGH			STALLS HIGH			STALLS HIGH			STALLS LOW		
1	2.8		1	2.3		1	1.6		1			1	1.4	
2	1.4		2	1.1		2	1.6		2			2	2.0	
3	0.0	1.5	3	0.8	1.3	3	0.2	1.0	3		1.1	3	0.7	1.3
4	0.9		4	1.1		4	0.9		4			4	1.9	
5	2.3		5	1.1		5	0.7		5			5	0.7	
6	2.8		6	1.5		6	0.7		6			6	1.0	
7	0.9		7	1.5		7	0.9		7			7	0.7	
8	0.5	1.2	8	1.1	1.2	8	1.1	1.2	8			8	1.7	1.2
9	1.4		9	0.0		9	1.3		9		1.1	9	1.1	
10	0.5		10	1.9		10	1.8		10			10	1.5	
11	0.0		11	0.0		11	1.3		11			11	0.8	
12	0.0		12	0.0		12	1.6		12			12	1.3	
13	0.0	0.3	13	0.4	0.5	13	0.6	1.0	13			13	0.5	0.6
14	1.5		14	1.0		14	0.4		14			14	0.0	
15	0.0		15	1.1		15	0.9		15		0.8	15	0.0	
16	0.0		16	0.7		16	0.9		16			16	1.0	
17	0.0		17	1.4		17	0.0		17			17	0.0	
18	0.0		18	0.0		18	0.0		18			18	0.9	0.4
19	3.0	0.7	19	1.0	0.8	19	0.7	0.6	19			19	0.0	
20	1.5		20	2.3		20	0.8		20			20	0.0	
21	0.0		21	0.0		21	1.1		21		0.9			
22	0.0		22	0.0		22	2.8		22					
LIMITED EVIDENCE									23					
									24					

EPSOM

DISTANCE 5f		DISTANCE 6f		DISTANCE 7f			DISTANCE 8f			DISTANCE 10f		
STALLS HIGH		STALLS LOW		STALLS LOW			STALLS LOW			STALLS LOW		
1		1		1	2.4		1	1.5		1	1.7	
2		2	1.9	2	0.4	1.2	2	1.1		2	0.0	
3	1.3	3		3	1.2		3	1.5	1.2	3	1.7	1.0
4		4		4	0.8		4	1.5		4	0.7	
5		5		5	1.6		5	0.7		5	1.0	
6		6	0.6	6	1.2	1.3	6	1.1		6	1.3	
7		7		7	1.2		7	0.7		7	0.3	
8	1.0	8		8	1.2		8	0.7		8	1.0	1.0
9		9		9	0.9		9	0.4	0.7	9	0.7	
10		10	0.8	10	0.0	0.6	10	0.0		10	1.5	
11		11		11	0.7		11	1.6		11	2.7	
12		12		12	0.8		12	0.6		12	0.6	
13	0.9	13		13	0.9		13	0.8		13	0.8	1.1
14		14		14	0.0		14	2.3		14	0.0	
15		15	0.4	15	0.0	0.3	15	1.4		15	0.0	
16		16		16	0.0		16	0.0	1.3	16	1.2	
17		17		17	0.0		17	0.0		17	0.0	
18	0.0						18	3.0		18	0.0	1.0
19							19	0.0		19	3.0	
20										20	0.0	

FOLKESTONE

DISTANCE 5f			DISTANCE 6f			DISTANCE 7f			DISTANCE 9f		
STALLS LOW			STALLS LOW			STALLS LOW			STALLS HIGH		
1	2.0		1	1.3		1	2.1		1	2.5	
2	1.0	1.6	2	1.5	1.2	2	1.0	1.4	2	1.8	
3	1.5		3	0.3		3	1.3		3	0.7	1.3
4	1.9		4	1.7		4	1.0		4	0.7	
5	0.0		5	1.2		5	1.1		5	0.7	
6	0.0	0.5	6	1.3	1.2	6	0.9	0.6	6	1.1	
7	1.1		7	0.6		7	0.3		7	0.0	
8	1.0		8	1.6		8	0.0		8	1.4	0.8
9	0.5		9	0.7		9	0.7		9	0.0	
10	0.8		10	0.4		10	1.0		10	1.8	
11	0.0	0.8	11	0.5	0.6	11	1.1	1.1	11	0.4	
12	0.0		12	0.5		12	1.5		12	0.5	
13	3.8		13	0.0		13	2.1		13	2.2	0.8
14	0.0		14	1.3		14	0.0		14	0.0	
									15	0.0	

GOODWOOD

DISTANCE 5f STALLS LOW		DISTANCE 6f STALLS LOW		DISTANCE 7f STALLS HIGH		DISTANCE 8f STALLS HIGH		DISTANCE 9f STALLS HIGH	
1		1		1	1.4	1	1.4	1	1.2
2		2		2	2.0	2	1.4	2	0.9
3	1.2	3	0.6	3	0.8	3	2.9	3	0.9
4		4		4	1.1	4	1.1	4	1.8
5		5		5	0.8	5	1.8	5	1.2
6		6		6	1.1	6	0.4	6	0.3
7		7		7	1.1	7	0.0	7	1.5
8	1.1	8	1.5	8	0.6	8	0.7	8	1.5
9		9		9	1.1	9	1.4	9	0.3
10		10		10	1.1	10	0.7	10	0.3
11		11		11	0.6	11	0.4	11	1.4
12		12		12	0.9	12	1.1	12	0.9
13	1.1	13	1.2	13	0.4	13	2.0	13	0.0
14		14		14	1.0	14	0.4	14	1.8
15		15		15	1.8	15	0.0	15	1.2
16		16		16	0.0	16	0.5	16	0.0
17		17		17	0.0	17	0.0	17	0.0
18	0.5	18	1.2	18	0.0	18	0.7	18	0.0
19		19		19	0.0	19	2.0	19	0.0
20		20				20	0.0		
21		21				21	0.0		
22		22							
23	0.0	23	0.3						
24		24							
25		25							
26		26							
		27							
		28	0.0						
		29							
		30							

HAMILTON

DISTANCE 5f		DISTANCE 6f		DISTANCE 8f		DISTANCE 9f	
STALLS LOW		STALLS LOW		STALLS HIGH		STALLS HIGH	
1		1	0.7	1	1.2	1	1.3
2		2	1.4	2	1.5 **1.2**	2	2.2 **1.6**
3	**1.6**	3	1.0 **0.9**	3	0.6	3	1.3
4		4	1.4	4	1.8	4	1.6
5		5	0.4	5	0.6	5	0.3
6		6	0.7	6	0.9 **1.0**	6	0.3 **0.6**
7		7	1.3	7	0.9	7	1.3
8	**0.6**	8	1.3	8	1.5	8	0.6
9		9	1.1 **1.1**	9	0.9	9	1.3
10		10	0.4	10	1.8 **1.0**	10	0.0 **0.7**
11		11	1.1	11	0.9	11	0.6
12		12	1.4	12	0.5	12	0.9
13	**0.8**	13	0.5	13	0.6	13	2.0
14		14	1.4	14	0.0 **0.3**	14	0.0
15		15	3.0 **1.1**	15	0.0	15	0.0 **0.8**
		16	0.0	16	0.0	16	0.0
		17	0.0			17	0.0
		18	0.0			18	0.0

HAYDOCK

DISTANCE 5f			DISTANCE 6f			DISTANCE 7f			DISTANCE 8f			DISTANCE 10f		
STALLS HIGH			STALLS HIGH			STALLS LOW			STALLS LOW			STALLS LOW		
1	1.4		1	0.8		1			1	0.9		1	1.0	
2	1.0		2	1.6		2			2	1.7		2	1.6	
3	1.0	1.3	3	0.4	0.8	3	1.2		3	0.2	1.1	3	0.6	1.0
4	1.7		4	0.8		4			4	2.0		4	1.0	
5	1.0		5	0.4		5			5	0.7		5	1.0	
6	1.0		6	0.4		6			6	0.9		6	1.7	
7	1.0		7	0.4		7			7	1.4		7	0.9	
8	1.4	1.0	8	1.6	1.4	8	0.7		8	1.4	1.1	8	1.0	1.1
9	0.0		9	2.8		9			9	0.7		9	0.7	
10	1.4		10	1.6		10			10	1.1		10	1.3	
11	0.0		11	2.0		11			11	0.8		11	1.2	
12	0.9		12	1.6		12	1.2		12	0.3		12	0.4	
13	0.5	0.6	13	0.8	1.0	13			13	1.2		13	1.0	1.0
14	1.3		14	0.0		14			14	2.4	0.9	14	0.5	
15	0.8		15	0.0		BASED ON			15	0.8		15	1.9	
16	3.0		16	0.0		LIMITED EVIDENCE			16	0.0		16	1.4	
17	0.0		17	0.0					17	0.9		17	0.0	
18	0.0	1.2	18	0.0	0.0							18	0.0	0.6
19	0.0		19	0.0								19	3.0	
20	0.0		20	0.0								20	0.0	

KEMPTON (AW)

DISTANCE 5f			DISTANCE 6f			DISTANCE 7f			DISTANCE 8f			DISTANCE 10f		
STALLS	HIGH		STALLS	HIGH		STALLS	HIGH		STALLS	HIGH		STALLS	HIGH	
1	2.0		1	1.5		1	2.5		1	0.5		1	0.3	
2	2.0	1.6	2	1.7	1.4	2	1.4		2	0.3		2	0.9	
3	0.9		3	1.3		3	1.1	1.5	3	1.3	0.9	3	0.3	0.6
4	1.6		4	1.1		4	1.2		4	1.6		4	0.9	
5	0.2		5	1.1		5	1.4		5	0.8		5	0.6	
6	0.7	0.7	6	1.1	0.6	6	0.2		6	1.3		6	1.8	
7	1.3		7	0.0		7	1.6		7	0.5		7	1.5	
8	0.7		8	0.2		8	0.5	0.9	8	0.3	1.0	8	0.9	1.4
9	0.7		9	0.6		9	1.2		9	1.8		9	1.5	
10	0.9	0.6	10	0.4	1.0	10	0.9		10	1.3		10	1.5	
11	0.0		11	1.3		11	0.3		11	1.3		11	1.8	
12	0.5		12	1.7		12	0.5	0.4	12	1.0	1.1	12	0.6	0.9
						13	0.6		13	1.0		13	0.6	
						14	0.3		14	1.0		14	0.7	

LEICESTER

DISTANCE 5f STALLS LOW		DISTANCE 6f STALLS LOW			DISTANCE 7f STALLS LOW			DISTANCE 10f STALLS HIGH		
1		1	1.8		1	1.3		1	0.0	
2		2	0.7		2	0.8		2	1.0	
3	1.3	3	1.8	1.3	3	0.7	0.8	3	0.7	0.8
4		4	0.9		4	0.7		4	1.0	
5		5	1.5		5	0.7		5	1.3	
6		6	0.7		6	1.5		6	1.3	
7		7	0.7		7	0.7		7	1.3	
8		8	1.1	0.9	8	1.1	1.4	8	1.0	1.3
9	1.0	9	0.8		9	1.1		9	2.0	
10		10	1.4		10	2.2		10	1.0	
11		11	0.9		11	0.7		11	0.4	
12		12	0.6		12	0.6		12	1.6	
13		13	1.8	0.9	13	0.0	0.7	13	0.0	0.9
14		14	0.5		14	0.8		14	2.5	
15	0.3	15	0.5		15	1.9		15	0.0	
16		16	0.0		16	1.7		16	0.0	
17		17	0.9		17	0.6		17	2.8	0.6
18		18	0.0	0.2	18	1.4	1.0	18	0.0	
		19	0.0		19	0.0		19	0.0	
		20	0.0		20	1.8				

LINGFIELD (AW)

DISTANCE 5F STALLS	LOW		DISTANCE 6f STALLS	LOW		DISTANCE 7f STALLS	LOW		DISTANCE 8f STALLS	LOW		DISTANCE 10f STALLS	LOW	
1	0.6		1	0.8		1	1.2		1	0.7		1	0.7	
2	0.5		2	1.5	1.1	2	0.8		2	1.3	0.8	2	1.3	
3	1.6	1.1	3	1.4		3	1.2	1.0	3	0.4		3	1.5	1.0
4	0.8		4	0.9		4	1.0		4	0.6		4	0.7	
5	1.9		5	1.5		5	0.8		5	0.8		5	1.0	
6	1.1		6	0.8	0.9	6	1.2		6	1.2	1.1	6	0.7	
7	0.6		7	0.7		7	1.0		7	1.6		7	1.6	
8	1.1	0.9	8	0.6		8	1.3	1.1	8	0.9		8	0.7	1.0
9	0.6		9	0.7		9	1.0		9	1.8		9	1.2	
10	1.3		10	1.1	0.9	10	1.0		10	0.8	1.2	10	1.0	
			11	1.1		11	1.0		11	0.7		11	1.2	
			12	0.8		12	0.4	0.6	12	1.6		12	0.5	0.8
						13	0.3					13	1.0	
						14	0.7					14	0.4	

MUSSELBURGH

DISTANCE 5f (GOOD, GOOD TO FIRM)		DISTANCE 5f (GOOD TO SOFT, SOFT)		DISTANCE 7f		DISTANCE 8f		DISTANCE 9f	
STALLS LOW		STALLS LOW		STALLS HIGH		STALLS HIGH		STALLS HIGH	
1	1.0	1	0.0	1	1.1	1	1.6	1	
2	1.2	2	2.0	2	0.4	2	1.3	2	1.0
3	2.0	**1.2**	3	0.5	**1.3**	3	1.5	**0.9**	3	1.3	**1.2**	3	
4	0.6	4	2.7	4	0.6	4	0.5	4	
5	0.5	5	1.0	5	1.3	5	0.8	5	
6	0.9	6	0.5	6	1.0	6	1.3	6	1.4
7	1.0	**1.0**	7	0.6	**0.7**	7	1.3	7	0.5	7	
8	1.8	8	0.5	8	1.4	**1.2**	8	0.8	**0.9**	8	
9	0.9	9	0.6	9	1.2	9	2.1	9	
10	1.0	10	0.0	10	0.6	10	0.0	10	0.4
11	0.4	**1.0**	11	4.2	**1.1**	11	0.0	11	0.5	11	
12	1.8	12	0.0	12	1.0	**0.7**	12	0.7	**1.0**	12	
13	0.6	13	1.0	13	1.4	13	0.7	13	
14	0.4	14	0.0	14	1.4	14	0.3	14	1.0
15	0.0	**0.4**	15	0.0	**0.8**					15	
16	0.0	16	3.0					16	
17	0.0	17	0.0					BASED ON LIMITED EVIDENCE	

NEWBURY

DISTANCE 5f		DISTANCE 6f		DISTANCE 7f		DISTANCE 10f		DISTANCE 11f	
STALLS HIGH		STALLS HIGH		STALLS HIGH		STALLS LOW		STALLS LOW	
1		1		1		1		1	
2		2		2		2		2	
3	1.2	3	0.9	3	1.2	3	1.6	3	0.8
4		4		4		4		4	
5		5		5		5		5	
6		6		6		6		6	
7		7		7		7		7	
8		8	1.2	8	1.0	8		8	
9	1.2	9		9		9	0.5	9	1.1
10		10		10		10		10	
11		11		11		11		11	
12		12		12		12		12	
13		13	1.0	13	1.0	13		13	
14		14		14		14		14	
15	0.0	15		15		15	0.0	15	1.4
16		16		16		16		16	
17		17		17		17		17	
18		18	0.7	18	0.7	18		18	
LIMITED EVIDENCE		19		19		LIMITED EVIDENCE			
		20		20					
				21					
				22	0.0				
				23					
				24					

NEWCASTLE

DISTANCE 5f		DISTANCE 6f		DISTANCE 7f		DISTANCE 8f		DISTANCE 10f	
STALLS HIGH		STALLS HIGH		STALLS HIGH		STALLS LOW		STALLS LOW	
1		1	2.3	1		1		1	0.5
2		2	1.5	2		2		2	1.3
3	0.9	3	1.9 / 1.5	3	1.5	3	0.9	3	1.2 / 1.1
4		4	1.2	4		4		4	1.6
5		5	0.8	5		5		5	1.0
6		6	1.2	6		6		6	0.7
7		7	1.2	7		7		7	1.3
8	1.0	8	0.4 / 0.9	8	0.6	8	1.3	8	1.7 / 1.2
9		9	1.2	9		9		9	0.3
10		10	1.5	10		10		10	1.9
11		11	0.0	11		11		11	0.8
12		12	1.2	12		12		12	0.3
13	1.0	13	0.5 / 0.7	13	1.0	13	0.6	13	0.8 / 0.6
14		14	0.5	14		14		14	0.8
15		15	1.6	15		15		15	0.5
16		16	0.7	16		16		16	1.9
17		17	1.0	17		17		17	0.8
18	1.4	18	0.0 / 0.4	18	0.5	18	1.5	18	0.0 / 1.1
19		19	0.0	19		19		19	0.0
20		20	0.0	20		20		20	0.0
						BASED ON LIMITED EVIDENCE			

NEWMARKET (JULY)

DISTANCE 6f		DISTANCE 6f		DISTANCE 7f		DISTANCE 7f		DISTANCE 8f		DISTANCE 8f	
STALLS HIGH		STALLS LOW		STALLS HIGH		STALLS LOW		STALLS HIGH		STALLS LOW	
1		1		1		1		1		1	
2		2		2		2		2		2	
3	1.2	3	1.2	3	0.9	3	1.0	3	1.3	3	0.6
4		4		4		4		4		4	
5		5		5		5		5		5	
6		6		6		6		6		6	
7		7		7		7		7		7	
8		8	0.7	8	0.9	8	0.9	8	0.5	8	1.0
9	0.9	9		9		9		9		9	
10		10		10		10		10		10	
11		11		11		11		11		11	
12		12		12		12		12		12	
13		13	1.1	13	1.7	13	1.3	13		13	1.3
14		14		14		14		14	1.4	14	
15	1.0	15		15		15		15		15	
16		16		16		16		16		16	
17		17		17		17		17		17	
18		18	0.5	18	0.0	18	0.7			18	1.8
		19		19		19				19	
		20		20		20				20	

NEWMARKET (ROWLEY)

DISTANCE 6f		DISTANCE 6f		DISTANCE 7f		DISTANCE 7f		DISTANCE 8f		DISTANCE 8f	
STALLS HIGH		STALLS LOW		STALLS HIGH		STALLS LOW		STALLS HIGH		STALLS LOW	
1		1		1		1		1		1	
2		2		2		2		2		2	
3	1.3	3	1.2	3	1.5	3	1.3	3	1.1	3	0.6
4		4		4		4		4		4	
5		5		5		5		5		5	
6		6		6		6		6		6	
7		7		7		7		7		7	
8	1.0	8	0.8	8		8		8	1.3	8	1.9
9		9		9	0.9	9	0.6	9		9	
10		10		10		10		10		10	
11		11		11		11		11		11	
12		12		12		12		12		12	
13	0.4	13	1.0	13		13		13	0.3	13	0.3
14		14		14		14		14		14	
15		15		15	0.3	15	0.7	15		15	
16		16		16		16		16		16	
17	0.8	17		17		17		17		17	
18		18	1.3	18		18		18		18	0.8
19		19		19		19		19	1.0	19	
		20		20		20		20		20	
		21		21	0.0	21		21			
		22		22		22	2.7	22			
		23	0.6	23		23					
		24				24					
		25				25					
		26				26					
		27									
		28	1.7								
		29									
		30									

NOTTINGHAM

DISTANCE 5f STALLS HIGH			DISTANCE 6f STALLS HIGH			DISTANCE 8f STALLS LOW			DISTANCE 10f STALLS LOW			DISTANCE 14f STALLS LOW		
1	1.6		1	1.0		1	1.6		1	1.0		1	2.5	
2	0.8		2	1.9		2	1.1		2	1.1		2	2.2	
3	0.8	**1.0**	3	0.6	**1.15**	3	0.7	**1.0**	3	0.6	**0.9**	3	0.9	**1.5**
4	1.0		4	1.6		4	1.0		4	0.6		4	0.4	
5	1.3		5	0.6		5	0.7		5	1.4		5	1.3	
6	0.8		6	1.9		6	2.1		6	0.0		6	0.0	
7	0.5		7	1.0		7	1.5		7	1.8		7	0.4	
8	1.3	**1.0**	8	1.3	**1.15**	8	1.1	**1.7**	8	1.8	**1.3**	8	0.8	**0.8**
9	1.3		9	1.0		9	1.4		9	1.8		9	2.3	
10	1.0		10	0.6		10	2.5		10	0.9		10	0.5	
11	1.2		11	0.3		11	0.4		11	2.0		11	0.0	
12	0.4		12	1.6		12	0.0		12	0.3		12	1.3	
13	1.7		13	1.0	**0.8**	13	0.4		13	1.0	**0.8**	13	0.0	
14	1.6		14	0.6		14	0.0	**0.3**	14	1.0		14	0.0	**0.6**
15	0.7	**1.0**	15	0.4		15	0.0		15	0.4		15	0.0	
16	0.9		16	0.0		16	0.6		16	0.0		16	1.2	
17	0.0		17	0.9		17	0.6					17	4.0	
18	0.0		18	1.6	**0.7**									
			19	2.0										
			20	1.0										

PONTEFRACT

DISTANCE 5f			DISTANCE 6f			DISTANCE 8f			DISTANCE 10f		
STALLS LOW			STALLS LOW			STALLS LOW			STALLS LOW		
1	0.8		1	0.5		1	1.0		1	1.4	
2	0.8		2	1.9		2	2.3		2	1.3	
3	0.0	1.1	3	1.5	1.0	3	1.1	1.3	3	0.2	1.4
4	0.8		4	0.9		4	1.4		4	1.8	
5	3.4		5	0.5		5	0.7		5	1.6	
6	0.8		6	1.0		6	1.2		6	1.6	
7	0.8		7	1.0		7	1.0		7	1.0	
8	0.8		8	1.0		8	1.2	1.0	8	0.8	
9	0.0	1.0	9	0.3	0.8	9	1.2		9	0.7	0.7
10	2.0		10	1.2		10	0.4		10	0.6	
11	1.8		11	0.6		11	1.0		11	0.4	
12	0.5		12	0.9		12	0.0		12	0.0	
13	1.6		13	1.3		13	0.3	0.5	13	1.0	
14	0.6		14	1.5		14	0.5		14	0.6	
15	0.6	0.7	15	0.7	1.3	15	0.4		15	0.0	0.5
16	1.0		16	1.8		16	1.2		16	0.9	
17	0.0		17	1.8		17	0.8		17	0.0	
18	0.0					18	0.0	0.7	18	0.0	
						19	0.0				
						20	0.0				

REDCAR

DISTANCE 5f STALLS	LOW	DISTANCE 6f STALLS	LOW	LOW	DISTANCE 7f STALLS	LOW	DISTANCE 8f STALLS	LOW	LOW	DISTANCE 10f STALLS	LOW	LOW
1		1	0.0		1		1	1.0		1	0.5	
2		2	0.6		2		2	1.0		2	0.3	1.0
3	0.8	3	1.7	0.8	3	0.5	3	1.3	0.9	3	1.4	
4		4	0.8		4		4	1.3		4	1.8	
5		5	0.8		5		5	0.3		5	1.0	
6		6	1.4		6		6	1.0		6	2.2	1.0
7		7	0.3		7		7	1.7		7	0.5	
8	1.2	8	0.3	0.9	8	0.8	8	0.3	0.8	8	0.4	
9		9	1.7		9		9	0.3		9	1.3	
10		10	0.8		10		10	0.7		10	0.8	0.8
11		11	0.6		11		11	0.7		11	0.3	
12		12	1.6		12		12	2.4		12	0.9	
13	1.2	13	0.7	1.0	13	1.7	13	0.9	1.4	13	0.9	
14		14	0.8		14		14	1.6		14	1.3	
15		15	1.5		15		15	1.2		15	1.2	1.1
16		16	3.0		16		16	0.7		16	0.7	
17		17	0.0		17		17	1.6		17	1.5	
18	0.8	18	0.0	1.9	18	1.0	18	1.9	1.1			
19		19	3.0		19		19	0.0				
20		20	0.0		20		20	0.0				
21							21	0.0				
							22	0.0				
							23	0.0	0.0			
							24	0.0				
							25+	0.0				

RIPON

DISTANCE 5f STALLS LOW			DISTANCE 6f STALLS LOW			DISTANCE 8f STALLS HIGH			DISTANCE 10f STALLS HIGH		DISTANCE 12f STALLS HIGH	
1	0.9		1	0.7		1	2.1		1		1	1.1
2	0.9		2	1.1		2	1.4		2		2	
3	0.9	1.1	3	1.7	1.2	3	1.4	1.6	3	1.0	3	
4	0.8		4	2.4		4	2.5		4		4	
5	1.7		5	0.3		5	0.4		5		5	1.0
6	1.7		6	1.5		6	0.7		6		6	
7	0.0		7	0.7		7	2.1		7		7	
8	2.0	1.0	8	0.3	0.9	8	0.7	0.8	8	1.2	8	
9	1.0		9	0.0		9	0.0		9		9	0.7
10	0.0		10	2.2		10	0.4		10		10	
11	0.0		11	0.9		11	0.0		11		11	
12	2.1		12	0.9		12	0.8		12		12	
13	1.1	0.7	13	0.0	0.8	13	0.0	0.2	13		13	
14	0.0		14	0.7		14	0.0		14	0.6	14	
15	0.0		15	1.9		15	0.0		15			
16	0.0		16	1.2		16	0.0		16			
17	4.0		17	0.0		17	0.0		17			
18	0.0	1.8	18	0.0		18	0.0	0.0	18			
19	4.0		19	0.0	0.9	19	0.0					
20	0.0		20	0.0		20	0.0					
			21	0.0								
			22	4.0								
			23	4.0								

SALISBURY

DISTANCE 5f		DISTANCE 6f			DISTANCE 7f			DISTANCE 8f			DISTANCE 10f		
STALLS	HIGH	STALLS	HIGH		STALLS	HIGH		STALLS	HIGH		STALLS	HIGH	
1		1	2.0		1	1.2		1	0.3		1	0.5	
2		2	1.4		2	1.5		2	1.0		2	0.0	
3	1.1	3	1.4	1.3	3	0.4	1.0	3	1.6	0.9	3	1.5	1.1
4		4	1.1		4	1.5		4	1.3		4	2.0	
5		5	0.6		5	0.4		5	0.3		5	2.0	
6		6	0.3		6	0.8		6	1.6		6	0.5	
7		7	0.6		7	1.9		7	1.9		7	1.5	
8		8	0.6	1.0	8	0.8	0.9	8	1.3	1.1	8	1.0	
9	0.9	9	1.7		9	0.8		9	0.3		9	0.5	1.0
10		10	1.7		10	0.4		10	0.3		10	0.0	
11		11	0.9		11	0.8		11	1.3		11	0.6	
12		12	0.8		12	0.5		12	0.7		12	3.1	
13		13	0.0	0.7	13	1.1	0.8	13	0.9		13	0.0	
14		14	0.0		14	1.4		14	1.9	1.0	14	0.0	
15	1.1	15	1.5		15	0.0		15	0.9		15	0.0	0.0
16		16	0.0		16	1.6		16	0.0		16	0.0	
17		17	0.0	0.5	17	1.1		17	0.0		17	0.0	
18		18	2.1		18	2.6	2.1	18	0.0		BASED ON		
		19	0.0		19	3.0					LIMITED EVIDENCE		
					20	0.0							

SANDOWN

DISTANCE 5f			DISTANCE 7f			DISTANCE 8f			DISTANCE 10f		
STALLS	HIGH		STALLS	HIGH		STALLS	HIGH		STALLS	HIGH	
1	1.2		1	2.3		1	0.2		1	1.2	
2	1.8		2	0.3	1.3	2	1.2		2	1.7	1.2
3	0.8	1.1	3	1.3		3	0.5	0.8	3	0.7	
4	1.0		4	1.3		4	0.5		4	1.2	
5	1.0		5	1.3		5	1.5		5	1.4	
6	0.4		6	0.0	1.1	6	1.5		6	1.0	1.0
7	0.2		7	1.6		7	1.7		7	0.7	
8	0.6	0.7	8	1.6		8	1.5	1.4	8	1.0	
9	1.0		9	0.3		9	1.2		9	1.4	
10	1.6		10	1.3	0.7	10	1.2		10	0.7	0.8
11	0.3		11	0.5		11	1.0		11	0.5	
12	1.3		12	0.6		12	0.0		12	0.4	
13	0.5		13	0.0		13	0.0		13	0.0	
14	0.8	1.4	14	0.0	0.0	14	1.9	0.7	14	1.3	
15	1.4		15	0.0		15	1.5		15	0.8	0.8
16	3.0		16	0.0		16	0.0		16	3.0	
17	3.0					17	0.0		17	0.0	

SOUTHWELL (AW)

DISTANCE 5f			DISTANCE 6f			DISTANCE 7f			DISTANCE 8f			DISTANCE 12f		
STALLS	LOW		STALLS	LOW		STALLS	LOW		STALLS	LOW		STALLS	LOW	
1	1.8		1	0.3		1	1.0		1	0.4		1	0.2	
2	0.9		2	0.7		2	0.7		2	0.9		2	1.0	
3	1.5	**1.4**	3	1.8	**1.0**	3	0.9	**1.1**	3	0.4	**0.8**	3	0.0	**0.6**
4	1.4		4	1.0		4	1.5		4	1.1		4	0.2	
5	1.4		5	1.3		5	1.5		5	1.4		5	1.4	
6	1.3		6	1.4		6	0.6		6	1.4		6	1.4	
7	0.4		7	0.9		7	0.6		7	1.5		7	0.8	
8	1.0	**0.9**	8	1.1	**1.1**	8	1.5	**1.0**	8	1.5	**1.2**	8	0.6	**1.4**
9	1.0		9	1.2		9	1.8		9	0.7		9	2.2	
10	0.5		10	1.1		10	0.6		10	0.5		10	2.0	
11	0.5		11	0.5		11	0.7		11	0.5		11	0.4	
12	0.0	**0.2**	12	0.3	**0.6**	12	0.6	**0.8**	12	1.8	**1.0**	12	1.0	**0.7**
13	0.0		13	0.8		13	0.7		13	0.7		13	1.0	
14	0.0		14	0.9		14	1.1		14	1.0		14	0.5	

THIRSK

DISTANCE 5f STALLS HIGH			DISTANCE 6f STALLS HIGH			DISTANCE 7f STALLS LOW			DISTANCE 8f STALLS LOW			DISTANCE 12f STALLS LOW	
1	2.3		1	0.6		1	0.7		1	0.6		1	
2	2.3		2	1.8		2	1.1	1.2	2	0.9	0.7	2	
3	1.8	1.6	3	0.6	1.1	3	1.4		3	0.6		3	1.0
4	0.5		4	2.1		4	1.7		4	0.8		4	
5	1.0		5	0.6		5	1.1		5	1.3		5	
6	1.0		6	0.9		6	0.4	1.1	6	2.4	1.4	6	
7	0.5		7	1.2		7	0.7		7	0.7		7	
8	0.5	0.6	8	0.6	0.8	8	2.3		8	1.1		8	1.1
9	0.5		9	0.6		9	1.1		9	1.4		9	
10	0.5		10	0.9		10	0.7	0.7	10	1.0	1.0	10	
11	0.5		11	0.0		11	0.8		11	0.5		11	
12	0.5		12	1.0		12	0.5		12	0.8		12	
13	2,8	0.9	13	2.0	1.0	13	1.4		13	0.6		13	0.5
14	0.7		14	0.4		14	0.6	0.7	14	1.6		14	
15	0.0		15	2.1		15	0.0		15	1.3	1.0	15	
16	2.0		16	0.6		16	0.0		16	0.6		16	
17	0.0		17	1.2					17	0.0		17	2.0(?)
18	0.0	0.8	18	1.5	1.0				18	0.8		18	
19	0.0		19	1.1								19	
20	0.0		20	0.0									

In 5f handicaps of twelve or more runners only one horse in the last five years (Westbrook Blue) has managed to win on the stands' side when exiting one of the lowest four stalls. Unsurprisingly, he turned out to have been well-handicapped and went on to win his next race by two lengths off an eleven pounds higher mark at odds of 15/2. All the other low drawn winners went across to the far rail and most of them 'made all'.

WARWICK

DISTANCE 5f			DISTANCE 6f			DISTANCE 7f			DISTANCE 8f			DISTANCE 10f		
STALLS	LOW		STALLS	LOW		STALLS	LOW		STALLS	LOW		STALLS	LOW	
1	1.5		1	3.5		1	2.7		1	2.6		1	3.9	
2	1.6		2	1.0		2	1.6		2	1.3		2	0.4	
3	0.4	1.3	3	1.5	1.4	3	0.5	1.5	3	2.1	1.6	3	1.4	1.9
4	2.4		4	1.0		4	1.0		4	0.9		4	1.2	
5	0.7		5	0.0		5	1.5		5	0.8		5	2.4	
6	1.1		6	1.5		6	0.8		6	0.8		6	0.8	
7	0.7		7	0.0		7	0.8		7	0.8		7	0.4	
8	1.0	0.8	8	1.9	0.8	8	0.0	0.7	8	1.4	0.9	8	0.4	0.7
9	0.0		9	0.0		9	0.8		9	0.9		9	0.8	
10	1.0		10	0.0		10	1.0		10	0.5		10	1.2	
11	0.0		11	1.4		11	1.2		11	0.0		11	0.4	
12	0.0		12	0.9		12	0.9	0.6	12	0.6		12	0.5	
13	1.7		13	0.0		13	0.0		13	0.6		13	0.0	
14	1.2	0.7	14	0.0	0.7	14	0.0		14	0.0	0.5	14	1.2	0.4
15	0.0		15	1.9					15	0.7		15	0.6	
16	1.8		16	0.0					16	1.4		16	0.0	
17	0.0		17	0.0					17	0.7		17	0.0	

WINDSOR

DISTANCE 5f			DISTANCE 6f			DISTANCE 8f			DISTANCE 10f		
STALLS		HIGH	STALLS		HIGH	STALLS		HIGH	STALLS		HIGH
1	0.3		1	2.2		1	1.5		1	1.6	
2	2.0		2	0.4		2	0.2		2	1.0	
3	1.7	**1.2**	3	0.7	**1.1**	3	1.7	**1.1**	3	0.5	**1.1**
4	1.7		4	0.9		4	0.9		4	0.5	
5	0.3		5	1.1		5	1.5		5	2.1	
6	0.7		6	1.1		6	0.9		6	0.5	
7	2.0		7	2.0		7	0.9		7	1.0	
8	0.3	**0.9**	8	0.7	**1.1**	8	1.5	**1.0**	8	1.0	**0.9**
9	0.7		9	0.7		9	0.9		9	1.6	
10	1.0		10	1.1		10	1.1		10	1.0	
11	0.8		11	0.9		11	0.9		11	1.0	
12	0.0		12	0.7		12	1.1		12	1.6	
13	0.0	**0.5**	13	1.1	**0.9**	13	0.6		13	0.5	**1.2**
14	0.9		14	1.1		14	0.9		14	2.1	
15	1.2		15	0.7		15	0.9	**0.6**	15	0.8	
16	1.6		16	0.5		16	0.0		16	0.0	
17	3.2		17	0.0		17	0.0		17	0.0	
18	0.0	**1.6**	18	0.0	**0.3**	18	0.0		18	0.0	**0.0**
19	0.0		19	0.0					19	0.0	
20	0.0		20	0.0					20	0.0	

WOLVERHAMPTON (AW)

DISTANCE 5f			DISTANCE 6f			DISTANCE 7f			DISTANCE 8½f			DISTANCE 9½f		
STALLS	LOW		STALLS	LOW		STALLS	LOW		STALLS	LOW		STALLS	LOW	
1	1.4		1	1.2		1	0.9		1	1.6		1	0.8	
2	1.4	1.2	2	1.3	1.1	2	1.4	1.2	2	1.2	1.3	2	0.6	1.0
3	1.6		3	0.7		3	0.9		3	1.2		3	1.1	
4	0.3		4	1.2		4	1.4		4	1.0		4	1.4	
5	1.5		5	0.8		5	1.4		5	1.0		5	1.2	
6	1.6	1.1	6	1.5	1.1	6	1.2	1.1	6	1.4	0.9	6	1.3	1.2
7	1.3		7	1.4		7	0.9		7	0.8		7	1.4	
8	0.2		8	0.9		8	0.9		8	0.4		8	1.1	
9	1.0		9	1.2		9	0.5		9	1.0		9	0.9	
10	0.4		10	0.5		10	0.8	0.7	10	1.0		10	0.6	
11	0.8	0.6	11	0.5	0.8	11	0.6		11	0.7	0.8	11	0.7	0.7
12	0.0		12	1.0		12	0.8		12	0.9		12	0.2	
13	0.4		13	0.4					13	1.5		13	1.2	

YARMOUTH

DISTANCE 5f			DISTANCE 6f			DISTANCE 7f			DISTANCE 8f			DISTANCE 10f		
STALLS	HIGH		STALLS	HIGH		STALLS	HIGH		STALLS	HIGH		STALLS	LOW	
1			1	1.6		1	1.0		1	0.6		1	0.0	
2			2	0.9		2	0.8		2	1.0		2	1.6	**1.2**
3	**1.1**		3	1.2	**1.2**	3	0.6	**0.8**	3	0.9	**0.9**	3	1.1	
4			4	0.9		4	1.3		4	1.0		4	2.0	
5			5	1.6		5	0.3		5	0.9		5	1.5	
6			6	0.9		6	1.6		6	0.6		6	1.0	**1.3**
7			7	1.6		7	0.0		7	1.0		7	1.0	
8	**0.6**		8	0.9	**0.9**	8	1.0	**1.4**	8	0.3	**1.0**	8	1.5	
9			9	0.0		9	2.8		9	1.3		9	1.0	
10			10	1.2		10	1.6		10	1.6		10	1.5	**0.9**
11			11	1.0		11	1.0		11	1.0		11	0.6	
12			12	2.0		12	0.7		12	1.3		12	0.0	
13	**1.6**		13	0.0	**1.0**	13	0.5	**0.9**	13	1.4	**1.2**	13	0.7	
14			14	1.6		14	0.9		14	0.8		14	0.0	**0.7**
15			15	0.0		15	1.3		15	1.8		15	0.8	
LIMITED EVIDENCE			16	0.0		16	0.9		16	0.0		16	0.9	
			17	0.0		17	0.0		17	0.0				
			18	0.0	**0.0**	18	0.0	**0.4**	18	2.6	**0.9**			
			19	0.0		19	0.0		19	0.0				
			20	0.0		20	0.0		20	3.0				